INSPIRING
CREATIVITY

INSPIRING CREATIVITY

An Anthology of
Powerful Insights
and Practical Ideas
to Guide You to
Successful Creating

EDITED BY RICK BENZEL, M.A.

Creativity Coaching Association Press

Published by
Creativity Coaching Association Press
8180 Manitoba Street, #151
Playa del Rey, CA 90293

For information about quantity purchases of this book or to inquire about publishing your manuscript on a creativity-related subject with the Creativity Coaching Association Press, please visit our website at
www.creativitycoachingassociation.com
or contact us at publisher@creativitycoachingassociation.com

Cover Design and Book Design
Cherryl Moote
www.mootepoints.com

FIRST EDITION
International Standard Book Number (ISBN): 0-9767371-0-8

Printed in the United States of America
10 9 8 7   6   5   4   3   2   1

TABLE OF CONTENTS

❖

III: CREATE BIG IDEAS AND WORK SUCCESSFULLY

IV: LIVE YOUR CREATIVITY EVERY DAY

V: EXPRESS AND HONOR YOURSELF

VI: CHALLENGE YOURSELF TO HIGHER CREATIVITY

PUBLISHER'S NOTE

Dear Reader:

Welcome to this first creativity anthology, *Inspiring Creativity*. This book was borne out of a creative moment. One minute the idea was not there, the next minute, it was. The concept came to me during conversations I had sharing coaching experiences with many of the contributors in this book. I realized that my coaching cohorts -- and others like them around the world - possessed a wealth of insights to share with artists and creators of all kinds. It dawned on me that many readers could benefit if each of these practicing creativity coaches would write their wisdom in a book... and then it hit me, why not make a single book with all their tips and advice?

Inspiring Creativity is thus intended to offer you a diverse range of thought and insight into how to develop your creative potential. The 22 articles are grouped into six categories, or sections, which address fundamental issues that creative people face at some point in their careers: the need to give themselves permission to create; the drive to find and hone good ideas; the lessons to learn about overcoming fears and blocks that interfere with deepening one's work, the difficulty of finding time and space every day to do your creative work; the importance of honoring your creative soul; and the challenge of going on a creative journey wherein you finally understand your inner creative essence, your guide...your own creative hero.

You are welcome to read this book article by article in sequence or you can dip into it by individual articles as you wish, seeking insights as they pertain to your specific interests or situation in the moment.

On behalf of all 22 contributors, it is our collective hope that this anthology will inspire you in powerful ways and that your work will slowly but surely begin to move you toward realizing your full creative potential.

Rick Benzel
Publisher
Creativity Coaching Association Press
Email: publisher@creativitycoachingassociation.com

ACKNOWLEDGMENTS

The Publisher would like to gratefully thank two special people who worked tirelessly and with great creative effort to make this book an attractive, professional publication:

- Cherryl Moote, who threw her amazing design talents into developing the cover and interior design of the book, and who went above and beyond the call of duty in laying out the pages and making the whole publication process go smoothly.

- Julie Simpson, who helped nurture the idea and contributed her valuable expertise and extensive volunteer time copy-editing and proofreading the entire manuscript and participating in several important decisions in this book's publication.

In addition, I want to thank Eric Maisel, whose writings and approach to creativity coaching have mentored all of us in this book, and who provided guidance to me during the course of this project.

Finally, I thank all contributors. This anthology could not exist without their intelligent, inspiring articles.

FOREWORD

BY
ERIC MAISEL, PH.D.

❖

Creativity coaching, a brand-new twenty-first century service profession, has attracted individuals from the arts and from the helping professions who understand that the human impulse to create is both a magnificent attribute and a harbinger of great challenge. If you get it into your head that you must write novels, compose symphonies, prove or disprove string theory, or in some other way really manifest the potential of your heart, mind, and hands, you have set yourself on a journey that traditionally you have had to navigate alone. Now you need not feel completely alone: creativity coaches are available to help.

Since the field of creativity coaching is so new, most creative people know nothing about it, not even that it exists. I believe that this will change as more people enter this embryonic field and begin to work as practicing creativity coaches and as our new profession draws more attention to itself. To date, hundreds of creativity coaches have trained with me and started working with clients all over America and around the world. The essays in this collection reflect their attitudes, expertise, and understanding of the creative life. It is exciting to think that this book may be your first introduction to this new field.

What do creativity coaches do? They help clients make and sustain meaning. They investigate issues of blockage, self-doubt, anxiety, fear of failure, worries about mistakes, and other process issues and personality issues that interfere with creating. They help creators deal with marketplace issues, career issues, issues of isolation and alienation, and other problems that inevitably arise for people who choose to create. They cheerlead, listen, educate, respond, and help their clients produce deeper work and adapt better to the realities of the world.

Creativity coaching is the activity of one person helping another person with the psychological, emotional, existential, and practical problems that arise as a person tries to create. Virtually nothing is out-of-bounds as a creativity coach endeavors to help his client write, paint, invent, or compose and lead a rich life that centers around creating. I can't think of a more interesting or valuable vocation for a new century and a new millennium. It is beautiful work; it is needed work; it is one of the few new things under the sun, and it is its own work of art.

Creativity coaches also become much more effective self-coaches. The creativity coaches I train find it impossible not to look at their own creativity issues as they work with clients and ponder what hinders creative expression. A coach-in-training begins to see why she never finished her mystery novel as she works with a blocked painter or composer. A coach-in-training discovers that her negative self-talk has caused her to stand on the creativity sidelines. Coaches-in-training learn that they can be of great help to their clients and they also learn how to help themselves. Participants begin to understand, not abstractly but viscerally, what it takes to create.

Because of the Internet and phone contact, people separated by vast geographic distances can work easily and effectively with one another. A creativity coach in Ireland can work with a client in Israel. A writer in Georgia and a painter in Delhi can work with the same creativity coach in Chicago. One of the many advantages of this cyberspace opportunity is that creativity coaches who could not build a practice in their locale, because it is home to too few working artists, can build a practice by reaching out across the country and around the world. We shall see if this new cyberspace ease aids the growth of this profession. What I know for certain is that the work we do is soul-stirring and vitally needed.

As more individuals see themselves as creativity coaches, train to become creativity coaches, and begin to coach, it is natural that we will begin to hear from them. In this collection you will hear from 22 creativity coaches. The subjects they have chosen to write about include ways of unblocking, balancing creative work with the demands of everyday life, committing to your creative work and your creative nature, and other topics that will become perennials in the creativity literature. Some of the topics are broad and general, some are as specific as creating while living with a chronic illness, all are informative and engaging.

I look forward to more essays and more anthologies. It will be fascinating to read concrete pieces that relay, for instance, how a coach worked with a would-be novelist to help her begin, write, finish, and sell her novel. It will be eye-opening to see how a coach helped a painter move from his current painting style to one he'd been itching to try for a decade. I hope that you find this first collection of creativity coaching essays fascinating and I also recommend the anthologies to come in the future, anthologies to which you may want to contribute should you choose the path of creativity coach.

Creativity coaches have the opportunity to write about creativity in new and fresh ways, as befits a brand-new profession made up of practitioners who are creative themselves. I hope that in the future we see dialogue pieces, where a coach and her client write jointly about the coaching experience. I hope that we see pieces that dig deeply into the split second when a writer decides that this isn't a day to write. I hope that we see pieces that follow the creation of a mural from first idea to completed commission and the creation of a symphony from first melody to premiere performance. I hope that we really get inside the experience of people who create and that creativity coaches continue to bring their creative self to the task of exploring this territory.

The early days of psychotherapy, when Freud, Jung and Adler vied for the mantle of leader, produced a great deal of abstract theory and precious few human-sized vignettes. It will be good if, as creativity coaches explain their methods and share their ideas, we get to experience how one person worked with another person to solve problems and affect change. I can imagine that we will see excellent investigations that are grounded more in reality than in theory and that deepen our understanding of the challenging issues that all creators face. I look forward to these human-sized, intimate investigations grounded in the reality of two people working together, creativity coach and creator.

I recommend this essay collection to you on three scores. First, it will give you a sense of what creativity coaches are doing and thinking and how they conceptualize the territory in which they work. Second, something you read may help you with your own creating. You may discover that you never really had permission to create or that you've become better at suppressing your voice than heralding it and, startled by that discovery, experience an epiphany. Third, these essays may open a door for you and entice you into thinking about creativity coaching as a profession worth pursuing.

If you are interested in doing some unique, heartfelt work that can also become a revenue stream, creativity coaching may be just the ticket. If you are an artist, a helping professional like a therapist, a coach in another discipline, a teacher, or just someone excited by the vision of supporting, educating, comforting, and coaching creative and would-be creative souls, I invite you to think about training as a creativity coach. Please visit www.creativitycoachingassociation.com for information about creativity coaching, how you can train to become a creativity coach, and how you can gain certification in creativity coaching. And visit my website, www.ericmaisel.com, which contains additional information.

Let me end this brief foreword by sharing with you a letter I received not too long ago.

Dear Dr. Maisel:

Your books have meant a great deal to me in working through a lifetime of creative anorexia. The power of that self-withholding has been difficult to face and fear itself is the first and most massive desert that I feel I am still crossing. The temptation to escape into dreams of 'if only' are so warm and comforting and the distant mountains of mastery seem so remote and, when glimpsed, such cold and solitary comfort (though not without beauty) that I have been tempted more than once to go the way of the little match girl. But, as you point out, there is a force so compelling and so instinctual to create meaning in one's life, that with rather hobbled steps I'm still trying.

With that preamble, I come to the reason for my letter. I wonder if you know of any practitioners like yourself in Miami whom I can contact and get some personal support from in this effort to regain my ability to create? I am 50 years old and not unaware that my mid-life transition is making the process all the more urgent. And I imagine that I am also right in the middle of a fat demographic in this regard. But none of that discourages me. I look forward to your reply and I thank you for any time you can find to respond to my request.

This artist is not looking for a psychotherapist, a marketing guru, a painting class, or a class in creativity. She is looking for the kind of support and direction that is not offered in art schools, counseling clinics, pastoral offices, or career centers. She is one of countless people who feel an inner necessity to manifest potential and make meaning but who come up against inner and outer obstacles and become blocked and thwarted. She is looking for a creativity coach. In this anthology you will hear from some of the people who stand ready to help.

GIVE YOURSELF PERMISSION TO CREATE

IT'S NOT WHAT YOU CREATE,

IT'S THAT YOU CREATE

❖

BY KATE R. QUINLAN

We've all heard it. Many of us have muttered it in frustration, or silently surrendered to the anguished thought. "I'm just not very creative."

When I hear someone say this (or hear the words drag dejectedly through my own mind, like the losing team leaving the field), I politely but firmly repudiate this damaging admission.

True, some of us have been criticized and discouraged. We may have been told we should find something more practical to do with our spare time or our lives. Some of us lacked opportunity or a role model and have just assumed that we are in fact missing that particular speck of DNA that blesses some people with great creative genius, and passes by the rest. Regardless of why, if you think you are without creative ability, I think you're wrong.

I am intent on convincing you of two concepts. One is that you have creative ability regardless of your doubts. The second is that you should apply your creativity to enjoy its process, not solely its product.

Let me start with what I offer as proof that you, whoever, wherever you are, undeniably possess creative ability. You are innately creative by the very fact that you are human! Plants mutate. Animals adapt. But the human species manipulates the resources on this planet to meet its needs and desires. Look around! We have evolved from small foraging tribes seeking shelter in caves to tenants of high rise condos with a view to enjoy while we order our groceries online. One can simply list the creative trials and achievements that have contributed to meeting our basic human physical needs and provided for psychological well-being

3

and spiritual fulfillment. This is the legacy of our inexhaustible creative ability from all humanity, not just a select few. So to the lament, "I'm just not very creative," my response is, "That's just not very likely."

Now, it might take you some time to nudge your thinking from, "I'm just not very..." to "Oh, yes I am!" It is unlikely you will become an artist of great renown overnight. It's even unlikely that you will pick up the tools to create anything at the first blush of positive self talk about your innate ability to create. But when you do, you face the challenge of how to manifest your creativity.

This is actually a challenge similar to parenting. Those who raise children well don't try to force them into a model of what they think their children should be. Wise parents give way to each child's individuality and thereby guide, direct, and set examples. Optimally, parents enjoy the process of watching their children grow to become well adjusted adults worthy of admiration and respect.

The same holds true for nurturing your creativity. If you can view it as your child, you will begin to enjoy and fully experience the process. Like children, your creative efforts will go through stages, some thrilling, some disappointing, some causing you to want to pull your hair out, some rich with satisfaction and reward. It's a journey of hills and valleys; a timeline of events and feelings that grows to become a part of yourself that you are comfortable with and proud of.

Inevitably you will encounter notions that add to the challenge of nurturing your creativity. At the same time, you need to seek practices that enhance your creative development. Let me point out five notions you must resist and five practices to embrace in order to give your creative prodigy its best opportunity to flourish.

FIVE NOTIONS TO RESIST

Everyday you are subjected to attitudes and notions that influence your life, your thinking, your creating. Some of these attitudes are necessary cultural norms. Some are encouraging and liberating. But unavoidable are the damaging notions and opinions that can undermine your confidence. Whether a quick comment overheard, or firmly ingrained dogma, it is too easy to take on attitudes that do your spirit harm. It is paramount that you resist these notions and fortify yourself against the opinions that are not true to your thinking. They will not enhance your creating. In fact they will stifle your creative exploration. Think of it as damage control and resist taking these notions on as your own.

Assumption: As you nurture your creative self, you will often feel the nag of self-doubt. When you are in this vulnerable state, it can be easy to assume that the creative work of others is better than your own. You see the creative accomplishments of artists and crafters in the media, in galleries, on the Internet, at exhibits, workshops, and classes. This constant exposure to a variety of art and artists can lead you to assume that others have been blessed with bountiful creative abilities and you are fooling yourself to think you have any.

The assumption that the creativity of others is better than yours is false and must be resisted. In fact, the creative accomplishments of others have no reflection on your work. Discovering and exploring your creativity is not a competition. Your creative work stands alone as your creative work.

When setting out on your creative path, determining whose is better is a false destination. Your goal is to learn about your own abilities and limitations, discover and play with materials, and to thoroughly enjoy the process. When you completely engage in these moments of creating, your work is as worthy as any other. Don't make assumptions about your creative work based on the works of others.

Intimidation: When you've worked hard putting your resolute spirit into creating, it feels good to be received with resounding praise. But showing your work to others can be unnerving. Sometimes when you reveal your work to family or peers or to public view, the reception is mixed. But if you let even a single disparaging remark – even something as banal as "What's that?" – undercut your confidence, it hinders your willingness to try again. Echoes reverberate from childhood telling you to stay in the lines or that the sky should be blue.

Plentiful is the advice to just ignore what other people think (yeah, right!). It can be very difficult to ignore the reaction of others, but it is worth objective analysis. Opinion about your work will always come from a variety of sources. Ask yourself: Is this opinion coming from someone you know or respect? Do you know from where this person's attitude about your work comes? Is it experience? Ignorance? Could it be envy?

It may very well be that a dubious opinion emanates from someone who is herself intimidated by your work, and is simply responding critically in self-protection. I am not suggesting you become defensive when someone's opinion of your work is less than glowing. But I am suggesting you keep in mind the possibility that the reactions of others are not always about your work, but rather about the person voicing the opinion. This may sound like an early chapter from your Psych 101 textbook, but it is nonetheless valuable to remember. You are in a vulnerable moment when you seek compliments and get something less. This can bring on unpleasant emotional and even physical reactions. What you interpret as negative criticism can scare and intimidate. You must process others' perception of your work carefully and not let them wound your creative energies.

On the other hand, constructive criticism, critiques from peers or a master, is a wonderful gift to seek, albeit carefully. You can gain from the expert whose work you admire and whom you trust to give valuable feedback. You must trust yourself to resist being intimidated when someone is willing to risk delivering an honest appraisal.

Ironically, praise can also be intimidating. You've worked hard, all the while yearning for recognition and praise. And when the adulation arrives…whammo! Regardless of how much you wish and hope and pray for it, favorable judgment can be daunting. With acclaim can come self-doubt about the authenticity of your work or the ability to reproduce the same quality next time. A looming deadline, should your work be in demand, can intimidate anyone into a dandy of a creative block. The long sought praise, when it finally arrives, can be a double-edged sword.

It may take some personal soul searching and coaching to get you past your feelings of intimidation. Whatever it takes, you must resist intimidation and find better ways to process reactions, negative and positive, that others might express.

Implication: Sometimes those who are near and dear to you will invoke their ideas about what you "should" be creating. Comments like: "How about something to match the sofa?" or "Can you draw / paint / write something like what I saw on television or in a magazine?" These implications of how you should be doing your work, suggestions that clearly come from outside your creative exploration, are best ignored. Politely and firmly, ignored. I'm not referring to feedback or assistance you might ask for from a mentor or coach or fellow artist who knows you and your work. I'm referring to the so-called advice from someone who cares enough to offer their ideas, but has no clue what your work is really about. You need to be familiar, comfortable, and grounded in your work, and not be vulnerable to implications otherwise.

No doubt even the likes of Van Gogh, Picasso, Pollock, and other groundbreaking artists received well-meaning comments implying that they really ought to make their paintings a bit more realistic. Probably many more unknown artists endured creative lives of frustration as they let themselves be influenced by well-intentioned suggestions about their work or the trends of their time. It takes practice to develop skin tough enough to resist such advice from others, particularly when it comes with sincere amenity. But once you allow yourself to be influenced by errant implications…well, that heavy thunk you just heard was the door of a creative adventure slamming shut. Offer a simple thank you. They were, after all, just trying to help. Then stop listening and continue your creative work.

Expectation: The visionary work that occurs before getting your hands involved can take you into imagining all kinds of wonderful possibilities. A vision of what you're going to create is necessary to the task. However, expecting a singular result can obliterate your view. If you are rigid in what you are working toward, you will bypass the process and miss out on the exploration of options.

Think of all the creativity lost when an assignment is given with the words, "It should look like this when you're done." If you've heard these words (haven't we all?), abolish them from your thinking. It is the side-winding and veering off the path that takes you to new creative places. Perhaps what you thought was going to be a painting becomes a collage.

What you started as an embellished piece of clothing becomes a tapestry to hang on the wall. Or vice versa. You could end up taking on a lead role in the play when you thought you were auditioning to be in the chorus. Maybe your family expects you to complete your training in architecture, but you've discovered animation to be far more exciting. Don't charge forward hell-bent on getting to one place fast. Meander. Notice where you've been and where you might be heading. Having a single pre-defined destination reduces the many possibilities that could take you further than you expected.

Imitation: It can be tempting, particularly when your ideas are not flowing or your confidence is teetering, to look at someone else's creative accomplishments and endeavor to do the same. Sure, you might come up with something to show for it, but if it's meant to be like the work of another, it's lacking in your true and unique creative input. The effort will probably also lack in personal gratification. If you're only striving for praise, you can fool some of the people some of the time, but it's a nasty business to fool yourself!

Viewing the work of others is certainly a wonderful source of inspiration, motivation and stimulating ideas. We all study artists past and present for an overview of possibilities. It's exciting when the work of other artists spur you to explore your own creativity. But you must translate your exploration into the realm of your own creativity, doing more than adding your mark to an imitative effort. Your creative work needs to come from your inner core, your mental imagery, your exploration. In your yearning to create, you only trip yourself up by duplicating the creative efforts of others. Bypass the personal creative journey and you cheat yourself of the personal gratification, and you cheat the world of your potential.

FIVE PRACTICES TO EMBRACE

It's as important to recognize attributes that you must resist as it is to determine the behaviors to take with you on your personal creative adventure. Many will give the advice that it is essential to not be afraid of failure. They are right, but they are also oversimplifying the dilemma of feeling uncreative. It's easier to say don't be afraid than to figure out what to do with your fear. To act courageously is not to be without fear; rather, it is to go forward in spite of fear. That's the start of the adventure, taking that first step and daring to begin.

Daring: You must have the courage to begin anywhere, anytime. Better yet, you must dare to begin creating here and now. Dare to follow an unexpected direction, to take a side road that appears, to create the unforeseen. Dare to make the sky yellow. Dare to tear rather than cut the paper. Dare to photograph out of focus. Dare to put a bit of yourself into your work.

When you are creating, you are exploring what you see and feel, playing with ways to use materials and tools, combining what you discover, and creating something that didn't exist before. That takes some nerve! And it takes trial and error, and trying over again. But daring will take you to the discovery of new entities, visually, audibly, tactilely, and emotionally. In the process, you will learn great things about yourself, your vision, your heart, your endurance, perseverance, stamina, and your sense of joy.

If you never create anything that takes the art world by storm, wouldn't you still gain great things? Wouldn't you still benefit from the experience? You can't make mistakes, because there are none. So dare to begin. Think about it, talk about it, gather the materials. Pick up the brush, dab it in paint and make a mark. Now keep going. Keep trying, exploring, and daring. It will get you much further than being afraid of making a mistake.

Inkling: You simply cannot be fully aware of all that your mind holds. You can't hear every message your brain sends. Many messages you act on automatically, many are pondered, and many are dismissed or ignored. It's easy when life gets too busy to miss some of the quieter messages, the zephyr of thought that is barely perceptible with all else that is going on. But those little whispered suggestions, echoed bits of self knowledge and kernels of wisdom you've filed away are the inklings, the keys to unlocking information and ideas that reside in the back of your mind. From these inklings emerge ideas from which you can create. They are the non-automatic, the less expected, the stuff from which you can generate the extraordinary.

You need to silence the pragmatic voice and listen carefully to the more fanciful, the less reasonable, the impish, obscure and outrageous. It is definitely there, even when seemingly silenced. Listen for the voice that has ideas. Honor your intuition. Quiet the boisterous brain that says, "We should do it like this!" Hear the timid whisper that says, "What if we tried it another way?" As you practice such listening, the voice of inkling will develop the courage to speak up more frequently. You will learn to hear it more clearly, and grow more appreciative of what it has to offer.

Doing: This is the quintessence of it all. You've planted the seeds, watered, fed, and eliminated the weeds. Your creativity must blossom. The clay hits the wheel, the chisel strikes the stone, the glass goes into the flame. The creation is created.

Planning to create, yearning for it, dreaming of it, collecting the materials for it – these are the preparations to create. At some point, you must take the risk, listen to your intuition, get your hands dirty, make a mess, and create something. Create anything! All of the notions that get in your way, the intimidation, the expectations, the fear of not making the mark must be thwarted, and you must pick up the pencil and draw. Open your mouth and sing. Thread the needle and sew. Whatever it is you've wanted to do, you must get to the beginning of it and do it.

It won't be quick or easy. Life will interfere. Time and money will run short. At times you will be overwhelmed, frustrated, and discouraged. This is an integral part of the process. It makes you no less capable that you face adversity. But it does make you less productive if you don't forge ahead in spite of the adversity.

Creativity is instinctual; nevertheless it requires time, space, and commitment. Despairing that you cannot create is using energy that could be applied to creating something. Creating anything is better than perpetuating your own despair. Feeling "I'm just not very creative" is more likely an excuse for "I'm just not willing to do it."

When observing a piece of art work, we've all overheard someone say, "Sheez! I could have done that." My response is "Yes, you possibly could have done something like that!" But "could have" is not the point. The point is that someone did it! They took the time, gathered the materials, put their ego on the line, took a leap of faith and did it! We don't have to appreciate the creative efforts of everyone. But we do have to honor that the artist took steps in their personal creative journey, made their mark, and dared to display it. That's a whole lot more than saying, "I could have done that!" Doing it is the difference.

Experiencing: The reason to create artistically is to experience the process. What you create is not necessarily the objective. That you create is the profound proof of your process. You must feel the process physically and emotionally. Get your hands dirty. Feel your muscles ache. Watch the colors blend and contrast. Touch the textures you're creating. Write down and tweak and rewrite and revise and start over and try again. You want to experience getting lost in the work, totally engrossed in the task at hand.

Merriam Webster defines creativity as "to bring into existence something new." The crucial point is that creativity is not defined as the new thing produced; it is the act of bringing forth.

Do not procrastinate nor rush through the process, but savor it and tend to it with delight. If you've ever been told to hurry up and finish or to not make a mess, you will benefit by deleting those words from your memory. Linger. Thrash about. Daydream. Get things in a jumble. Be there in the Zen sense of living every moment. Mentally leave the everyday world and become oblivious to time and place. Be fully engaged. You will experience something new as it emerges before your eyes. And therein lies the bliss. Therein lies the frustration, and the excitement, and the tedium, and the gratification, and the joy. Feeling the diverse emotional range that is the process of your creating is confirmation of your being fully alive. Looking forward to the process can make you want to live a little longer and with greater satisfaction. Experiencing the creative process can get your endorphins flowing, uplift, heal, and energize you. Sharing your creativity will connect you to people and places you would not have known otherwise. The experience can expose qualities about yourself that you were previously unaware of. This is the pay-off. Installation in a gallery is fantastic. Rave reviews, hundreds sold, reprints, and repeat commissions are exhilarating and perhaps profitable. But what you create is the simply the evidence. That you live the experience is the true reward.

Rejoicing: By all means, celebrate your creative efforts! Set aside modesty and revel in a bit of self appreciation. Be pleased! Be proud! Show some excitement that you've created something! Hang your work on the living room wall. Wear your art when you're out and about. Say "Thank you! I made this!" Have an open house to show your work. Approach a gallery. Submit to a publisher. Toast your accomplishment. Giggle over it a bit. Pat yourself on the back and acknowledge a job well done. You have earned the privilege to indulge. Take pleasure in what you experienced and what you have to show for it. You resisted the intimidation, ignored the assumptions and implications. You kept your mind open and your hands busy. You dared to take the leap and enjoyed your journey. You created your own work. Congratulations are definitely in order!

THE ULTIMATE TRUTH

It is imperative that we all discover and encourage our own creativity. We must be wary of that which becomes an obstacle and embolden that which will open the doors. Creativity is waiting to seep out, to flow, and to tumble forth in torrents. We are healthier and happier when we dare to act on our creativity, when we foster the creative ability within us – and all around us! While nurturing our own creative instincts, by example we encourage the creative abilities of others. Much psychology can be explored as to why we lose our creative vitality. Imagine how wonderful if throughout our lives we were encouraged to pursue our ideas and enjoy our creative experience. All of us need to recognize and hold on to the truth that it's not what we create, it's that we create.

❖ ❖ ❖

Kate Quinlan is a creativity coach with a background in education, social work, interior design, and art history. Having spent much of the first half of her life clinging to her creativity in spite of feeling intimidated and assuming that everyone else's work was better than hers, she will dare to follow her inklings and experience the rest of her life as an artist, writer, and coach encouraging everyone in her path to partake on their own creative journey. She welcomes email at krquinlan@yahoo.com.

Kate is grateful to her husband, Roger for his steadfast inspiration and corroboration. Also for the boundless support from her children, who are undoubtedly her finest creative accomplishment.

CREATIVITY IS YOUR BIRTHRIGHT

HOW TO GET OVER FEELING YOU DON'T HAVE "PERMISSION" TO CREATE

❖

BY DAVE STORER

Several common lines of thought lead many people to the false conclusion that they don't have the right, or sufficient "permission" to create. Some examples:

- Only the "true" artists – the really talented ones – get to create. All the rest of us are amateurs and dilettantes and should be embarrassed to admit to any artistic interest or ambition.

- If you don't demonstrate great talent, or at least serious potential, pretty much right from the beginning of your engagement with an art form, then you're clearly not one of the above mentioned "true" artists and so you better not embarrass yourself by going any further.

- Someone with acknowledged authority to judge talent in a given art form must "anoint" you as one of the chosen few soon after you start. For example, you need to get published impressively, or you need to be accepted into an art school or MFA program, etc. at a young age, or the professionals in your art form will forever consider you an outsider and the rest of society will look on you as a poser.

In some ways, these thoughts reflect a harsh reality for many artists, writers, musicians, and movie makers in our society, especially for those who want to be considered professionals in a given creative field. But in most cases, these attitudes are purely myth and keep far too many people from acting on their creative needs and pursuing their artistic dreams.

We are all born with incredible creative abilities, and few things in life make us happier than fully engaging those abilities. To let a belief that we haven't the proper "permission" – from either society, family and friends, or ourselves – stop us from developing our creative abilities and expressing our deepest, truest selves in the best creative way we know how would be a terrible loss. The choice to create is yours; no one else should be given the power or authority to stop you.

The various messages we get that tell us we haven't the right to create can be separated into three categories:

- What society as a whole tells us
- What our family and friends tell us
- What we tell ourselves

Let's take a close look at these and bust the myths behind them.

HOW SOCIETY TELLS US NOT TO CREATE

What are the societal forces arrayed against creativity? For one, our society is highly competitive – we seem to want to make everything we can into a win/lose proposition. Today's reality television especially takes this to a ridiculous level. The networks give us competitive tourism ("The Amazing Race"), competitive camping ("Survivor"), competitive dating ("The Bachelor" and "The Bachelorette"), and even competitive plastic surgery ("The Swan"). Even the singing competition, "American Idol," while not evil in itself and in some ways almost democratic, nonetheless creates just one winner and hundreds of thousands of losers a year.

What we must remember is that at a very basic level of the human psyche, we are all strongly encouraged by winning versus strongly discouraged by losing. For many, it takes just one loss to stop creativity cold. My own writing career is a case in point. Just out of college, I wrote one short story, sent it to one magazine, got one rejection note and didn't write seriously again for years. Many writers I've met tell a very similar story.

Some might counter this by saying competition makes us stronger. This is true to some extent, but in the end, competition does more harm than good. Hyper-competitiveness most often creates a small handful of lucky people with extremely fragile, over-blown reputations, behind which stand legions of dispirited "losers."

You might say that everyone is free to create in the so-called privacy of their own home, because clearly everyone who wants to be published in the New Yorker or exhibited in the Louvre hasn't the right to be. Yes, but the question isn't whether everyone who wants it should have the right to succeed commercially with their creative efforts, but rather whether everyone should feel they have the right to embark on a creative enterprise regardless of their perceived talent or commercial potential. To that, the answer is a resounding YES.

We can easily see the effect of competitiveness on creativity in the schools. In the public school art classes of my youth ('60s and early '70s), the teachers often seemed to be looking for the one or two kids in the whole school whom they thought were really talented, the ones they could encourage just as one of their own early teachers had clearly encouraged them. The rest of us, who didn't take immediately to drawing or painting or sculpture, were essentially ignored. We weren't encouraged, or given the chance to start by making a real mess, or to fail and yet not give up if that's what we really wanted.

I was never actively insulted by my art teachers, but neither was I truly encouraged. For example, in junior high school, I made a polar bear (and the seal he'd just caught!) out of clay. It wasn't brilliant – but I loved it. The success I felt I'd had with it thrilled me. (Okay, it was a little over-the-top adolescent male; the bear's eyes didn't really need to be blood red.) But the point is, my art excited me and I wanted to do more. The teacher didn't seem to notice though, saying nothing positive or negative, and thus a great interest in working with clay died. I suppose if my interest had been greater, or if I'd had more inherent confidence, I would have tried harder to do more of it. But the point is, teachers, parents, and everyone else who fail to engage kids deeply enough to see, feel, and nurture their creative needs engender negative effects on kids' creative lives.

I believe many art teachers are afraid to encourage any but the most wildly promising young artist because of what they see as the risks involved. If I were teaching art, I wouldn't want to give any of my students false hopes either – such as telling them they should not bother getting a"real " job because they are wildly talented and are destined to become a great genius if they simply dedicate themselves completely to their bottle cap art. After all, let's be honest, many young people are only too eager to latch onto any praise and use it as the basis for some pretty wild dreams.

But this leads me to announce one of the bedrock truths of creativity coaching: People are always to be encouraged and supported in their wildest creative dreams, yet grounded in reality. It's desirable and possible to say to a budding artist, "It's clear that your bottle cap art is deeply important to you, and I think you should dive as deeply into it as you feel you must, and here are some ideas that might help you do that, but it might not be a good idea to quit your job just yet. What do you think?" In other words, *all* children (and adults!) can be encouraged to create without making them dangerously impractical, or giving them a greatly exaggerated sense of their own chances of commercial success.

Our society emphasizes competition between creatives in the marketplace as well. Critics love to tell us how very few of the books, paintings, movies, and CDs are"worth " the price. There is a valuable service in this – after all, who wants to spend money on a bad movie or book, etc. – but again this type of competition creates artificial winners and losers. The five to ten movies that receive major Oscar nominations a year get a bonanza of free publicity that convinces millions more people to pay to see them, but what happens to all the other movies? Only five movies a year can be nominated for "Best Picture," but does that mean that only five movies a year are truly worthy? Again, the outcome seems to be that by raising up the few, you suppress the many.

Consider also that keeping a tight lid on the number of individual artists who are generally thought to be"worth the price " keeps the price for those chosen few unnaturally high. The more a gallery owner is able to convince the art-buying public that their artist is a"genius " far above anyone else, the more money they'll be able to get for their art.

HOW FRIENDS AND FAMILY MAY CONVINCE US NOT TO CREATE

There are other forces at work in our immediate social circle of family, friends, and co-workers that often stop us from creating. These include various "attitudes" that such people aim at us, including:

The"Puritan Work Ethic " Attitude

This attitude suggests that we must work very hard every waking hour of our lives (except on Sundays), but more to the point, there's the added suggestion that work can't be fun. There would seem to be something immoral about loving your job, not to mention spending a significant part of your life deep in the "play" of creating. My wife once heard someone say,"My brother hasn't worked in thirty years. He's a sculptor." Rodney Dangerfield got more respect than the average, truly hard working artist.

The "Work Must Pay" Attitude

This is the attitude that the only possible benefit from acting on our creative urges should be monetary, or "If you can't sell it for a lot of money, then what's the point of doing it at all?"

As I'm sure many of you already know, if you tell a stranger that you're an artist or writer, most likely the first thing they'll ask you is how much money you've made doing it, or where have you been published or displayed that they might have seen? This perception is deeply embedded in our culture and ignores the many huge personal rewards of creating that have nothing to do with money, as well as the fact that every art form requires a very long apprenticeship before the artist can come anywhere close to being paid good money or appearing in a widely circulating form. To paraphrase Yogi Berra, it takes many years to be an overnight success. But our culture seems to forget that, which puts undue pressure on beginners and even intermediate level artists to feel they need to succeed, long before they should even be thinking about it.

The"What Kind of a Thing is that to Do? " Attitude

It can be very hard to maintain your identity as an artist if you embark on a pursuit that seems completely alien to your friends or family. This is partially why many successful people in many fields simply come from families who've been doing the same thing for a long time. For example, star quarterbacks are often the sons of football coaches, stock-brokers spawn stockbrokers, artists spawn artists and writers spawn writers – Martin Amis, the Cheever family, the Fondas and Douglas's, and others.

This is more than chance, and more than genetics. It's cultural. If your family values art and self-expression highly; if there are successful people creating all around you as you grow up, modeling every day the skills and attitudes needed to succeed in art, you will be much more inclined to think you have the "right" to do it, and you'll probably get a lot of good help and encouragement along the way.

For example, consider how Jane Yolen described her support, in her wonderful book for writers, *Take Joy*:

> When I was growing up, I thought all adults were writers. My father was a journalist, my mother a short story writer. Their friends were all authors, and my father was president of the Overseas Press Club. More writers. We lived first in New York City, then in Westport, Connecticut. Even more writers.

> If I thought about adults at all, I thought of them as writers. Of course I knew there were teachers and doctors and librarians and butchers (this was a long time ago!) Those were their everyday jobs. But at home, late at night, I knew all those grownups were scribbling away.

> It came as quite a shock to me to discover, rather late in my elementary school life, that most adults were actively afraid of writing.

Don't we all wish we were raised in such a family and social circle? How much more comfortable might we feel in our creative skins?

HOW WE CONVINCE OURSELVES NOT TO CREATE

All the above issues regarding how others try to stop us from creating only affect us if we let them. Your identity – who you are and what you do – resides inside you; it doesn't come from anyone or anywhere else. It is like the creative process itself. So you might say, if you can't look to someone else to do your creating for you, then why should you look to others for permission to create?

The most important permission you can give yourself when it comes to creativity is the permission not only to try, but also the permission to fail. One failure, as we've seen, does not and should not convince you that your creative dreams and goals must be given up. Failure is a very big part of every successful person's life. Remember that Edison tried *thousands* of different alloys as filaments for a workable light bulb before he came up with one that actually did work. Think of it – he didn't let thousands of failures stop him.

Yes, it can be quite challenging to continue to see yourself as a creative person if no one else is willing to see you in that way, but this simply comes down to a chicken and egg situation – most people in our culture will not let you easily claim a creator's identity. They will push against you and demand "proof" of your creative talent. When that happens, many of us give up simply because we get tired of having to push back against this sort of pressure. We end up feeling like impostors:"I say I'm an artist, but no one seems to be buying it. It must all be a sham. I'm not sure I can keep this up. "

In these situations, the best philosophy to live by is "fake it 'til you make it." That's true whenever you enter into any kind of new identity. It happens when you graduate and start your first "real" job, it happens when you change overnight from a worker to a boss; it happens when you get married or when you have your first child. These are times when you just have to grow into your role before the identity involved seems completely real to you, let alone those around you.

When I say "fake it 'til you make it," what I should more accurately say is, "even though your chosen creative identity feels unreal somehow, if you keep doing it – keep working at your art with all of your heart and muscle – sooner than you think, you will be perfectly comfortable with that identity and so will most everyone you know." The identity comes from the doing of it.

Similarly, many of us worry that we aren't passionate enough to be "real" artists or writers, etc., but again, this is chicken/egg thinking. Your passion for a creative activity may be dampened by the internal and external resistance that keeps you from the actual creating. I promise you that the more deeply and often you get into your art, the more passionate about it you'll become. The equation is *not*:

NO PASSION = NO PERMISSION

The true equation is:

DEEP CREATIVE INVOLVEMENT $\longrightarrow$ PASSION FOR YOUR ART

Finally, let me discuss the issue of "talent." Clearly, there is such a thing as talent in every art form. I have no doubt that some artists have more raw talent (genetic "giftedness") than the rest of us, but I think the idea of talent, or the lack thereof, is one of the easiest excuses people use to avoid the hard work necessary to achieve their creative dreams.

Most of us couldn't become concert pianists no matter how hard we tried, but on the other hand, how many of us try that hard? How can you be so sure you're not"gifted " enough to achieve your creative goals? A fair number of successful artists, musicians, and writers downplay how very hard they've worked to get where they are, and if they do this, it may be just to enhance their image as"naturals. "

But "talent" is nothing more than a predisposition to do something well. At best, it's a head start, at worst it becomes a curse of impatience, arrogance, and over-confidence. Remember the fable of the Tortoise and the Hare! It applies here precisely. Some successful artists promote their own genius myth because it sounds a lot better than, "I just worked my butt off." And it keeps the rest of us from realizing we could do it too, if we truly dedicate ourselves to the art forms we love, and put in the necessary time and effort.

Another problem is that we're often afraid to reveal our true selves – our deepest dreams and wishes – afraid to put them out there in public where a stranger's rejection or ridicule can chop off our dream as quickly as a guillotine blade slicing through a neck bone. So we seek creative permission in order to feel safe in our creating, safe from rejection and ridicule, but the hard truth is that we're never completely safe when we're creating something new. We may try to hedge our bets various ways, but whenever we create, we are going out on a limb. In fact, we're launching off into the unknown without any guarantee of success whatsoever.

Even experienced, long-successful, wildly celebrated novelists still write the occasional clunker. You never know for sure what the result will be. The best you can hope for is that with time, experience, and artistic growth, you'll improve your ratio of good works to bad. So if you think that some expert's approval of you as an artist somehow guarantees the success of your next project, you're wrong.

The long and short of it is, don't give anyone sovereignty over your own true creative needs and interests. The creative process is everyone's birthright; artistic skills are everyone's to acquire and develop and, most important, as we create, we heal psychic wounds, forge deep connections, and create meaningful wholes, for ourselves and whomever we touch with our work. Being creative is truly"soul food. "

PRACTICAL SUGGESTIONS FOR GIVING YOURSELF PERMISSION

What are some specific, practical things you can do to get to a place where you feel you absolutely have the right to create and can begin to connect deeply with your own creative process and start to actively pursue your creative dreams?

- **Look deep within yourself** to discover who you really are and what you really want to do. The answers to these questions are *inside* you. The more strongly and clearly you see yourself, the less vulnerable you will be to the opinions and attitudes of others. Meditate. Clear the chatter of your mind and get to the bedrock truth of your creative essence.

- **Be BOLD.** Declare your identity to the world. Decide what your artistic ambitions and intentions are, and tell everyone you know. If you are confident and decisive, you will get much better responses than you expect. As Goethe said,"Whatever you can do, or dream you can, begin it. Boldness has genius, power, and magic in it. "

- **Change your culture.** Do what you can to drop from your everyday life people who seem to feel they have the right to tell you what you can and cannot do and who you can and cannot be – the people who seem threatened by your possible success and happiness. Surround yourself instead with people who give you strength through their own honesty while keeping you honest with yourself. Seek out an artist's group that supports your creative goals, or start one yourself. Few things are more invigorating than truly helping other people with their own dreams. Read biographies of your favorite artists and other successful creators.

- **Dedicate yourself to skill building in your chosen form.** Take classes, on-line or in person. Dive into a skill building book like *Drawing on the Right side of the Brain*, or *Writing Fiction*, by the Gotham Writers' Workshop, or *The Creativity Book*, by Eric Maisel. Dedicate yourself to an artistic mentor in your field who is willing to take you under her wing and pass on her own hard-won skills. This is an ancient and honorable practice, and very rewarding for both apprentice and master.

- **Learn more about the creative process.** Read books on creativity, take a workshop, or hire a creativity coach. Join or start a group dedicated to exploring the creative process in your chosen form. Get together with like-minded people to make, do, create – just to see what happens. Groups can be very liberating, instructive, and a whole lot of fun.

- **Commit to your creating.** When you finally get over worrying about whether you can or should do it, and manage to commit fully to your creative goals, you will really start to get into "flow." That is when your passion will kick in. That is when the magic will start to happen.

The key to successful creating is easy to state (though not always easy to achieve): Clarify your goals, commit to them fully, and start to act on them with all of your heart and mind. That is what every "genius" and otherwise satisfied creator discovers sooner or later. And there's nothing stopping you from doing the same.

Good luck and joyous creating!

❖ ❖ ❖

Dave Storer has been writing fiction for many years and, among other credits, has published a short story in *American Way*, the in-flight magazine of American Airlines. He has degrees in Biology and English, and Technical Writing and lives in his home town of Ann Arbor, Michigan after having completed the requisite ten-year vagabondage on the West Coast. As a creativity coach, he focuses on helping beginning and intermediate writers and other creators, with classes and workshops that support all phases of the creative life, from setting and achieving goals, to skill-building and effective marketing. He can be reached at davidstorer@msn.com or at 734-646-1101.

BECOMING AN "IMPERFECTIONIST"

HOW TO STOP LETTING PERFECTIONISM KEEP YOU FROM BEING THE ARTIST YOU FEAR

BY EDWARD B. KURPIS

The article you are about to read is not perfect. I wanted very much to make it an ideal piece, replete with deep insights, embellished with powerful words and startling images that would amaze you and make you wish you too could be artistically brilliant. That was my vision for this writing, as it had been for most creative endeavors I undertake.

Fortunately though, I have learned that ideal articles don't get written, so I wrote this one instead. It is an example of the fact that many people have excellent creative ideas that never get off the ground or go anywhere because they believe their finished work has to be perfect. After all, how can wanting to be perfect be detrimental? Think of the phrases:

"If I can't do it right, I might as well not do it at all."

"My work is not ready to be seen."

"As soon as I perfect my idea, I'll get it started."

"You don't really want to read my story; it's not all that good."

"No one will ever buy my work, I'm just a beginner."

In my years of experience as a creativity coach and consultant to individuals and companies looking for ways to become more innovative, I have found that the goal of creating something perfect holds back many would-be artists from being productive individuals. Perfectionism unknowingly creates false expectations. It helps to plant seeds of doubt and stifles even the most imaginative and talented people.

19

IS THIS HAPPENING TO YOU?

Perfectionism sounds like a terrific ideal. Shouldn't it be something to strive for?

Yes, it can be good to reach for excellence. Producing your best work is an understandable and productive goal. But when the quest for perfection derails your creative process, something else may be going on. Understanding the true meaning of perfectionism and the influence it may be having in your creative life may be the first step in freeing up the blocks you have when you are seeking to create.

My own awareness of the hidden meaning of perfectionism was awakened one groggy morning over a cup of coffee and a serious contemplation of my refrigerator door. I had not noticed, until that moment, that this surface had become a veritable annex to the Guggenheim, literally transformed into a gallery of modern artwork from my precocious six year-old niece Gabrielle. Hers were colorful scribbles – dozens of abstract paintings of people and animals I was supposed to have known but did not recognize – and other mysterious inventions from her imaginative mind. Gabby was a veritable artwork factory. Each day she happily produced scores of new drawings that pushed the bounds of creativity, which she shared with everyone around her. She did not really care if you liked her work or not; her personal goal was to create the art and get it out into the world to be seen. Her obliviousness to what others thought or whether they even understood her art resulted in a huge portfolio of creative work that told us more about her ideas, personality, and spirit than we could ever have learned from any other source. Her art, in her own mind, was always perfect, the ideal expression of herself.

On that day, Gabby's "perfect" work caused me to reflect on why many would-be artists who strive to create meaningful stories, pictures, or music are not always able to approach their creative work with the same sense of fearlessness and abandon.

Years ago I had a creativity coaching client, Sylvan, who wanted very much to begin writing a novel he had been dreaming about for years. But he had great difficulty getting started on it and sought my help in motivating him to press forward on his project. When I first met him in his office, I noted how it was filled with how-to books on creative writing, tips for agent hunting and book publishing, and marketing ideas. He also had a large collection of beautiful writing journals designed to artfully memorialize his creative thoughts, yet they were all completely blank. Files he had set up for the work he had completed on the novel project consisted of some very studied (yet unfinished) outlines and a few notes he had taken over the years sketching out his ideas for yet more novels, screenplays, articles and poems that he intended to write one day. Plus he had lists of other "legitimate ideas" that he was sure "would sell" as soon as they were developed. All of these projects were duly documented on his perpetual to-do list.

Sylvan was organized and efficient, but not producing the work he longed to create. When I asked him why he was unable to take any meaningful steps toward beginning his dream project, he had only one explanation: he was a perfectionist. For years he had been fiercely rationalizing that his work had to be more complex, more difficult and more demanding. It had to be carefully crafted and full of precious intent and meaning. It had to display his talents in the most perfect light so that he would be taken seriously as a writer by those in the writing establishment. He craved for other professionals to see just how talented he was. He felt that it had to be perfect before it was done. And he swore it would be…as soon he could get around to working on it.

As you might imagine, Sylvan's perfectionism was at the core of his inability to create. As we spoke further over the months of my consulting work, we began to observe what perfectionism really meant to him. Believing he was a perfectionist was actually Sylvan's way to avoid those very painful moments that most artists experience at some point of their development: the fear of being judged.

Whenever an individual seeks to be perfect – in their home, their work, perhaps in their personal grooming or their creative endeavors – this is frequently an attempt to make oneself immune to criticism. When the products of one's personal efforts are open to being observed, analyzed, or criticized, the possibility always exists that others will indeed see the negatives and speak out against the results. Holding out for perfection thus becomes a way to shield oneself from criticism. If what I do is perfect, then I am beyond reproach.

At the heart of this avoidance of criticism are both a fear of rejection and a desire to be loved and accepted by others, powerful social needs in all human beings. The noted psychologist Abraham Maslow explained how these forces clearly impact behavior in his acclaimed theory of the human "hierarchy of needs." His well-accepted theory explains, in part, that in order to develop a true sense of self-esteem and thefull realization of one's potential, certain lower-order needs must be protected and resolved first, including the fulfillment of a sense of belonging, social acceptance, or love. Criticism is a form of rejection that serves to negate feelings of acceptance. In a sensitive or insecure individual, this may result in a loss of productivity, a creative block, or a desire to avoid the very type of work that would have personal meaning for that person.

This is particularly true of the personal work done by most artists and creatively inspired people. The act of creating something – an idea, a character in a play, a song, even a chocolate cake – is usually a powerful representation of oneself. Artists and creators in all fields often seek a measure of personal fulfillment, recognition, or admiration through their private efforts and expressions of art. Seeking that kind of acceptance from those efforts is fraught with potentially devastating consequences, particularly if the need for such reinforcement is personally meaningful to the artist.

The quest for perfectionism itself can lead to self-critical behaviors. In the avoidance of rejection or criticism of others, artists frequently end up rejecting or criticizing *themselves*, the very action they seek to avoid! "We run toward that which we fear most," a noted psychotherapist in New York once recounted to me, meaning that many people can identify their anxieties but are powerless to stop themselves from creating the very conditions for their anxiety to blossom.

Another creativity coaching client of mine, David, was a would-be actor who suffered from paralyzing stage fright. After many discussions about the genesis of his fear, we saw that it came down to David's desire to be the perfect actor in front of his audience. He was powerfully afraid of forgetting his lines and breaking character, a sign of his incompetence, as he explained it. Yet on stage, before any lines were spoken, staring into the eyes of that audience, it made him feel the heat of their potential judgment of him and his craft, which caused him to freeze up and forget his lines. That, of course, made David experience the fear he had initially only imagined. In criticizing himself before the audience did, David created the very conditions he feared most.

THE IMPERFECT ANSWERS TO PERFECTIONISM

Although your awareness of the problem of perfectionism may be enough to get you back on track, most artists need to take additional productive steps to control and counteract the blocks they may have created from an overemphasis on perfectionism. Here are four ideas to help you deal with this dilemma:

1. **Secure greater confidence in your skills or abilities.** Often the fear of being improperly judged stems from a lack of security in the amount or type of training an artist has had. People who begin creative projects without some formal training, education or professional experience often suffer from the fear of being criticized as amateurish. This anxiety can lead to a hyper-sensitivity to the potential for error and thus a reliance on the expressed desire to want to be perfect.

   If you lack training, experience, or even an understanding of how the rules of the game are played in your industry, seek to enhance your natural abilities with some measure of authentic training. Look for continuing education courses or other refresher classes in acting, painting, creative writing, design, or whatever your field of art is. Seek groups functioning at your level or below and find environments where it's OK to be less than perfect. Introductory classes are typically designed to allow for the grooming of talent through safe criticism.

2. **Practice making mistakes.** Give yourself permission to do "bad work." Not everything you create needs to be Mozart, Monet, or Mamet. In fact, set out to be the *anti-master*. Be messy on pur-

pose; intend to write bad poetry; make a soufflé and then jump around your kitchen to make sure it falls. In other words, as an exercise, strive to be human. Most importantly, share these failures with everyone you know. Just don't tell them you failed on purpose. Have a few good private laughs as you put everyone in the uncomfortable position of examining the worst of your worst. Feel what it feels like to hear the less than perfect reactions you get – and not care about what's being said – since you directed this experiment. Do this until you develop the understanding that you can divorce yourself from any harsh reactions of others.

3. **Actively seek criticism by taking control of it.** Kelly, a coaching client who feared displaying her artwork because it was not perfect in her eyes, sought some coaching on how to overcome this resistance. We addressed the issue by taking small, incremental steps to control the amount and level of exposure, and therefore criticism, she would get.

I asked Kelly to take one of her completed pieces she was most reluctant to show, and to hang it on a wall for one week only, in a place where no one other than she would see it. Just knowing that it was hanging up somewhere was enough to start her. After a week, we hung the painting on a different wall, this time when the chances were remote, but not impossible, that someone else might see it. In another week, we moved it again to a slightly more populated area. Each week we continued to increase the level of exposure of the artwork and thus the potential for someone else to see and even comment on it. As the days went by, the fear of making the work public was gradually desensitized. Through this experience, Kelly's fear of criticism was diminished since she was controlling the amount of exposure the work received over time. After a month of seeing her work hanging on the wall, she became less aware of it and the reactions it was getting. After two months, Kelly decided to show the painting to the women at her workplace and later took it to a sidewalk art fair. The painting was sold within the week.

4. **Understand what you need from your creative work. Seek intrinsic rewards.** Many people do things for the rewards they offer. What type of rewards are you seeking from your creative work? Are they primarily extrinsic rewards – money, recognition, fame, acceptance from others? Whenever individuals seek externally generated rewards, that is, rewards that rely on others to confer them upon you, they put their long term satisfaction in the hands of others. The motivation to pursue your work under those circumstances can be easily derailed because external rewards offer less genuine satisfaction in the long run than intrinsic, or internal, rewards. The problem with extrinsic rewards is that the good feelings they provide are usually temporary and often only fuel the pursuit of more external acknowledgements, which can become

unattainable. Furthermore, people will always measure the level of rewards they receive against the rewards received by others. When the amount of your reward is not perceived to be equitable when compared to others, you feel cheated, or "less than" another, and your performance will likely suffer from it. Motivation is hard to maintain when you don't see yourself being treated equally.

Intrinsic rewards, on the other hand, are long lasting and ultimately more satisfying. An internal feeling of pride, satisfaction and achievement, not conferred by others but derived from your own true sense of self, is the real nirvana we seek as artists. Living up to your own standards of perfection – for achieving a goal you longed to complete, for starting a project dear to your heart – doesn't require trophies, ribbons or medals to mark accomplishment and a sense of personal fulfillment. Seek to do work that has that kind of personal meaning to you. The rest will follow.

And wouldn't that be the perfect way to create?

❖ ❖ ❖

Edward B. Kurpis is a nationally-respected strategic marketing and media authority, who is credited with being the co-founder/co-developer of cable network CNBC, the premiere world-wide business news channel that broadcasts globally to over 100 million homes today. Mr. Kurpis has developed a strong reputation for innovation in the media industry, as a dynamic and creative force in business development, with a long string of innovations, including creating and/or developing over 20 successful network and other new media business ventures for NBC. Today those "ideas" are valued at over $3 billion.

Ed is currently an active writer and artist, and the President and CEO of the New York Institute for Creativity. His services include education and training, public and motivational speaking, management consulting and creativity coaching for individuals and businesses across the U.S., specializing in the fields of personal artistic and creativity development and innovation management insights for business.

If you are interested in hearing more about Ed's workshops, seminars, professional consulting opportunities or other ideas, insights or guidance, he may be reached at the New York Institute for Creativity via e-mail at CreativityInstit@aol.com. Ask to sign up for his unique free e-newsletter!

CHOOSE
A MUSE
FOR
INSPIRATION

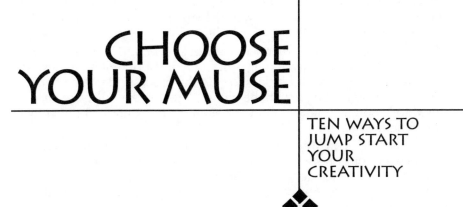

CHOOSE YOUR MUSE

TEN WAYS TO
JUMP START
YOUR
CREATIVITY

STACEY RASFELD

The Ancient Greeks explained the world around them by attributing power and influence to a pantheon of gods and goddesses. They worshipped gods of thunder, the sun, war, and love. They also honored goddesses that governed the arts – The Muses.

The nine Muses are the daughters of Zeus (King of the Gods) and Mnemosyne (Titan Goddess of Memory). Each Muse personifies a particular human desire or emotion leading to a different expression of creativity. Although each Muse inspires a specific art form, each also represents basic creative ideals that apply to all of the arts.

Even today, the Muses can be powerful guides to an exploration of the different facets of creativity. Angeles Arrien, in her book, *The Nine Muses*, writes, "Muses are divine forces ... that guide us in the making and remaking of the human spirit and the world."

Let's consider how each Goddess' specialty can inspire us to look at our own creative process in new ways. The following tricks will call down their assistance and trigger Divine a-Muse-ment!

MNEMOSYNE

Mnemosyne is the Goddess of Memory and the mother of the nine Muses. She embodies creation, synthesis, innovation and imagination. Just as the Muses were born from the union of Intention (Zeus) and Imagination (Mnemosyne), so too is a creative act born from a combination of personal passion and will.

Art is cut of the cloth of one's personal life experience, burnished and enlivened by detail and texture. Put your unique point of view, your life experience into the mix. What does Life look like from behind your rose-colored glasses? How does it feel to walk in your loafers / Mary Janes / Sketchers / Manolo Blahniks? Embrace your own imagination, innovation and creativity.

Natalie Goldberg, in her seminal book, *Writing Down The Bones*, devotes a chapter to developing a personal a list of writing topics. Ms. Goldberg provides a list of ideas to start the process. Idea Number Two admonishes us to "begin with the phrase, 'I remember.'" We are encouraged to keep going and to fall back on the catch phrase "I remember" when bogged down.

What do you remember? Remember with all your senses. Remember someone who inspired you: their voice, the texture of their skin, their idiosyncratic habits. Or, recall a childhood memory: the smells, the sounds. For me, the smell of popcorn sends me reeling – specifically, movie theater popcorn.

> Friday nights, in Chicago, in the early '70s. My sister and I meet my mother at the "El" after work. It's hot. It's dusty. The concrete floor of the station is damp. We've scanned face after face until she FINALLY appears. We three run across the street, under the tracks, to Johnny's Dog Town. The air is heavy with salt and hot oil. We stuff Mom's big purse with hotdogs, fries and tamales. We hurry back across the street to the Bryn Mawr Theater and pay our $1.60 to the ticket taker.

> The lobby is cool and dry. The air is buttery sweet, stronger than the hot dog smell from my mother's purse. The concession stand is a brilliant blue-white oasis in the long dark carpeted lobby. We buy one large Coke and small buttered popcorn. Tonight, Mom buys a box of Jr. Mints and a Butterfinger. We find seats, and dig in. Cartoons. Two different movies.

> This is a really good night: we leave after the second feature and go to the bookstore on the corner. Two comic books and a novel later, we snuggle together on Mom's enormous queen-sized sofa bed and read until our eyes droop shut.

This memory transports me to the safest haven I've ever known – Heaven from one whiff of movie popcorn! Where will your nose take you? How far can you travel on the touch of silk or the feel of sand between your toes?

CALLIOPE

Calliope is the Goddess of Eloquence, Epic Poetry, Drama, Performance, Communication, Transmission and Storytelling. Think *The Iliad* and *The Odyssey* or Huckleberry Finn's journey down the Mississippi.

What are your stories? Where have you wandered? What was your Great Adventure? Write, paint and dance to find your way home.

Write an epic poem to one great love, your first pet, a kindergarten playmate, your 'Nana or Uncle Joe. Be overly dramatic, bombastic. Break all the rules of grammar and punctuation you learned in school.

Or make like Michelangelo and paint your own Sistine Chapel on the bedroom ceiling.

CLIO

Clio is the Muse of History and Writing, the impulse to ferret out Truth and celebrate Knowledge.

Feed your need to know what happened and why. Proclaim yourself a witness to Joy and celebrate the people around you. Cultivate a perspective of all the events that have transpired throughout time. Let human cruelty and foolishness drive you mad. Be wise and grow a compassionate heart.

Dig into your own history. Do you have a genealogy chart of your family? If not, start one. Drag out old photo albums, sit down and have a beer with your grandfather. Listen to his war stories. Visit your aunt for afternoon tea and record her memoirs.

ERATO

Erato is the Goddess with many faces: she is the Muse of the four aspects of Love. Her compassionate face is called Agape; her drive to procreate and create, Eros. Libido expresses sensuality, sexuality and physical desire and Philia navigates the rules of friendship.

Open yourself to love in all its forms: sex and heart and emotion. Be open to the thrall of love, to twisted and hysterical love, thwarted love, jealous love, love left-behind, adultery and deviation. Discover spiritual love.

We decide what is left to show for our finite parade of days: material possessions, worldly achievements… and the love given to others.

Create art designed to be given away: a card, a coupon book of comfort, hugs and backrubs, a drawing of your niece's secret smile. Write a song and help a friend through her divorce. In the end, all we have is what we are every day. We are what we do, share, give and love every hour, every minute and every second.

EUTERPE

Muse of Music and Lyric Poetry, Euterpe wields the power of intuition, beyond words.

Music can put you in a trance. Music is healing, and creates a bridge through pain and suffering. Music is magic. Music is personal. Music reminds us we are alive and connected to something larger than ourselves. Music inflames, incites, and provokes. Holding onto the dragon as it flies is a heady experience. As musicians, we strum, strike, stroke, pluck, pick, sing and blow through that crazy energy. We try to fashion a life out of these singular, sonic moments.

Set aside a couple of hours one weekend afternoon to honor the Composer, Musician, Performer, Diva, Conductor, Singer, Guitarist, Rocker or Rapper within you.

Not musical, you say? Well...

Get into the shower and belt out an aria. Buckle yourself into your car and drive down the highway, radio blasting. Wander down to the ocean and chant into the waves.

My sister and I used to scream Beatles songs into hairbrush microphones. Go out tonight and give it your karaoke best.

Pay attention: there is music all around you. The wind whistles. Feet slap against pavement. Tires screech. A billboard calls to you. The grace of a traffic cop makes you weep. Notice that stockbroker at the front of the line tapping his leg impatiently. What is the rhythm of newspaper against khaki?

Stop trying – just listen.

Stop right now and close your eyes. Go ahead. Do it.

Take a deep, slow breath. Then another. And another.

Let your shoulders fall, and your jaw unclench and listen to the sounds around you at this moment..

In this second of stillness, hear the opening strains of your favorite piece: let Satie, Monk, Billie, Miles, Lennon & McCartney or Snoop seep into your consciousness. Follow the line, breathe in the harmony.

Remember again that we PLAY music. Music is joy, light, whimsy. Don't try to harness the laughter so much as ride the wave.

MELPOMENE

In the midst of sorrow, Melpomene, the Muse of Tragedy, shows us the way to overcome adversity, to be the Hero in our own drama. We can be very strong but still melancholy. We can be wise but still full of sadness. We can hope against hope that there is light at the end of the tunnel. Examples of hope in the face of heartbreak surround us, if we open our hearts to them.

Hope is taking action without certainty. Take a risk and extend yourself in your own community. Bring soup to an ill neighbor. Cook a pot of homemade chili for your local firehouse. Create an ikebana floral arrangement for a single mother you know. Eulogize a mentor. Dance in tribute to a lost lover. Cross your fingers and hope.

POLYHYMNIA

Polyhymnia is the Muse of Oratory, Sacred Hymns, and Poetry. She also rules over Passion, Contemplation, Illumination, and Symbolism.

Sit in silence to explore the mystery of daily living. Cultivate a ritual, a regular habit of contemplation. Create a private mental space in which ideas can well up into your conscious mind from the depths of your being.

Quiet reflection allows you an opportunity to commune with the divine, the sacred. Discover The Vedas, the Bhagavad Gita, the Torah, the Koran, the Bible. Tackle the big questions: where did we come from? What is your purpose? Debate the crucial issues. Energize others with an inspirational and inclusive speech.

TERPSICHORE

The Muse of Dance, Terpsichore is also known as the mother of the Sirens. She governs movement expression and vitality; she celebrates the Body's rhythms, power and grace.

Enjoy your body, its flexibility and movement.

Dance.

Strut.

Take your CD player into a room alone. Close the door, take off your shoes, close your eyes and move! Feel your body loosen and your pulse quicken. Stamp your feet. Wave your arms and do the Hokey Pokey. Grab a broom and do a slinky tango across the floor. Jump around and do the twist or tie a gauzy scarf around your waist and swirl in a sinuous belly dance.

Today, be active; instead of daydreaming, take a walk. Skip. Play hopscotch. Run along the beach. Cleanse your mental house and clear out your physical space.

THALIA

Thalia is the Muse of Comedy. She reminds us how to play, celebrate and laugh. She is a mischievous goddess, delighting in serious fun. Give yourself up to her deliberate chaos and mindless abandon.

Be silly.

Rent your favorite comedy and watch it upside down. Laugh, loudly. Pretend you are auditioning for a TV laugh track.

Have a picnic in your backyard. Serve punch, peanut butter sandwiches and Oreos. Wear a big hat and white gloves or a vest. Play croquet.

Stroll through a museum wearing a beret.

Buy a coloring book and new box of crayons. Sprawl on the floor and color all night.

URANIA

The Muse of Astronomy and Mathematics, Urania reminds us that the sciences are also arts.

Become aware of the natural world around you. Let your whole being swell with wonder as a butterfly emerges from its cocoon. Be curious about the world in front of your nose. Plant a bean in a styrofoam cup and watch it sprout.

Take a photo safari through your neighborhood; shoot only the things that are red or blue or yellow. Shoot everyone from a mouse's viewpoint. Shoot one picture for every letter of the alphabet. Take an entire roll of things that are round or liquid. Make copies of your results and construct a mobile out of hangers and string.

FROM INSPIRATION TO INTENTION

The Muses inspire. That is their job. Yours is to have the intention and take action. One step….and the next.

Sometimes we wonder, how? When? Sometimes we say, "I can't, I have no time. I have no talent for it."

The answer is right now, you can, and you do. And so what.

Simple, no?

First, gather your energies. Close your eyes and be still for 30 seconds. Breathe a real breath, one you feel down into your toes. Again. Once more. You can do anything for 30 seconds.

Now pick up your pen, your brush, your notebook, your guitar. Just PLAY, pretend you are everything you dream to become, pretend you have enough time, money, and resources to live your dreams. Pretend and just do the work for five minutes.

Be a creativity guerilla, an artistic terrorist. Let art strike at any moment; defiantly insert random creative acts throughout your day. Notice the windshield wipers slapping back and forth? What's the rhythm? Can you snatch a song from this pattern of tapping? What worlds unfold from the contents of the shopping cart idling in front of you? Who is that mysterious stranger, fuming impatiently before you in the checkout line? An undercover spy?

Five minutes is not the answer. You deserve sustained time to do real work, deep work. But take the time whenever you can snatch it. Take it in bits, several times a day.

If you treat yourself often, taking little creative bites all day, how will you resist taking mouthfuls of creativity?

Don't resist. Overindulge in creativity, grab handfuls of creative time. Take an hour, take an afternoon, take the whole day. Call down the Muse who fits the moment.

It's better than chocolate.

❖ ❖ ❖

A-Muse-ing Resources

The Nine Muses by Angeles Arrien, Tarcher/Putnam, New York, NY

Magic Mandala Coloring Book by Martha Bartfeld, Mandalart Creations, Santa Fe, NM

The Artist's Way by Julia Cameron with Mark Bryan, Tarcher/Putnam, New York, NY

Writing Down the Bones by Natalie Goldberg, Shambhala Publications, Boston, MA

Art and Soul by Pam Grout, Andrews McMeel Publishing, Kansas City, KS

The Creative Artist by Nita Leland, North Light Books, Cincinnati, OH

The Van Gogh Blues by Eric Maisel, Ph.D., Rodale, New York, NY

A Creative Companion by Sark, Celestial Arts, Berkeley, CA

Stacey Rasfeld originally trained as a musician but was ambushed by painting and collage later in life. She developed the "Choose Your Muse Workshops," a series of multi-disciplinary play dates using the ancient Greek Muses of Inspiration as a framework for exploring creativity. The workshops include theater games, writing exercises, and painting activities to help students get their creative juices flowing in a non-competitive, non-judgmental atmosphere. The Workshops strive to create an environment where participants have permission to let loose and have fun – something many people have not done since kindergarten. No special skills or experience are necessary, just a willingness to play! To share your thoughts and comments, to schedule a presentation for your group, or for current workshop information, email her at creativitymuse@yahoo.com.

CREATIVE COURTSHIP

LEARNING TO LOVE, HONOR AND CHERISH YOUR MUSE

❖

BY KYLE MORRISON

If you've ever been married, you know these occasional feelings of disillusionment: the days your mate comes to you complaining that things just aren't the same; the times you notice that your partner's once charming ways have turned annoying; those painful moments when you wonder why you ever got married.

This disaffection, sometimes called the end of the "honeymoon period," is a natural and inevitable part of being in partnership. Its unexpected arrival throws the uninitiated for a loop. They wonder, *Isn't it supposed to be easier, better than this?* Even those with a more realistic outlook can be caught unaware: *I thought we could handle our problems; I thought we were different.*

Call me crazy, but I am secretly excited when couples hit this stage because it's where the rubber meets the road, where real growth and potential begin. Though painful and distressing, problems are an inevitable part of any relationship. It's the way they are viewed and handled that makes all the difference.

Did you ever stop to realize that the same is true for problems in your relationship with your muse – your creative spirit – the part of you that urges you to be or do something more expressive? This may not be a romance you take seriously or even acknowledge, but you and your muse are as tied together as you and your significant other.

Perhaps you are among those who feel the call, whether it's evidenced by the sweet ache in your heart upon seeing a beautiful painting, the pang of jealousy at someone else's artistic success, or the musical instrument you long to take up again after decades of neglect. These messages are asking you to pay attention, to show up at the altar of your partnership with that mysterious and creative force within you.

What does it really mean to show up? The innocent and easy answer is that it starts with vows to love, honor, and cherish – a good beginning for any marriage. What comes after, though, can be either pure hell – or pure alchemy (the transformation of lead into gold) if you're willing to keep your eyes and your heart open and learn from what you discover.

FALLING IN, THEN OUT OF LOVE WITH YOUR MUSE

Remember what it's like to be newly in love? Apply these delicious feelings to your relationship with your inner creator. How natural and easy to get lost in dreams, wishes and longings about the perfection you could achieve together! Just think: your novel could get published and become a bestseller, your photographs might hang in the city's premier gallery, or maybe you could sell a ton of your work at the local crafts fair – enough to quit your day job, even. These imaginings are akin to the infatuation stage of a romance, in which we do not yet see the imperfections and frailties of our beloved. There is nothing wrong with this phase; in fact, it's an essential ingredient in forming a bond between ourselves and the desired other.

But you know the story: while a chosen few seemingly go on to live happily ever after (one of many myths in the world of creative success), the rest of us crash to earth pretty quickly. Whether it's a mate with habits that no longer charm, or the boilerplate rejection letter that sends your muse into a tizzy, it's jarringly apparent that your agenda and reality do not match. Suddenly you become unsure of your commitment to your creative spirit, your vision for wedded bliss, or your ability to continue for even one more day – a natural reaction to shattered illusions.

But difficult as it may be, this is not the time to abandon your dreams. Instead, you must begin to form a different relationship to your partner, focusing on the vision as the most desired and best possible outcome while acknowledging the daily, sometimes tricky course adjustments it will take to get there. It also means being open to outcomes other than the vision you had planned or hoped for.

For many, it's much easier to react out of habit, from closely held beliefs about what should or shouldn't be. Some people silently give up or pretend the struggle isn't important, while others throw in the towel and head for new distractions and less demanding "affairs." All of these reactions assume that loving relationships are supposed to be continually pleasing to the heart or the eye. Wouldn't it be liberating to learn that this is a lie?

THE INTIMACY KILLERS

So how do we begin such an arduous task, when bad feelings, dashed hopes and heavy hearts block the path? We start by gradually creating true intimacy, which is the uncovering, over time, of our deepest nature – for better or worse – and the shared knowledge and acceptance of that nature between you and your partner. Intimacy accepts the dark and light, the easy and hard, and the up, down and inside out. Whether in partnership with a person or with your creative spirit, creating and sustaining intimacy is hard work.

To build true intimacy with your creative inner partner, you need to first understand how not to do it by unlearning some natural behaviors. Getting familiar with these intimacy killers will put new tools in your pocket – tools designed to foster authentic communication and accept- ance and even rekindle the desire you fear has been irrevocably lost among so much disappointment. These are the same tools marital ther- apists have developed to improve even the most difficult or hopeless- sounding relationships.

Among the most well-known of these therapists is Dr. John Gottman, author of several popular books on marriage and director of The Gottman Institute in Seattle. His oft-quoted studies reveal the con- sistent elements of a relationship headed for the rocks as well as strate- gies for altering a collision course. The most common unhelpful behaviors he identified are called "the Four Horsemen of the Apocalypse," for if they are allowed to flourish, they will erode and even- tually destroy a partnership.

The Four Horsemen – contempt, criticism, defensiveness, and stonewalling – are no doubt familiar to your intimates, and you've like- ly also employed some or all of them as you struggle to relate to your muse. We are all guilty of creating potholes on the road to connubial and creative bliss.

For example, not long ago I was the queen of *contempt* when it came to artistic endeavors. From as early as fifth grade – when I made a colorful apron in home economics with a crooked seam and, mortified, tore it to shreds in front of my teacher – I loathed any imperfection that came from my hands. My face flushed with shame and anger at each botched attempt at expressing myself. This included my inability to wrap presents with perfectly square corners, the childish marks that came from summer camp paintbrushes, and the clunky notes I pecked out on the piano with Mrs. Rosenbloom every Tuesday afternoon. These and other episodes were proof positive I lacked talent and had no business thinking I would ever succeed.

At the time, nobody tried to convince me otherwise, so my percep- tions were never challenged. In the face of such self-contempt my muse nearly shut down completely, as would any partner subject to such dis- dain. It's only now, from the perspective of adulthood, that I know tal- ent had nothing to do with it. Replacing self-hate (as deep and dark a contempt as you can find) with self-esteem and consistent support from others would have gone a long way in helping me see myself as an artist with potential.

Criticism is just a milder form of contempt. My mother makes her first oil painting – a very pleasing, if rather unfinished looking still life of fruit in a bowl–and apologizes that it's "not very good" when she shows it to people. My husband insists he can't sing, even when I hear him do it all the time. "I'm not creative" is one of the most common phrases we hear when the topic of self-expression arises.

If contempt is cold rejection of one's own or another's efforts, criticism is its slightly warmer cousin. Criticism implies that you expect better of your other; you expect adherence to lofty standards of right and wrong or good and bad, creating what is sure to be an uneasy peace between you and your partner. Your muse, with its tender offerings from your deepest being, reacts no differently to such stringent demands.

Defensiveness is nothing more than the ego's attempt at self-protection. What if images or sounds of fury and death inhibit you from further creative pursuit because you insist you're a cheerful, happy person? What if you're chaste and proper, but your beloved shows sudden signs of juicy, robust sexuality? What if you are accused of not being a good companion? *This wasn't our deal!* you may think. *I can't do this – you're not who I thought you were, and if I follow you, I may not be who I thought I was either.* But if you close yourself too tightly against the moods or manifestations of your mate or your muse because it's uncomfortable, you are protecting yourself from the true spirit and potential of your relationship.

Although all of Dr. Gottman's horsemen are defensive strategies in their own right, *stonewalling* is the ultimate defense. It is the adamant refusal to allow creative or personal growth into consciousness or practice. Whether you are too busy indulging in one modern distraction or another, or you have consciously decided that your efforts at creating are fruitless, you are defending against your own genius, the core that defines your higher self and your potential. Couples who spend too much time in this stage, says Dr. Gottman, are nearing the end. Whether you're scared, stubborn, or just don't know what else to do, stonewalling sends the message: *I refuse to discuss it, argument over, end of story.* Unless you find a way around this very destructive strategy, your mate – inner or outer – will eventually abandon you in favor of self-preservation and self-respect.

TAKING TIME OUT TO KNOW YOUR FEELINGS

As clear-cut as Dr. Gottman's concepts may be, how do you know when you're subjecting yourself (and thus, your creative partner) to one or all of the Four Horsemen? While some people are good at being honest with themselves, most of us aren't. Our emotions simply get in the way.

In these cases, giving some distance to the voices by getting them out of your head and into objective space can help clarify things. This is the equivalent of a time-out during a heated disagreement. You can do this by free association writing, journaling, story telling, drawing or dancing out the energies, or even singing. (This last idea came to me one day when, depressed and frustrated, I erupted into an original song: "You're trying too hard, you're trying too hard, *you are trying too hard!*" Entirely unplanned, it seemed to come from a different place inside of me. My muse, perhaps?)

Take a time-out with the intention to reflect and learn and then come back into the discussion – i.e., to your artwork, music, or blank page – with the new learnings. Were you expressing from your vulnerable heart or from your habits? What are you afraid of? Did your partner or muse feel heard? If not, why not?

NEGOTIATING WITH YOUR MUSE

Dr. Gottman stresses the importance of allowing the other to influence you. Are you open to what your muse is trying to tell you? Maybe you'll find she is whiny and inert because you are unable to simply quit your job and be at her beck and call around the clock. If so, you may have to strike a compromise and talk her into cooperating within the boundaries of your modern daily life – as long as you follow through by giving her regular attention. The key is listening with an open heart and being willing to stay open to what you learn even if you don't like it or can't yet see how things will work out. As with any meaningful change affecting two intimate beings, this takes time, practice, and the occasional two steps forward and one step back.

It's also essential to make the time you two spend together as respectful and fun as possible. Your creative partner wants to know you take her seriously and that you are not going to abandon her. She longs to be important to you because you are terribly important to her. Without your cooperation, she is voiceless and trapped with no way to contribute her vitality and color to your life and the lives of others. Martha Graham said:

> There is vitality, a life-force, an energy, a quickening that is translated through you into action, and because there is only one of you in all of time this expression is unique. And if you block it, it will never exist through any other medium and be lost. The world will not have it! It is not your business to determine how good it is nor how it compares with other expressions. It is your business to keep it yours clearly and directly, to keep the channel open …

Though their approaches may differ, the experts all agree on one thing: good relationships take consistent work and re-commitment. Building trust, respect and true union is not something achieved with a vow and a shift into cruise control with good intentions. To evolve in your relationships and within yourself, you must be willing to poke around in the dark corners that Bruce Springsteen sings about in his *Tunnel of Love* song: "Then the lights go out and it's just the three of us; you, me and all that stuff we're so scared of."

The intent to learn, rather than protect ourselves from the truth, is what saves us from identifying too strongly with our fears – fears of not being good enough, of disappointing others, of not living up to our often too-high expectations. The late Reverend Joseph Barth, of Harvard Divinity School, said, "Marriage is our last, best chance to grow up." To be receptive to learning about the challenges and callings of being in a relationship requires us to examine why it's so threatening to let something as precious as truth enter our hearts and lives. For this kind of deep knowing and acceptance is not only the greatest gift we can give ourselves, our partners and the world, but is perhaps the most courageous thing we humans are capable of. And when bound to your mate or muse by mutual trust, support and intimacy – hard-won though it may be – you have entered the realm of the Divine and the original source of creation. Who could ask for a better marriage?

❖ ❖ ❖

Kyle Morrison is a writer and life coach who assists those in search of the authentic path with the everyday realities of self-expression and intimacy. Closest to her heart is the subject of the poignant and difficult human search for wholeness at midlife. An avid photographer, her publications include *The New York Times, Fine Gardening, Cape Cod Life* and *Today's Photographer* magazines, as well as articles published in *Backpacker* magazine and the *Seattle Times*. Kyle lives in Seattle, Washington with her husband and three neurotic cats. She welcomes email at kylemorrison@yahoo.com.

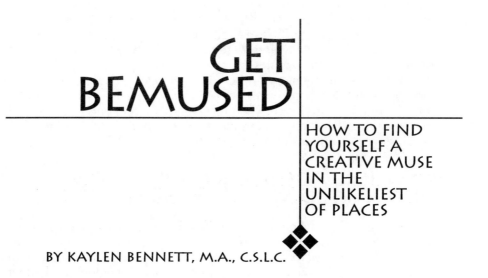

GET BEMUSED

HOW TO FIND YOURSELF A CREATIVE MUSE IN THE UNLIKELIEST OF PLACES

BY KAYLEN BENNETT, M.A., C.S.L.C.

What if there really are muses? What if you could find one? There are! You can! Read how one woman found hers unexpectedly in the middle of a personal journey...but first, a slightly twisted little story about the original Muses...

A SLIGHTLY TWISTED GREEK MYTH

The two teams lined up, vying for supremacy and the right to claim they were "king of the mountain." In a fierce competition, the Olympians beat the Titans hands down. The hometown crowd was exuberant and clamored for a permanent cheerleading squad who would forevermore extol the virtues of the Olympians and sing songs to glorify their victory.

And so Zeus, captain of the Olympians, wanting to pass down his godly genes, made love to Mnemosyne, the Titan goddess of memory, on nine consecutive nights, after which she gave birth to nine daughters. These gorgeous creatures indeed sang about the beautiful earth, the stars in the heavens, and the victorious Olympian team, bringing joy to all who heard them. They became known as The Muses.

According to Greek mythology, if you were a singer or a poet you might be blessed by one of them with the gifts of insight and talent in order to further glorify the Olympian victory. Each Muse had her area of specialty: Clio (History), Calliope (Epic Poetry), Erato (Love Poetry), Euterpe (Lyric Poetry), Melpomene (Tragedy), Terpsichore (Dance), Thalia (Comedy), Polyhymnia (Songs to the Gods), and Urania (Astronomy).

As long as you honored and respected your Muse, she would continue to inspire you. On the other hand, it was said that a Muse, if not held in the highest regard, could ruin your life with a mere thought. A king boasted that *his* daughters were better than The Muses, and he was instantly turned into magpies. A singer and poet once mocked The Muses. He lost his memory and could no longer remember his songs and poems. But for those who honored The Muses, their gift of inspiration was much desired, and when received, the recipients could spend the rest of their lives achieving success by carrying on the traditions of their history and culture through the arts.

SO WHERE *DOES* A CREATIVE PERSON FIND A GOOD MUSE THESE DAYS?

Since the days when gods and goddesses mingled with mortals around Mount Olympus, not much has changed for creative souls. Writers, musicians, actors, poets, songwriters, painters, and artists of all persuasions long for the kind of inspiration, encouragement, and talent that The Muses bestowed upon mortals.

Fortunately, you don't have to sleep with the enemy or bear nonuplets in order to find a muse! One could be closer than you think, but don't be surprised if your muse doesn't look like what you might expect. Mine surely didn't.

You see, there are no rules about how a muse should look or be – none at all. Gender, age, appearance, and character are all variable, but I can tell you this: Muses are like angels. They come to you when you need them, even if you are unaware of their presence. You can set out on a search for one, but most likely you already have one in your life. Maybe you've had several that have come and gone, staying with you only as long as you needed them. Maybe you were aware of their gifts, and maybe you weren't, but you are a different person because they were there. You can have an inner muse or team of muses, too, but having a muse with whom you can share a cup of coffee is just downright fun.

How I found my muse is a story that weaves itself into a rich tapestry that, when viewed from the bottom seems like unconnected threads, but when viewed from the top is a beautiful landscape of lush trees, all bearing delicious fruit ready to be picked.

OF CATS AND MUSES

Anyone who knows me knows one thing for certain, that I love animals and they are part of my soul. My cat Baranof was 15½. It had been just the two of us for eight years after my other cat, Presley, and my dog Corky died. Baranof, who had been on the sidelines for the first eight years of his life, stepped into his new role without hesitation. He was my friend, my comforter, and my spiritual teacher, and now he was slowly dying of chronic renal failure.

My life's purpose was to get to work and back home to take care of him. I remember the first time the vet wanted me to stick the 18-gauge needle under the skin in my cat's neck to give him subcutaneous fluids. It looked like a sewing machine needle. "You want me to do what?" I felt hot, began hyperventilating, and almost passed out, but finally I did it. And that was the easy time because someone was there to help me do it.

There came a time when I had to do it alone at home because I couldn't afford $60 a week to have the vet do it. And then there were injections for anemia, cooking special food, giving him pills, and trips to the emergency vet in the middle of the night by cab.

The only creative thing I did during that time was to figure out new ways to get myself up in the morning and to work. I had to because I was running out of money and running out of credit, even with the pet insurance and help from family.

I was sinking into a deep, dark void day by day, yet Baranof persevered. He almost died twice. We became even closer than we had been. My animal communication skills were launched to a new level with Baranof. He was a very good teacher. Lying on the bed I could call him to me in my mind, and within 30 seconds he would appear.

I spent hours on internet discussion lists with other animal lovers who were all looking for the same miracle that I was. We laughed and cried over each other's posts and grieved over every cat that died. We all knew that the next batch of condolence e-mails could be coming our way. It was only a matter of time, and time was short.

So there I was riding the bus home every day thinking of what I needed to do when I got home. Was it vet day? Was it sub-q fluids day? Was it shot day? Did I have the strength to keep going? Did Baranof? How would I pay for it all? Some days I would distract myself by observing people and listening in on their conversations.

I began to notice a couple of men who talked a lot about music, history, and Vienna. Some days the elder of the two was there alone, and I was drawn to him. Although I didn't know why, I felt that I should talk to him sometime. That's what I call getting a nudge from Spirit. When you get one, pay attention. It's always worth it.

One day I passed him as I was getting off at my stop. I smiled and said, "Hello," and made some neighborly comment. We greeted each other a few times after that and eventually we began to sit together. "Buck" as I call him, was 80. He was hard of hearing, which meant our conversations were broadcast all over the bus, at least my end of them was until I learned he was reading my lips and I didn't need to shout. Slightly stooped over, he always carried bags of books, often one bag slung over his arm with no hand, with more books in his backpack. He had a twinkle in his eyes that I later came to know as his ornery side, and he had already outlived the prognosis for a terminal illness. In warm weather he wore a baseball cap, in cool weather a beret; but rarely was he *sans chapeau*.

Buck left home early every day and made his rounds – to the libraries to do genealogy research, to the coffee shop for lunch, and to bookstores to buy, sell, and trade. He once owned a used bookstore and had a keen sense of what was valuable and sought after. It was typical to hear him say something like, "I bought four books at Store A for $10.00 and sold two of them at Store B for $15.00, traded one at Store C and bought one for $2.00, and then sold one to Store A for $3.00 more than I paid for it." He had a trade credit of over $200.00 at Store C. Having a routine and purpose for the day seemed to serve him well. He walked 30-40 blocks a day and his mind was sharp. As much as I dislike routine, there is a place for it.

He often showed me his purchases covering everything from archaeology to UFO-ology. And how many times did he ask me if I'd read this or that book or author? Hundreds, but I can remember only once saying, "Yes." I felt somewhat intimidated. He must have thought I'd never read a book in my life, but I had to remember that he had 30 years more time in the world than I did. If I had given him my reading list, chances are he'd not have read one title on the list, or so I thought!

It didn't stop at books, though. He also bought classical music and had a special liking for contemporary classical music that I found cacophonous. If I were on "Who Wants to Be a Millionaire?" Buck would be my lifeline for music, history, modern art, literature, science fiction, the Mafia, Austria, and genealogy.

Books and CD's weren't the only treasures in Buck's backpack. One day he pulled out a dog-eared priority mail envelope, inside of which were drawings that he did every night before he went to bed. He had "good paper" at home, he said, but he preferred the backs of envelopes, bills, and college book covers. His favorite medium was a ballpoint-inked piece of cotton on lightly sanded frozen food packages. Try sticking a broom straw down a pen refill, drawing out the ink, swabbing it onto cotton, and then drawing with it, all with one hand! I was mesmerized by the smudge-filled pages of drawings, some of which were comparable to Picasso.

Baranof was declining week by week, and so was I. Buck went on a trip to Austria for a few weeks, and then Baranof died in late July at the age of 16. Even though he could have passed any time during the night he held on until morning when we went to the vet. You see, one of his purposes in life was to help me make peace with death, especially that of my animals. When I was growing up it was always my mother that was designated to take the animals to the vet and drop them off, never to be seen again. We were never there at the end to say good-bye.

As an adult, there were various reasons I had not been present at the end. One cat died at the vet when I was at home. Once a vet discouraged me from being present because I was crying, and he told me things to scare me away. Twice I stayed in the waiting room until it was over but didn't view the body, and when my dog died I smelled his sweet spirit waft through the room. Baranof was going to take me through that experience and that's all there was to it.

On an internet discussion board devoted to animals, I had once asked people to tell me the truth about their euthanasia experiences. Some stories were wonderful, some horrific. I vowed that I would never again let an animal die alone. When the time came, I wish I'd been calm and centered. I wasn't, but Baranof was. My face and eyes were red from crying all night. He was almost gone, and then he was. My brave best friend had left, and I prayed that all my angel animals had come to help him over. I went home numb, and for the first time in nearly 30 years, I had no animal in my life, nothing to do after work, and nothing to live for.

I sat in a pit of deep despair for weeks, waiting for God to take me, too, because there was no point in living without an animal companion. It was stinky, smelly crap in that pit, and I wallowed in it. Truthfully, I don't remember much about the first seven weeks until my new kitty Tobee Wan Kenobe came into my life. He was a 14-week-old feral kitten, scared of everything and everyone. He was a wild child, and he was all black while Baranof had been all white. He made me get up every day. He made me focus on him and his needs. He made me laugh even though I would grieve the loss of Baranof for two years. I officially adopted him in late September. I bought a plastic trick-or-treat pumpkin, stuffed him in it, and took photographs for Halloween. Thank God, for animals. They save lives.

EXCUSE ME, ARE YOU MY MUSE?

Back on the bus, Buck continued to bring his drawings. Every once in awhile he'd offer a subtle comment, hinting that maybe I wanted to draw. I ignored him. Draw? Me? I couldn't even do a decent paint-by-numbers horse when I was a kid. And in high school I thought art was a "fluff" class for people who weren't going to college. I couldn't take the chance of not getting an "A" so I never signed up. Secretly, however, I had great admiration for people who could create things with their hands, whether it was painting, sewing, or whittling wood.

My motto, however, was "If I can't do it perfectly, I won't do it at all." I don't know if I was born that way, but it showed up early in my life. In first grade my parents thought I was a genius because all my papers had 100's on them. Then at report card time, I was, as they say, "busted." The teacher tattled on me and said I had been throwing away all the imperfect papers.

All these years later the perfectionist in me was still hard at work, and there was very little chance that I would start drawing, even if I wanted to, and even less of a chance that I would show it to anyone else. One thing about muses, though, is that what they do isn't always obvious. A good muse can inspire you subtly, over time, without you realizing it.

I guess I'm a slow study because it was almost three years later when I noticed I had started doodling during lunch and meetings. They were simple drawings; a four-year-old could have done better. Picasso said, "Painting is just another way of keeping a diary." That's how I felt about my doodles, and I kept every single one of them. My first-grade teacher would have been proud. One day I brought them to show Buck on the way home. He could have laughed but he didn't. He could have commented on their simplicity but he didn't. Instead, he found something of interest in them, and said, "You have a good hand."

From then on, almost every day we had our own form of "show and tell." Buck would show me his drawings and then ask, "Do you have anything?" I sheepishly showed him my doodles, risking my whole sense of self in the process. A good muse always honors the intimate breakthrough.

Within a few months, I was bored with my "diary" so I went to the art supply store and selected brushes, watercolors, colored pencils, and paper without having any idea whatsoever as to how to use them. If a brush felt good in my hand, I bought it. If I liked the way something looked, I bought it. If I liked the colors of paint, I bought them. Then I went home, cleared off the dining room table, and painted a really awful watercolor that looked like absolutely nothing. Gee, what a surprise.

But you know what? If you don't like what you've created, turn it into something else, and that goes for life, not just art. Much of life and art is merely perception. What it is, is what you make of it.

So I scanned the picture into the computer, loaded it into a graphics program, and viewed it pixel by pixel on the screen. This is like taking a leaf and looking at it under a microscope. I found sections of the picture that when enlarged and extracted, were actually interesting. I gave them titles like "Birth" and "Chaos" and printed them. I kept the original watercolor in a special place, and I put all of the computer art in a binder.

Then I discovered the art of tweaking, accidental tweaking actually. I didn't know what I was doing. I just experimented. Now I was able to turn a watercolor that was supposed to have been a Reiki symbol but had turned out looking like a signpost on a dirt road, into a glorious rainbow spiral that I called "Chakra Fire," and I used it on my website. Printouts went into my binder. I could hardly wait to show Buck, and he was aMUSEdly impressed by the *before* and *after* pictures. He encouraged me to continue, and said he wanted his son to see them.

Computer art changed my life. It changed the way I thought about everything. Nothing was as it seemed. You can never trust a photograph these days because it could have been created from unrelated objects. Two people in the same photo may not even know each other, and neither may have ever been to the geographical location, which may also have been made up.

So when something in my life looked like a stumbling block, was it really, or was that just what the computer program had made it look like? If it wasn't, then what was it really or what could I turn it into?

THE EYES HAVE IT — PROCESS VERSUS OUTCOME

I continued to experiment with art supplies and when I discovered fluorescent gel pens on black paper, I was hooked. I drew for hours at a time, often while listening to music with, as Buck said, "three-quarters of an ear." I told Buck, "I just draw lines. If it looks like something, that's a bonus."

Faces and eyes were all through the gel pen drawings. They would appear out of nowhere and often looked like people with tribal masks and huge headgear from Africa. A spiritual psychic once told me they were "shamanic." I wasn't sure what I was supposed to do with that piece of information, but I continued the drawings. For variety, I tried drawing with gel pens on white paper and could not do it. There was something special for me in the brightness of the colors against the black, of seeing the world from night instead of day, and finding out what was hidden that now wanted to be seen.

Of course I took all of these with me on the bus, even the ones that I didn't like, but wasn't it fun that I actually did like some of them? Buck and I would always turn each other's drawings in every direction to see what emerged. Often what looked like nothing, when turned upside down, would reveal some meaningful form. The human brain is always searching for pattern and familiarity. Occasionally, we burst out laughing, giggling like kids who had seen their first "dirty picture," when we realized what we had drawn subconsciously. The bus driver would look in the mirror and laugh, too. Sometimes I suspected he was able to read our minds, or maybe he had a secret mirror system and could actually see our drawings.

As I turned the pages of my "portfolio" at home one day, my inner muse tapped me on the shoulder and said, "Look, look at these. Do you see the difference?" Yes, I could see a sense of freedom and *laissez-faire* in the more recent drawings as the eyes peered at me out of the blackness. "Oh, I've finally gotten it," I thought.

Gotten what, you ask? I had gotten the *now*, baby. I had finally experienced the joy of *being* while *doing* without expectations of what was at the end. By enjoying the process I often was surprised at the outcome. Every now and then I would try to draw something specific and fail. My inner muse immediately reminded me that the purpose for my drawing was to know the *now*, to be so joyfully absorbed in what I was doing that I neither knew nor cared that it was, by my old definition, "imperfect," and then to appreciate what I had at the end, no matter what it looked like.

Had I just become a recovering perfectionist?

WHEN YOU'RE DONE, YOU'RE DONE...
OR MAYBE NOT

I discovered that sometimes there was nothing more to be added to a drawing, even though I felt a need to fill in a blank space, change a line, or add something. Every time I did it, I ruined the drawing. Why would I draw for an hour and then suddenly start obsessing over it? I'd lost the "now."

I asked Buck about it. "How do you know you're done?" I expected him to say, "When you're done, you're done." Instead he said, "Sometimes it isn't done, and I lay it aside. Later on I might see what it needs and add to it." "Oh," I said. "When I do that, I ruin it." "Well, if you have a lot of drawings, you can afford to do that. It gives you confidence to take a risk."

That wasn't what I was expecting, and I had to think about it for a few days. My supposedly tamed perfectionism was sneaking up on me again. Where in my life did it feel like something needed tweaking, but I wouldn't do it because I was afraid I would ruin what I already had? Oh, gosh, how about everywhere? Even so, there are those situations where you've done all you can, and then you have to let go. Sometimes you can go back. Sometimes you can tweak it. Sometimes you can't. And sometimes you realize it's OK the way it turned out after all, even when you didn't think so at the time.

I noticed in Buck's drawings when he experimented with color or strokes. It didn't matter if it "worked" or not. Buck said, "I don't expect anyone to like my art. Sometimes I don't even like my art." Creativity isn't just about producing what you envision. It's also about allowing the unknown to be born. Sometimes you don't even know what you have until many years later. The scientist who invented the adhesive used in Post-it® Notes was actually trying to create a very strong adhesive. It was many years before he found an application for the semi-tacky adhesive "mistake." You never know where a mistake could lead, but it always leads to where you're supposed to go next. In *The Joy of Painting*, Bob Ross said, "We don't have mistakes here, we just have happy accidents." I've had a lot of happy accidents!

BROKEN CRAYONS AND THE KITCHEN TABLE

Buck told me he started drawing in the 1970's using his kids' broken crayons. He used to bring modern art books home for them to look at. He did the same for me. On days when he didn't have any of his own art with him, he'd bring art books. I felt like I was sitting at his kitchen table learning to see life in new ways, through the colors, shapes, and textures of people whose minds certainly didn't work like mine did. I wondered what it was they were experiencing that came out in these odd pieces. Buck liked busy, chaotic, and colorful paintings in which you could see something new every time you looked at it. They made me dizzy. I liked sculptures and paintings that looked like something identifiable, especially animals. Buck was a sneaky muse indeed. I'd see the influence of these artists in his art, and once in awhile in mine.

TWO SIDES TO EVERY MUSE

Maybe it was because of his health or maybe it was just his ornery side revealing itself, but sometimes Buck was absolutely embarrassing to be around. When you get old, you can get away with some pretty obnoxious behavior, and people will just look disgusted or amused and dismiss it as just an old person who's not "all there."

Once he blurted out, "Today's music is completely worthless. Rock and roll has the same repetitive beat. It's boring." Several scowled faces looked in our direction, some of whom were high school kids who were probably in a band and later told their friends about the crotchety old guy on the bus.

Even worse was the time Buck loudly announced when a wheel-chair passenger was boarding, "They shouldn't allow wheelchairs on the bus because it slows everyone else up." This was more than just an opinionated comment. It was a serious breach of acceptable bus riding behavior, even in my rulebook. I hoped no one thought I was related to him. On the other hand, if they did think that, then maybe I'd be getting sympathetic looks instead of hateful ones.

That was Buck. He liked to be controversial. He liked to stir things up. After all, he was old and could get away with it. I figured after what he'd been through in 80-some years, he had a right to be curmudgeon-ly, and I rather envied his unabashed manner. Perhaps that's one of the fun things about getting old, but why wait? Maybe I should learn to spit now instead of keeping it on my list of things to do before I die. Picasso once said, "It takes a very long time to become young." As for Buck, if he were a Muse in ancient Greece, I could easily imagine him turning someone into magpies. But the next day he would probably stop by and feed them some tasty grubs that he'd dug out of his yard just for them, just like he brought food for the crows at the bus stop.

It's been six years since I met Buck. My appreciation of art has expanded so much that I have joined the art selection committee at work and visited museums. I share my art with co-workers. I put it on the web. I honor my art – and the artist. I became a creativity and spir-itual life coach. A client once referred to me as his muse. Baranof and my other animals still live in my heart. Tobee is a little braver. I'm still here. I didn't die after all.

TOBEE WAN KENOBE'S COACHING TIP

I leave you with a little tip that I learned from my cat recently. I've always bristled when someone tells me to do it in "baby steps." My resistance to that phrase was powerful. What image comes to mind for "baby steps?" A tottering baby who is always falling down? One who finally stands up and takes a step or two, but doesn't get very far? For me, it isn't very motivating. I, after all, want to make quantum leaps and forget everything in between, but then I'd be missing the *now* of the journey, wouldn't I? So I decided that instead of baby steps, I'll take kitten steps. Kittens take delicate little steps, but they also make a good leap now and then, and they have a whole lot of fun doing it!

My best to you on your creative journey. May you find your Muse and perhaps become one yourself.

❖ ❖ ❖

Kaylen Bennett, M.A., C.S.L.C., has an extraordinary ability to create for her coaching clients a safe and sacred space in which insights, ideas, and healing can occur. She frees them to remodel, refurbish, and rearrange their inner house and move toward a life of creatively expressing their soul's unique essence. Kaylen specializes in using meridian energy techniques to help animal lovers and creative people break free from limitations, bring their unique gifts to a larger audience, and create inner and outer health. She holds a master's degree in psychology from Antioch University, Seattle, and is a Creativity Coach, Certified Spiritual Life Coach, Certified Emotional Freedom & Healing Practitioner, Reconnective Healing Practitioner, and Shamanic Animal Communicator. She considers herself a recovering perfectionist, a writer, and an accidental artist who uses photography and mixed media to set her creative spirit free. Her poetry and non-fiction have been published, and she is now working on her first screenplay. Her website is www.SoulEtudes.com

OF FLYING MONKEYS & MODERN DAY MUSES

WHO YOU GONNA CALL?

BY JILL BADONSKY, M.ED.

Experts write that creativity is a timeless flow of peak experiences where fulfillment, generosity, and enlightenment abound. In the creative process, we get plugged into the splendor and satisfaction of our authentic nature. We express through channels that move, inspire, entertain or educate those who come in contact with our expression; we contribute something important to the world or at the very least amuse ourselves. So why not just be creative all the time?

It's the flying monkeys.

Flying monkeys are my term for the evil thwarters of the creative process. We encounter them as we attempt to take creative steps down the yellow brick road to the "land of Awes" – the awes of the creative flow. Flying monkeys block our path of good intentions with their devious ploys and distractions. They frustrate us and drive us into watching reality TV and eating Cheetos.

While facilitating workshops around the country to the creatively eager, I ask participants to share what flying monkeys stand in the way of their creative headway. What I didn't expect was similar monkeys constantly emerged:

1. Thinking the creative process is quick and easy, and so giving up too quickly when the normal stages of ambiguity and doubt arise.

2. Feeling that ideas are drying up – the same idea seems to be the theme of every work.

3. Taking creativity too seriously and therefore choking it in the process.

4. Having low self-confidence and self-esteem, constant negative self-talk and comparisons to others further along in the process.

51

5. Creating unrealistic expectations, or being caught in an epidemic of immobilizing or crazy-making perfectionism.

6. Applying creativity and ingenuity to procrastination strategies rather than to one's creative passions

7. Being overwhelmed with everything there is to do.

8. Believing there is not enough time to get to creative passions.

As for flying monkey number one, M. Scott Peck taught us in *A Road Less Traveled* that once we understand that life is difficult, for some reason it is not so difficult. When we surrender the delusion that life is supposed to be easy, we can free up the energy it took to uphold that illusion to find ways to be at peace.

The same thing happens in the creative process. When we get an idea, we feel an electric exhilaration and a drive to bring it into existence, but as T.S. Eliot says, "Between the idea and the reality falls the shadow." Creative manifestation is not always easy. Creative chaos comes up often and here is where many people quit thinking they are meant for creative expression.

But when creative individuals hear that the creative process can be inherently difficult and that encountering obstacles does not point to some character defect, their attention and energy can shift from the discouragement of "I'm just not cut out to be an artist," to "It's time to activate the Modern Day Muses."

THE MODERN DAY MUSES

In Greek mythology, the nine daughters of Zeus and Mnemosyne, the Goddess of Memory, were considered the keepers of creative inspiration, the Muses. The guardians of sciences were Clio and Urania. Terpsichore was the Muse of dance, Calliope the Muse of heroic and epic poetry. Erato was the Muse of love poetry. Euterpe was the Muse of instrumental music and lyric poetry. Her sister Polyhymnia was the Muse of vocal music. Melopomene was the Muse of tragedy, while Thalia was the Muse of comedy.

In my quest to find out more about why more mortals are not engaged actively in creative bliss, I went to Greece to interview the nine Muses. The visit resulted in the book, *The Nine Modern Day Muses (and a Bodyguard): 10 Guides to Creative Inspiration for Artists, Poets, Lovers and Other Mortals Wanting to Live a Dazzling Existence* (Penguin/Putnam 2003).

I ended up in France and this is what I found and reported in the book:

> Those Muses, they were in the middle of an extended sabbatical at the French Riviera, a rest place away from the think-tank-towers of Mt. Olympus. Okay, to tell you the truth, it really wasn't an extended vacation – let's get rid of the euphemistic cover-up. They were laid off in the Mt. Olympus downsizing that happened in June of last year.

A survey taken by Hercules indicated that their services had met with a critical decline since the invention of TV, the advent of the Internet, and the amplification of the mortal's preoccupation with other various and sundry addictions: swerving intentions, deliberate avoidance accented with chronic procrastination, never beginning, never finishing, ruthless self criticism, gummy bears, numbing agents of the rich and famous, street drugs of the roaming desperate, talking endlessly about nothing, Wild Turkey shooters, withdrawal from pursuits of passion, busy-ness that begets busyness, denial, denial of denial, immobilized good intentions, frozen interventions, Krispy Kreme donuts, free floating anxiety, enigmatic pain in the fifth vertebrae, allergies to wheat, dairy and tabby cats, incessant cleaning of kitchen counters, floors and outsides of drawers, and a hypnotic trance toward shows about survivors on islands. Modern day mortals want so badly to be creative but they are at the mercy of their own self sabotage...

The Muses were actually getting tired of the French Riviera, and they were ready to get back to what they loved the best ... inspiring mortals to blessed creative expressions of innovative solutions and delectable realities. The heck with the lay off - being the resourceful beings they were, the Muses knew they could get their posts back. But things would have to be different.

Things became different. After an extreme makeover and a revamping of the Muse mission with a lot of charts and graphs and a food fight late one Friday night, the Muses reinvented themselves to meet the needs of the modern day mortal. Now each new Muse is equipped with quotes, journal exercises, art exercises, rituals, and brainstorms to deal with Flying Monkeys. Additionally, a bodyguard has been added for the extra protection we need to stay true to our ingenuity and self-expression.

Allow me to introduce to you the names and domains of the Modern Day Muses:

- *Aha-phrodite*, the Muse of Paying Attention and Possibilities
- *Albert*, the Muse of Imagination and New Thinking
- *Bea Silly*, the Muse of Child-like Play
- *Muse Song*, the Muse of Encouragement, Nurturing and Good Company
- *Spills*, the Muse of Practice, Process and Imperfection
- *Audacity*, the Muse of Courage and Uninhibited Uniqueness
- *Lull*, the Muse of Pause, Diversion and Gratitude
- *The Shadow Muse*, the Muse of the Gifts of the Dark Side
- *Marge*, the Muse of Okay-Now-Let's-Get-Started
- and *Arnold*, The Bodyguard who protects us from blocks, fears, and abandonment.

DISPATCHING MUSES TO TAME FLYING MONKEYS

Last month, I met with the Muses to discuss which of the Flying Monkeys we should address to stay within the word limit required by this anthology. We ended up putting the decision off for several weeks until it dawned on us that procrastination seemed to be one of the most daunting creative blocks with which mortals grappled. A number of the other monkeys were first cousins of procrastination, so addressing this dilemma would in essence be a support for other creative afflictions. Additionally, taking ideas too seriously and feeling that ideas are drying up are just plain fun to banish, so the Muses wanted to address those two dilemmas as well. So here goes.

PROCRASTINATION

First, the Muses would like mortals to know that *procrastination* is a symptom. If you label yourself a procrastinator, it is like calling yourself a sneeze rather than saying you have a cold. Scan this list of procrastination causes and see if any sound familiar. When you know what the problem is, you can more easily implement the solution. If a problem does sound familiar, explore what the "Muse in charge" has to say about actions and thoughts that you can adopt:

- **The petrifying path of perfectionism:** You think you should be great at art immediately. The truth is that when we start a project we are NOT supposed to be good at it yet. We are beginners.

  Muse in Charge: *Spills* the Muse of Practice, Process and Imperfection

  Spills says use awareness, permission and surrender. Be aware that perfectionism does not work at the beginning of a creative endeavor. Give yourself permission to do bad or mediocre stuff so you will begin a project at all without such heavy pressure. Once you are in the process, the regular practice WILL move you toward excellence. Surrender your high standards for the joy of the process, the satisfying evolution of practice, and the unexpected happy discoveries that are guaranteed when rigid expectations are released. Some good news for perfectionists: You probably already are doing wonderful things - you just may not be able to see it because you have a rigid ideal you are not meeting. For example, have you ever not liked a project you did only to like it when you saw it again? You forgot your expectation and saw the result with appreciative new eyes.

  Mortal inspired by Spills: *While one person hesitates because he feels inferior, another is busy making mistakes and becoming superior.* - Henry C. Link

- **You have other unrealistic expectations:** You see someone else's work and think you should do, in the next hour, that which probably took that person years to master. Or you are overwhelmed by how much needs to be done so you end up doing something unrelated or nothing at all.

Muse in Charge: *Marge*, the Muse of Okay-Now-Let's-Get-Started

Marge says to break projects down so small it is hard not to get started, even as small as one minute of play. Often making the expectation this small gets you started and then the flow takes you with it. Also break the project down into preliminary steps such as thinking about it while driving, arranging the space for it, reading about it, exposing yourself to inspiration related to it. This is creative foreplay and will rev up your enthusiasm about going further.

> Mortal inspired by Marge: *It's a job that's never started that takes the longest to finish.* - J. R. R. Tolkien

- **You are stuck in time-consuming habits.** You find yourself watching TV, checking email, playing computer games, and doing everything but the art you want to be doing.

Muse in Charge: *Marge* again.

Develop a habit related to the creative process. Marge's favorite book is *The Creative Habit* by Twyla Tharp. In it she talks about how habit can be more important than talent in the creative process and habit does in fact result in increased talent. Do not underestimate the amount of energy it takes to free yourself from a non-creativity related habit. A force of will, a daily reminder of not wanting to regret how you spent your time on the planet, taking a class, forming a creative support group, enlisting a creative pal or a creativity coach will help yank you out of that habit. Little by little, as you gain respect for yourself with new patterns, you will feel you deserve to be immersed in the creative process rather than mindless distractions. However, as Muse Song, the Muse of Encouragement, Nurturing and Good Company will chime in, be gentle with yourself. Compassion will summon creative action more than beating yourself up will.

- **You fear you will be wasting time.** You worry that your art will not come out as you envision it.

Muse in Charge: *Spills* again.

Understand that engaging in the creative process is more than creating a singular art or writing project. Spills says the process can make you a better mortal, with fringe benefits including individuality, resourcefulness, patience, being more magnetic as a person, and problem solving that positively impacts every other aspect of your life. Enjoy the discovery involved in setting off in one direction and discovering a myriad of outlooks and possibilities, connections and manifestations.

OTHER FLYING MONKEYS TO TAME

The procrastination flying monkey has many relatives that the Muses can handle as well.

- **Difficulty coming up with new ideas.** Idea bankruptcy. You cannot seem to think of anything new. It seems the same theme comes up *ad nauseum*, and you wonder if that is it for you as far as new ideas.

  Muse in Charge: *Albert*, The Muse of Innovation and Imagination

  Take the subjects you have used before and think about them differently. Adrian, a woman I was working with, was stuck painting butterflies and seascapes. She wanted to deviate into new vistas, into something different.

  Albert promotes thinking differently by giving different perspectives and simple verbs to catalyze ingenuity into seeing differently. For example the verbs "exaggerate," "combine," "close," and "look" might trigger new seeing. The verbs can be loosely associated in any way, but here are some possibilities Albert used with Adrian. Exaggerate a butterfly's wing so big that it becomes an abstract; combine and make a sunset or a seascape out of butterflies; close your eyes and draw butterflies; look in a magazine, tear out images, and combine three of the images and see what happens.

  Albert advises associating possibilities from these additional words for new images: blur, dot, doodle, deviate color, subtract, add, confuse, mix, break the rules, forget perspective. Scan a photo into PhotoShop and modify with an artistic filter. This can inspire a new design for your art. Albert also encourages listing. Write a list of what you are in awe of; pick one or two ideas from the list and depict through art even if it is an abstract concept.

  > Mortal inspired by Albert: *Take the obvious, add a cupful of brains, a generous pinch of imagination, a bucketful of courage and daring, stir well and bring to a boil.* - Bernard Baruch U.S. businessman, statesman

  Other Muse in Charge: *Lull*, the Muse of Pause, Diversion and Gratitude

Lull says, take a break. Expose yourself to something different. Let new ideas incubate with a pause, relaxation and diversion. By slowing down, taking a break, releasing the process, and diverting your attention, you fill your soul, body and mind with the nutrients for the next step in the creative cycle. Ideas, inspiration, and motivation fulfill the creative cycle's promise of the return to spring. Go on an outing. As Julia Cameron would recommend, take an "Artist's Date," a festive excursion to refill your well. Explore a different creative outlet, and the result will feed your main passion.

Once we have surrendered to a break we will know when it has done its wonders - a surge of enthusiasm will send us into a delightful jump-start and we will once again be flabbergasted by our creativity. "There's a misconception that artists are constantly making things. We all go through cycles," says Carol Grape, a sculptor and instructor at the Art Academy of Cincinnati and Thomas More College, and author of *Handmade Jewelry*. "Sometimes that creative block scares people. But actually, maybe you're just observing things around you or taking care of other things in your life."

> Mortal inspired by Lull: *It takes a lot of time to be a genius, you have to sit around so much doing nothing, really doing nothing.* - Gertrude Stein

- **Taking the creative process too seriously**. The way-too-serious-flying monkey is devious. It convinces mortals that they must perform at certain standards in certain ways by certain rules for certain lengths of time. Creativity just doesn't require that much certainty. It is filled with play and spontaneity and in fact requires it.

Muse in Charge: *Bea Silly*, the Muse of Child-like Play

Bea Silly lobbies for play. She says fun is an elixir of spontaneous ideas. Solutions that seemed so evasive earlier appear effortlessly in the midst of play. To engage in the kind of play that stimulates ideas, mortals need to take themselves less seriously and make room for making things up, kidding, and goofing off. Bea Silly advocates the mortal prerogative to be silly, foolish, and frivolous, and thus, have fun. Have your work write to you what it wants to do next. Say to yourself that you are going to "play with" your writing or art rather than "work on it" and see what happens. Give yourself stickers and rewards for progress and action.

> Mortal inspired by Bea Silly: *The creation of something new is not accomplished by the intellect, but by the play instinct acting from inner necessity. The creative mind plays with the objects it loves.* - C.G. Jung

A WORD ABOUT THE BODYGUARD, ARNOLD

Fear comes up in the creative process. Arnold (yes, named after the Terminator, as in saying *Hasta la vista baby* to your creative fears) is like a protective spirit in bodyguard form. He takes this form because he gives you an image to conjure up when you come face to face with those forces that stop you from finding and acknowledging creative fulfillment. He reminds you that you have power inside yourself and that to give that power away to others by putting their opinions ahead of your own is a crime of unnecessary defeat.

Imagine having on your side the formidable attitude, intimidating physique and unwavering intention of both Arnold Schwarzenegger at his prime and many of the characters he plays in popular films. Imagine this figure on your side standing in front of anything that comes in your way. He stops it, or them, long enough for you to get refueled by the particular Muse you need for the reinforcement of confidence, perseverance, passion or whatever power seems to be missing. Place the bodyguard between you and both your internal and external predators.

As you go into the fear you are granted courage. Courage in the creative process translates as the essential ingredient of confidence. Confidence is a whirly-bird of power to convince yourself and others of the merit and credibility of what you believe to be your art and yourself.

Patience, practice, and confidence amend self-doubt. The bodyguard helps you defend yourself against your untrained mind. The mind is only an enemy when it torments you with fear's imagination. The trained mind can be your cheerleader. The truth is you can get good at what you want to get good at and no one can stop you but yourself.

> Mortal inspired by the Bodyguard: *We need to make the world safe for creativity and intuition, for it's creativity and intuition that will make the world safe for us.* - Edgar Mitchell, Apollo astronaut

CLAIMING YOUR MUSES

The clever creative tactics devised specifically and exclusively for mortals by the Modern Day Muses can tame your flying monkeys — and even train them to work for you rather than against you. The Muses are there inside of all of us. They are our strength, our wisdom, our will and our passion. Personified as Muses, we can more easily conjure up their energy with creative imagination, the energy that we want mobilized in the creative process. Be fueled by the voice of your creative potential. Go into the world and create. Remember to have fun. Be amused.

❖ ❖ ❖

Jill Badonsky, M.Ed. is a creativity coach, workshop leader, creativity group leader trainer, corporate drop-out, artist, playwright, daydreamer and international author of *The Nine Modern Day Muses and a Bodyguard: 10 Guides to Creative Inspiration for Artists, Poets, Lovers and Other Mortals Wanting to Live a Dazzling Existence*. Her background is in expressive therapies, education, marketing, art, performance and other obsessions of the creative mind. Visit www.themuseisin.com to be creatively fortified.

CREATE
BIG IDEAS
& WORK
SUCCESSFULLY

MINING
CREATIVE
GOLD

FIFTEEN WAYS
TO FIND YOUR
MOTHER LODE

BY DEBORAH BOUZIDEN ❖❖

What is creativity and how can it be accessed? This question has been pondered, discussed, and studied for years. Some people believe creativity is reserved solely for "artists" wearing berets and smocks. Others assume that it only comes in tidal waves to "geniuses" and that people of "normal" intelligence simply cannot have it.

To me, creativity is a gift given to *everyone*. To be creative, I believe an individual simply needs to experience what is around him, process his thoughts and feelings, and present them in a unique way to the world. In Rollo May's book, *The Courage To Create*, he defines creativity as "the process of bringing something new into being."

This doesn't mean that this 'something new' has to be an idea no one has ever had before. It only has to be something *you* have never thought of before. Each of us sees things in different ways. Take ten people out to watch the sunset and there will be ten different versions of how it looked.

In today's world, we live on the edge, always in a hurry, taking for granted the things around us, not enjoying our senses and the moments we've been given. We become so buried in the deep dark mine of life that we can't see the gold sparkling on the walls. It isn't that the gold's not there, it's just that we don't have the light of perception to see it.

Below are fifteen suggestions to help you discover your unique vein of creative gold. This list is in no way complete; you can try many others to discover your creativity, but these fifteen are a good place to start. Not all may be useful to you. The key is to be open and willing to experiment by listening, looking, and feeling to find which will work for you. Finding the mother lode takes time, energy…and a little bit of creativity.

1. Change Your Work Area

Look around your office or workspace. Have you been staring at the same four walls for so long you've memorized the curve of the sheetrock in the corner? Mark Twain said, "Familiarity breeds contempt." Sometimes all we need is a change in our work environment to spark a new thought. Perhaps by changing the direction your desk is facing or which window you look out, you will find a fresh perspective. Maybe by taking your work to the park, zoo, or simply outdoors, you'll have a flash of new insight.

An artist I coached, John, was frustrated. He wanted to dump his sculpture in the trashcan. The walls of his studio were closing in around him and the more clay he added to his work, the worse his piece became. The sculpture was hopeless. It seemed he couldn't find the depth of the piece. The shadows were all wrong and his creativity had stalled.

In a last ditch effort to 'get it right,' he moved his work to the patio outside his back door. Birds flew overhead, a slight breeze freshened the air, and sunlight brightened not only the nuances of his work, but also his mood. He finished his sculpture and now feels his best work is done outdoors.

2. Do Nothing at All

Have you ever been in the shower and ideas start streaming down all around you like water droplets? Or have you been ready to fall asleep, and suddenly the answer to a design problem you've been tormented with for weeks rolls out before you like treasure map?

We puzzle when this happens, yet it's a common occurrence and is one of the ways artists create. Perhaps the answer had been somewhere in your mind all along, but you couldn't tap into it because you were preoccupied.

Jules Henri Poincaré, the late nineteenth, early twentieth century mathematician, known for solving mathematical functions and discovering new theories, grew so stumped on one occasion, he felt as if his mind had shut down. In his biography, he tells of remembering the very moment when an answer broke through – he had just put his foot on the step of a bus he was boarding.

"… [R]est only serves to release the person from his or her intense efforts and the accompanying inhibitions," Rollo May says in *The Courage to Create*, "so that the creative impulse can have free rein to express itself."

The point is: turn your consciousness off. Get up and away from the desk, the canvas, or your project. Take a nap, make yourself a cup of tea, or sit quietly in a corner. Release your mind, so it can release its best ideas to you.

3. Experiment

Try something completely new. Learn or study a different medium than the one you are working in. If you paint landscapes, try portraits. If you paint with watercolors, try oils, collage, etc. If you write fiction, try non-fiction. Similarly, if you read business memos and newspapers all day, try looking at a magazine totally unrelated to your field. Trying something fresh and new will sometimes create exciting revelations.

My client, Carolyn, an oil painter, felt stifled by the limited outlets for her work. She wanted to stretch her skills, yet didn't know how or what to do beyond the canvases on which she painted. She found herself perusing the magazines at the local bookstore. There she discovered a unique angle for her work in a spinning and weaving publication. Years later, Carolyn is still painting landscapes on canvas, but has added silk scarves to her creative work.

4. Get Organized

Do you feel like you're going a million different directions at the same time? Do you forget what you should be doing from one day to the next? Do tasks sit undone because you're overwhelmed? Sit down, calm down, and then make a list of all the things you need to accomplish. List what needs to be done for the day or the week or the month. What's important is putting order in the madness and getting your life organized.

My friend, Ruth, couldn't complete one project, much less think about another. She rushed from here to there, redoing the same task over and over again and avoiding the creative work that really needed to be done.

Exhausted and frustrated, she sat down and took the time to list what she needed and wanted to do. Using the list as a guide, she completed one thing at a time, and then marked it off. After a week went by, she had accomplished more in that seven days than she had in the past year.

By organizing your time, space, and thoughts, you may just find you have more energy to be creative. Organization puts your world in order. It frees your body, soul, and spirit to create.

5. Listen to Music

In Elizabeth Miles' book, *Tune Your Brain*, she writes, "Using music is as natural as breathing or sleeping, and while many do so instinctually, recent research indicates that the systematic use of music can be an effective way to consciously manage your mind, body, and mood."

Music has been called creative energy. As you listen to the type of music you like, ideas often start to flow and you begin to create. Put on an upbeat tempo and you'll be zipping around the office or studio. Want to relax? Put on a Gregorian chant or the soft sounds of a harp CD.

"Music is a direct appeal to the emotions, and since [we] aim for much the same effect, listening to it while working is a natural," Jennifer Blake, New York Times bestselling romance author says. "My mainstay is a Mozart collection. The internal rhythms of his compositions mirror the alpha waves of the brain, which are associated with creative thought, or so I've read. It makes sense to me because having Mozart playing in the background while I work calms and centers me, helping eliminate the 'brain chatter' that interferes with concentration."

Try it. Play music that suits the mood you're trying to create. If you're frustrated or depressed, listen to songs that will improve your state of mind and move you toward a positive place where you can start fresh and relaxed. And don't hesitate to be bold and experiment with unfamiliar music styles and mixes. It just might open up a new area of creativity for you.

6. Make an Appointment with Nature

Whether it's hiking in a national park, jogging on a nature trail provided by your local city, or strolling through your neighborhood, sunshine, animals, and fresh air will revive your senses. Writers and artist have known and recommended 'time with nature' through the ages.

"We need the tonic of wildness," Henry David Thoreau wrote in his 1854 classic, *Walden*. "We can never have enough nature."

William Shakespeare knew that the beauty of the outdoors gives us all a commonality when he wrote, "One touch of Nature makes the world kin."

Spend time watching an ant gather his food, a deer graze in an open field, or a cloud drift across a crystal blue sky and you will know why St. Bernard penned, "You will find something more in woods than in books. Trees and stones will teach you that which you can never learn from masters."

7. Meditate

In today's world, we are surrounded by so much technology; our brains are stimulated and engaged all the time. Radios blaring, children screaming, horns honking and people wanting to engage in conversation are only a few of the assaults constantly hurled at our senses. We become so desensitized by these activities, it is difficult for a lot of people to get quiet and hear their own thoughts. Yet, to hear our inner selves, we must withdraw, and listen. We can do that with meditation.

"Meditation brings wisdom; lack of meditation leaves ignorance," Buddha said. "Know well what leads you forward and what holds you back, and choose the path that leads to wisdom."

Whether you meditate on Bible scriptures or you work on finding your center, it's a place to find peace and new ideas. "In deep meditation the flow of concentration is continuous like the flow of oil," Patanjali states.

8. Opposites Attract

Force two incompatible ideas together and see what happens. You never know what will come about when you begin playing with things that don't relate to one another. Years ago, people may have thought peanut butter and chocolate didn't sound compatible, but look what it's done for Reese's. Buttons and jewelry probably doesn't sound like a genius trend, but artists have taken the concept and made an exciting fashion statement.

What's the best way to add tension to a story? Put opposites together. For instance, what if you put a land lover out to sea? A country boy in the city? Put a farm boy in the same elevator with a society girl and her Pomeranian and you've got enough conflict for an entire series of books. Force two opposing impressions on canvas and people will gravitate to one or the other.

Consider Mel Gibson, the characters he's played, and his movie, *The Passion of The Christ*. A Hollywood celebrity of his magnitude taking on a project such as this was sure to turn heads. Millions went to see it for the message, but then we have to believe there were those who went to see it because of the dichotomy it represented.

9. Re-evaluate Your Goals

Take a realistic look at what you want to accomplish and see if it's doable within the time frame you have set for yourself. If you become anxious every time you sit down to work and it feels like you're reinventing the printing press, you might want to adjust. Perhaps your goals need to be cut down into smaller chunks. Perhaps you need to extend your deadline.

Carrie wanted to write the great American novel. Everyday, that goal loomed large in front of her and each time she sat down at the keyboard, she froze at the enormity of the task. When we spoke, I suggested she not look at the book in its entirety, but one chapter, one page, one scene at a time.

She spent the next several days, writing down all the scenes in her book onto index cards and planned them to be finished on a scheduled basis. A month later, I called to check her progress. Pleased with the way things were going, she estimated she would finish in six months – and she did.

10. Set Aside Time to Be Alone and Think

Become your own think tank. Take an hour a week to do nothing but ponder and brainstorm new ideas and new concepts. Be forewarned: thinking is difficult, exhausting, and requires processing. As Thomas Edison said, "There is no expedient to which a man will not go to avoid the real labor of thinking."

Brainstorm during this hour. Write down all your ideas whether you think they are good or bad, and agree to review them later. Sometimes we aren't the best judges of our inspirations at a given time. Moods may allow us to think everything is horrible, yet put a little time and distance in the mix and some wonderful concepts may emerge. Don't miss them.

A jewelry maker I worked with, Jane, was so involved in building her business that fairly soon the creative well went dry. She couldn't come up with any new ideas like she had when she first started. Not only was this frustrating for her, but her products, once unique and exciting, became assembly line productions.

She began setting aside two hours a week to do nothing but think. Time to mull about her products, the different forms they could take, and colors she could incorporate into the designs. At first it was difficult. Exhausted by the hours of divergent and convergent thinking, new ideas only slowly began to emerge. With time though, her thinking time has become energizing and she knows that's the time her mind is open and most accommodating to imaginative schemes.

11. Spend Time with Children

Children have a unique view of the world. They are honest, open, and their child's perspective can often give us pause at the automatic way we accept our hurried lives. Children are usually not jaded by bad experiences that lead to negativity. They do not worry about coloring out of the lines or how big a mess glitter makes. They've not learned to censor the things they say, the way they feel, judge what they create, or the time it takes to create it.

There's a lesson to be learned in spending time with children, as this anecdote shows. Linda helped her grandchildren roll out the play dough and showed them different shapes they could make with the different colors. While two of the children decided to make animals with their clay right away, the seven-year-old just kept rolling his glob between his hands.

"Aren't you going to make something?" Linda asked after a while.

"Yeah," he said as he looked down at the mound of modeling clay between his palms.

"When?"

"When it tells me what it wants to be."

12. Take a Class

Our minds seek new experiences, fresh knowledge, and like to stay engaged. Expanding what we know increases our ability to share unique insights with others.

One of the most valuable pieces of advice I have received came from my writing mentor, Kathryn Fanning. "Never think you know everything," she told me. "The minute you stop learning, you stop growing. That's deadly, not only for a writer, but for a human being as well."

For the last twenty years, I have followed that advice and offered it many times. Recently, having just finished creativity coach training, I read about a class being offered on creativity through the Rocky Mountain National Park Association. I wasn't sure how much more I could learn, but decided to give the class a try anyway. It turned out to be one of the most rewarding and insightful experiences of my life.

13. Look, then Take Another Look

We see colors, but do we really see them? How many things can you name that are yellow? Green? Are there ten? Twenty? Maybe just one? What about textures? Off the top of your head, can you list ten things with a rough surface? Smooth? Prickly?

Doing individual studies on color and texture will challenge your current perceptual outlook and will help expand the view of your immediate world. Just choose a color (green, yellow, blue, red, purple) or texture (rough, smooth, bumpy, hot, cold) and draw or list what you see or feel.

I give my students the following assignment from time to time. They draw a piece of paper with a color written on it from a hat. They must then find and draw ten objects of that color. Moans and groans are always heard from those who got brown, purple, or orange. But when these people bring in their assignments, I am continually amazed with their results. "I started seeing orange everywhere," "I didn't know there were so many purple things out there," and "brown is really a functional color" are a few of the comments I've heard over the years.

14. Turn off the Critic

Sometimes we begin censoring ourselves before we get to the good stuff. When the voice in our head starts telling us all the reasons a project is wrong, maybe what we should do is relax and consider our work practice. "It's not good enough," "It has to be perfect," or "It has to be finished today," are all things that can put a barrier between our creativity and us.

Nikki and I attended a five-day weaving workshop. I knew I wouldn't be able to finish my project in five days so I was taking my time, knowing any tidbit of knowledge I picked up would be worth the cost.

Next to me, tears welled in Nikki's eyes. Her hands shook as she tried to undo the fifth knot in less than an hour. She had told me earlier she needed to get the design finished by the end of the week and it had to be spectacular.

"We don't have time to make these perfect," I said taking the knot from her sweaty palms. "Why don't you just consider this as practice? You can always do another one later."

"You're right," she said returning from a short break. "This is practice."

The rest of the week, she worked calmly. By the end of the session, she wasn't finished, but her design and technique were beyond everyone else's.

15. Use a Different Approach

Present problems and questions to your thought process and think about them from a different angle. Look at a scene from a different character's viewpoint. Paint a tree orange instead of green. Take an object like an empty spool, a pinecone, or empty coffee can and see what you can make of them. These are only a few suggestions – try thinking up some of your own.

I gave my students one pine cone each. They were to take it and turn it into something different. Because it was Christmas time, I told them it couldn't be part of a wreath or centerpiece and it wasn't to be burned.

Five weeks passed. When the students began presenting their projects I couldn't have been more pleased. Brianna had made a horse out of hers, complete with furry mane and tail. Nathan took the liberty of using building blocks and made his cone into a car. Susan made a rose. Brenda's pinecone was the biggest surprise of all. Her pinecone became Nemo, the Walt Disney Company's fish creation.

There are as many ways to be creative as there are individuals on this planet. We must each find our own ways of giving birth to new realities. The measurement of success lies in our individual viewpoint, how much time we are willing to give to the creative process, and our abilities to mine our own experiences and introspections.

Believe in yourself, your ideas and your craft. That Eureka moment is only one creative notion away.

❖ ❖ ❖

Suggested Readings

Csikszentmihalyi, Mihaly, *Creativity*. HarperCollins Publishers, New York, USA, 1996.

May, Rollo, *The Courage to Create*. W.W. Norton & Company, Inc., New York, USA, 1975.

Steinbart, Alice, *Creating Brilliant Ideas*. Gildner-Reynolds, Winnipeg, Canada, 1999.

❖ ❖ ❖

Deborah Bouziden is an author, speaker, teacher, consultant, and creative coach. She has been writing and publishing since 1985. Her articles have appeared in such publications as *Writer's Digest*, *Woman's Day*, *Lady's Circle*, and many others. She has contributed to six books including the New York Times Bestseller, *In Their Name*, a book on the Oklahoma City bombing, and has five other books published ranging from historical fiction to non-fiction how-to. To learn more about Deborah, visit her website at www.deborahbouziden.com.

Note: If you have techniques that have helped you mine creative gold, Deborah would love to read some of your ideas. If the suggestions she's written about help you, she'd love to read your success stories. You may write her at Creative Ambitions, PO Box 2253, Edmond, OK 73083-2253 or email her at DBouziden@hotmail.com.

IGNITING THE CREATIVE SPARK WITHIN

HOW TO ESTABLISH CREATIVE FOCUS

❖

BY SUZANNE R. ROY, M.A.

When you were a child, did you ever use a magnifying glass to focus the sun's rays on a piece of paper? If you did, you no doubt remember seeing the paper ignite before your eyes. This result was perhaps unexpected and probably seemed like magic at the time, but I'm sure you wouldn't have been as surprised had you known that the word "focus" is, in fact, rooted in the meaning "to flame, to burn." Apparently, our ancestors were aware of the power inherent in the ability to focus energy on one spot. Unfortunately, this is a power that many people today, including those who aspire to become creative, often ignore.

In this article, we will explore what's inherent in the idea of "focus" and why focus is critical to creativity. You will then be given tips on how to sharpen your creative focus. After reading this article, you will have a greater sense of why and how to use focus to ignite the creative spark within you.

WHAT IS FOCUS (AND WHAT DOES IT HAVE TO DO WITH CREATIVITY)?

Many dictionary meanings are attributed to the word "focus," including the following:

- to settle on one thing
- to fix on one thing
- an adjustment (e.g., of one's eye) to bring things into clarity
- to concentrate on something
- starting point of an earthquake
- any center of activity

At first glance, some of these meanings may seem redundant or appear to be irrelevant to our topic, yet they each contribute some insight into what focus is all about and how we can make use of it in pursuing our creative endeavors. The first two concepts hint at how we might better approach our subject; the next two suggest how we can effectively handle the energy that will be the source of creative combustion; and the final two are a reminder of the faith we must bring to the use of this powerful "magnifying" tool that is focus, and of the need to act once a spark has been ignited. Let's explore each definition to see what it reveals to us about establishing creative focus.

To settle on one thing

This definition of focus as "settling" implies a cessation of movement, a stopping, an acceptance of one thing from among many as the subject or target of attention.

Clearly, the need to settle on one thing is simply common sense. We know that we can't focus a camera if we don't stand still long enough to direct the lens at one thing among the many things we see. We know that we can't adequately follow the action in our favorite TV program if we keep switching to the 120+ other channels we have at our fingertips. We also know that our children won't get the most out of their homework if they're playing video games, IM-ing with friends, and doing a dozen other things at the same time.

Why, then, would we assume that we can create without settling on one specific goal? If you've ever jumped from one idea to another because you weren't sure what you should be working on, you know that this unfocused approach usually doesn't produce much except procrastination and frustration. How can we ignite the creative spark within us if our own motion won't allow for the selection of a specific target toward which we can direct our energy?

The idea of "settling" goes further, however, and also carries with it the concept of being satisfied with something less than perfect. We know that if we wait for the perfect camera angle, the perfect idea, the perfect subject, or the perfect moment, we'll never settle on anything and never accomplish anything. Why, then, would we think we can be creative if we spend all our time and energy searching for perfection before actually taking action or completing a project?

To fix on one thing

This definition of focus as "fixing" goes beyond settling and implies being solidly glued to the one thing. It requires continued and deeper "still"ness than simply settling – "still" ness in the sense both of being motionless and of making sure that the target itself is still there if there's been any motion at all.

We've already established that we can't settle on something if we're constantly moving. We can't fix on something if we settle on it halfheartedly or abandon it prematurely. Our subject must be a stationary target for a long enough period of time to allow us to bring our energy to it, and it must "still" be in our sights even when we're momentarily directing our energy elsewhere. There must be a period of "still"ness, in both senses of the word, to allow the energy to build in one spot and get red hot.

Have you ever embarked on a project that you settled on but that you then had difficulty working on because of all the distractions around you or all the mental concerns you were dealing with at the time? The fact that you hadn't truly fixed on your target may have made true focus impossible. Your decision to work on the project was crucial, but "still"ness is what would have allowed you to establish true focus and to literally get "fired up" about your subject. In the midst of our daily routines, it is critical that we steal a few moments to sit with our idea or project each day to be sure our target is "still" there, even if we can't direct our energy to it at the moment.

To concentrate on something

This definition of focus as "concentration" addresses the need to bring energy to the point of focus and to concentrate that energy in the service of our goal. In other words, we must consciously and intensely think about, imagine, and/or physically and emotionally sense what we intend to do, and focus that "hot" energy in all its intensity specifically on our subject.

It's surprising how many people approach their creative work with the idea that it will magically define or reveal itself as they go along. Their sense of needing to generate, sustain, build, and focus energy is lacking. They see how easily more experienced artists appear to create, and they assume that they can do the same. What they don't understand is that even those gifted or extremely talented artists who have managed to internalize the creative process or tap into the creative subconscious to the extent that the works appear to literally spill out of them without much effort – even they have to concentrate and direct their human energy toward their goal if they want the creative spark to ignite.

Thinking, imagination, and physical/emotional involvement are critical creative tools, and the energy they generate must be tapped, fed, used, concentrated, and focused directly on the goal at hand every single day, no matter what, if we are to ignite that elusive spark of creativity.

An adjustment to bring things into clarity

This definition of focus as "adjustment" implies a movable quality to the process of focusing – a capacity and need to zoom in (or out, if we're standing too close to our subject) to capture and sharpen the most meaningful details. The adjustments we make in thinking about our subject, in analyzing it, in feeling it, in sensing it, will help to bring rich details into focus and will allow us to find meaning in our project. This, in turn, will feed and intensify the energies that we must bring to bear in pursuing our goal.

Our focus can be narrow or broad, depending on our purpose and intent and the amount of energy we can bring to our project. We must remember that focus is within our control. What we settle and fix on and concentrate our energy on can be narrowed or broadened at will. We are not stuck with our initial focal point, and this is, indeed, one of the areas where the subject itself – the details we focus on – may dictate how we should change or refine our focus. We must remain open to the possibility of change, as we would be if a rare bird strayed into camera range and we readjusted our aim to make it the focal point of our picture.

It's worth noting here that a narrow focus is usually more intense than an overly broad one. Our magnifying glass in the sun worked best when we were able to direct and sustain, in stillness, a small point of intense light on the paper. Don't be afraid to establish boundaries and parameters as you identify the subject you will focus on. Creative energy is usually stimulated by limiting restrictions.

Starting point of an earthquake

This definition of focus as "starting point" calls to mind its catalytic nature, that is, its ability to spark a reaction. This is the very thing we all hope for in trying to ignite our creative fire. However, the energy must be intense, and we must trust its power enough to let it take over when the moment is right.

Most people who have had real "eureka!" moments – be it in science or in art, with inventions or discoveries or startling new creations – will confess that the breakthrough came during moments of rest or sleep or at other times of letting go after periods of intense concentration. Focus is the starting point of an earthquake, whose effects will change our landscape if we really concentrate our energy and then allow it to proceed on its own. The energy that is harnessed when we consciously focus will intensify when we let go long enough to allow our subconscious to take over, and will create its own effects that contribute to our creative success.

Any center of activity

This definition of focus as "center of activity" is a reminder that activity is at the heart of the whole concept. If we focus, it is because we are actively seeking to capture a particular thing and actively choosing to stay still long enough to truly grasp it. As we focus, we are actively concentrating energy on one spot and actively refining our focus to be sure we see most clearly what we are aiming at. Once we've established a clear, intense focus, we are actively trusting, as evidenced by our persistence and our letting go, in the power of that energy to produce results. Finally, once the spark has been ignited, we must actively fan the flames to be sure the fire has truly taken hold and will continue to burn long enough to allow us to create.

What this means in terms of our creative activity is that we pay attention to the results of our focused effort so that we recognize the nascent flames and that we then work hard to capture the awesome power and beauty of that fire in our medium so that others may experience a new angle on creativity and the life force.

HOW TO ESTABLISH CREATIVE FOCUS

Now, let's see how you can incorporate these defining concepts into your own creative process to help ignite the creative spark within.

Step 1: Settle on one project and subject.

In order to focus, you have to make up your mind and decide on one project (for example, producing a painting or watercolor as opposed to writing a novel) and on the specific subject of that project (for example, painting an early morning view of your flower garden rather than a portrait of your favorite relative) out of the many possibilities that present themselves, even at the risk of making the wrong decision. You have to settle on one goal, no matter what, at least long enough to really become involved with it. No jumping from one project or subject to another; no double guessing yourself; no indulging in perfectionism. Settle on one thing, imperfect though it may seem, and don't change your mind. Commit to it so that you can focus on it.

Here's how you can accomplish this:

> a. Brainstorm what you think you'd like to work on. Do you want to create a painting, write a novel, assemble a quilt, or compose a piece of music? Think about the possibilities and tentatively choose a project. Then brainstorm the possible subjects or controlling effects you could deal with or create within that project. Repeat this process, if necessary, to be sure you've really explored your possible choices.

> b. Think about what really moves you about those subjects or ideas. What do you really want to express at this moment? What will excite you? What do you strongly desire to spend your time on?

> c. Choose one project and subject, and actualize that decision by committing your idea to paper. Explain your project and subject in as much detail as possible.

> d. Actively eliminate all other projects and subjects from consideration. Acknowledge that you've settled on this particular target. Actively banish all doubts and all fears and determine to stay fixed on your project till you've done something significant with it.

Step 2: Fix on your chosen subject.

In order to focus, you must bring your mind to your subject whenever you can – when you wake up in the morning, before going to bed at night, during spare moments when you're driving or waiting in line at the grocery store. You'll notice, I didn't say "bring your subject to mind."

That leaves room for forgetting. Get in the habit of consciously directing your mind to the subject you want to focus on.

Use the following ideas:

a. Explore your subject. Let it color your thoughts and ignite your imagination.

b. Use your time wisely. When you find yourself worrying about the past or anticipating the future, or otherwise wasting your mental energy, think about your subject.

c. Make your subject an active part of your daily routine. Commit five minutes of your time each day to free writing, followed by five minutes of focused free writing. The first technique is akin to meditation in that it helps you to get in touch with how noisy your mind is and to quiet it somewhat. It can help you to achieve the stillness you need in order to solidly fix your mind on your goal. The second technique allows you to brainstorm your topic and to delve more deeply into your subconscious for new insights about your subject.

Note: In case you're not familiar with free writing, it involves putting pen to paper and writing for a specified amount of time without lifting the pen from the paper. You try to capture the ideas that go through your head without concern for punctuation, grammar, logic, or sentence structure, letting go of one thought as soon as the next presents itself. If you do it the way it's meant to be done, you'll have trouble keeping up with your thoughts at first, but you'll eventually experience the blankness that is the goal of meditation. When you do, just keep writing "blank, blank, blank" until thoughts return. Keep the pen moving no matter what, until the time is up. It's a very interesting activity, and it can help you to get in touch with ideas and feelings that would otherwise just come and go without notice or that might never surface at all. (It also makes you aware of how active and intrusive your inner editor is.) In focused free writing, you pick a topic and use the same technique, but constantly force your thoughts back to your topic as you write.

Step 3: Concentrate your energy on your subject.

In order to focus, you must bring all your energy to your subject. Now is the time to approach your project from as many angles as possible.

Try the following:

a. Bring the power of your imagination to your subject. Daydream about what it will look or sound like, the dimensions it will take on, how it will be received, the impact it will make on others.

b. Bring the power of your intelligence to your subject. Do research, immerse yourself in related information, and analyze your approach. Thinking and creativity are not mutually exclusive.

c. Bring the power of your senses and your feelings to your subject. In addition to seeing it, try to hear it, smell it, touch it, or taste it, and anticipate how it will feel emotionally.

d. Spend at least 10 minutes each day actively jotting down ideas generated during these moments of concentration. Here again, focused free writing can be very useful.

Step 4: Adjust your focus to capture the most meaningful details.

In order to focus, you must adjust your view of your subject to establish clarity. You must also define it by separating it from what it is not. Contrary to what you might believe, defining and narrowing your boundaries will actually fuel the creative process and dictate more specific details than leaving your subject too broad.

Here are some recommendations:

a. Use available tools to help you find as many details as possible. Don't forget the dictionary and the library. The more you know about your medium and your subject, the more easily you'll be able to discover how to make your project unique and how to intensify your own energy toward it. You'll also be more aware of the details and background that can be worked in or removed from your focus.

b. Establish parameters and define specific criteria for your project. Make final decisions on the specific medium you will use and the genre you will adhere to. Make tentative decisions about such things as purpose, audience, format, and theme. Then, determine what specific restrictions these decisions will impose on you, or create restrictions of your own. This will help you to determine how broad or narrow your focus should be.

c. Zoom in and out of your subject. Based on the work you've done to this point, look at your subject from both close up and far away. Change your angle. Consider what background could be added or taken away. Remember that a narrow focus is often (though not always) more intense and meaningful than a broad one.

Step 5: After periods of intensity, allow your subconscious to take over.

In order to reap the benefits of focus, you must hold the focus long enough to get results and, at the same time, be willing to let the harnessed energy go its own way.

Some techniques for doing this are:

a. Actively think about and work on your project each day. Bring your full attention to it, preferably at the same time each day, if possible. Develop a vocabulary of words and images for your project so that your language is focused on your goal. Study the masters in your field and don't be afraid to imitate them as you develop your ideas.

b. Ask yourself questions about your project or subject. Verbally identify problems that you've encountered, and ask yourself how these can be overcome.

c. Follow up intense periods of work, thought, and questioning by actively letting go of your subject to allow your subconscious to take over. Turn away from your work for a short while. Sleep on your thoughts. Do some routine activity that will allow your mind to wander. Have faith that your mind will answer all your questions.

Step 6: Pay attention to the results and work on your project every day.

In order to reap the benefits of focus, you must work to nurture the spark and turn it into a blazing fire.

Try these approaches:

a. Jot down all the ideas that come to you about your project or subject, even if you have to do it on a napkin or a gum wrapper, and don't let your inner critic interfere with the flow of those ideas.

b. Focus on these new ideas and work to determine their value to your project. Stay on your topic and don't allow your focus to shift off course.

THE FOCUSING HABIT

As you can see, focusing is largely preparation work. Although it might seem complicated and involved, it's actually a simple process that can be internalized fairly easily and that can occur in a flash once you're really knowledgeable and enthusiastic about your subject. How long you should spend on each step depends on many factors, but it's likely that going directly to your writing desk or your easel or your quilting table without having established proper focus on a specific target will make it more difficult for you to ignite your creative spark and get the flames going. Focus is an element of the creative process that cannot be overlooked since it sets the stage and lights the fire that will make creative work possible. It is also part of the ongoing creative process, a tool at your disposal to keep the fire going and to make sure you stay on course.

Focus is such a powerful creative tool, however, that I must offer two notes of caution:

- Be careful where you consciously focus your mind and energy. Choose your target wisely because you may get hooked into a project that's not worth spending time on. If you find that you are "fixed" on something that interferes with your creative energy, reverse the steps in order to un-focus and free yourself of that fixation.

- Take stock of where you habitually and unconsciously focus your energy during the course of an ordinary day. Interestingly, you can be focusing even when you're not conscious of doing so. Notice what you devote the most time to in your schedule and in your thoughts. Remember that you have a limited amount of energy, so don't deplete that energy needlessly by focusing on useless targets. Finally, if you feel too tired to create or you find that you often berate yourself for being too lazy or distracted to pursue your creative goals, you may want to reexamine exactly where your energy is being spent and refocus it on what really matters in your life.

When we were kids, we sometimes thought the paper beneath our magnifying glass would never ignite. If you recall, you had to be patient and maintain the focus to see results. Keep that in mind as you follow the steps we've just discussed because, once you've ignited the creative spark and caused it to flare up, I'm sure you'll be awed by the unexpected and magical results.

❖ ❖ ❖

Suzanne R. Roy, M.A., a self-employed writer and business consultant, has taught basic writing, college writing, and technical writing at the university level, and creative writing for adult education. She has also written scripts, lyrics, and music for television and the stage, including a nationally-distributed children's television series for public television and a play that was showcased in NYC and produced in Australia. Suzanne lives in Maine and is a member of The Dramatists Guild of America. She offers services in creativity coaching, writing consultation, and editing, as well as a free newsletter on creativity and writing, and can be reached at SuzanneRoy@coachingthecreative.com.

GETTING UNSTUCK

NINE WAYS TO ESCAPE FROM CREATIVITY HALTING GOO

BY RICK BENZEL, M.A.

Every artist gets stuck from time to time in "creativity-halting goo." It can happen at any phase of your work: when you're beginning a project, in the middle, or close to completion. The goo can overcome you in many different ways – it can prevent you from finding an idea, or cloud your mind when choosing among many ideas, or pull you downwards into a creative void.

Whenever it happens and whatever form it takes, creativity-halting goo is frustrating, energy draining, and harmful to the self-esteem of the creative mind. It feels like a sticky poisonous tar that envelops you. No matter how much you try, you simply cannot escape from the gooey spot you have gotten yourself into – and your creative work stops dead in its tracks.

Keep in mind that there are times when losing your creative momentum is not because you are stuck, but rather that you are entering a valuable phase of the creative process referred to as an "incubation" period. During this time, your mind unconsciously processes new ideas and feelings that will eventually drive your project forward. Many creative people actually nurture such incubation periods, letting themselves remain fallow for days or weeks without trying to force ideas. They stop painting, writing, composing, dancing, acting – and instead sit back and attend to other business in their life, all the while letting their unconscious intelligence gently process images and thoughts in the background, without any attempt to track them.

How can you know if you are in an incubation period or a gooey mess? Actually, the most telling cues come from your body. When you incubate, your physical being is at ease. You feel calm, in a relaxed state of mind without nervous energy or anxiety. You eat and sleep well, and have no problems performing the other work of your life. You enjoy friends, reading books, going to movies – because behind the scenes, your mind is hard at work "considering."

When you are stuck, your body also lets you know it – but in very different ways! Your mind races, your stomach hurts slightly (or a lot), and your muscles become tense. The goo on your mind and body weighs you down, and at the end of a day, you feel like you need an expensive full-body massage. When you are stuck in goo for several days, your stress level mounts and often transforms into anger towards yourself or those around you.

Being stuck is no way to be creative – or to live. It saps your energy, your vitality, and your joy in creating. While artists and creators cannot get rid of all moments of stuckness, the solution is to minimize their effect on you. You need to learn techniques that allow you to break out of the sticky mass that holds you back, leading you back to health and productive creativity.

In this article, I present to you nine approaches that I have found to be useful in getting unstuck. They synthesize a range of ideas and techniques that I have used with my clients, as well as with myself. Think of these approaches as a toolbox that you can open whenever you need something with which to pry yourself free. Keep in mind that you may encounter various types of stuckness. Try out different techniques and see which are best for each individual situation.

THE REFRAMING APPROACH

This approach to getting unstuck is based on the psychological concept of "reframing" a problem, which means learning how to change your view of the problem. Given that your reality is shaped by your thoughts and interpretations, reframing is based on the concept that you can abandon negative self-talk, replacing it with positive statements and attitudes that lead you to a more fruitful interpretation of the moment.

Consider the following situation. You have just spent a week writing a chapter of your novel, but now you're stuck. Somehow your protagonist has ended up in a position that doesn't make sense for her character. You begin to curse at yourself, upset that the last week feels like wasted time. You can't figure out how to salvage the chapter you worked so hard to write. Your mind is going blank and the goo slowly begins to ooze all over you, making you feel like an author who's been tarred and feathered.

Many writers, painters, and other artists who invest large amounts of time on a project experience this type of gooey remorse. They become so invested in an idea that they find it difficult to accept when it doesn't work – and they become stuck trying to salvage the idea although they know it is taking them down an unproductive path.

This is when reframing can help. Rather than cursing yourself and viewing the experience as "wasted time" or as proof that "I lack talent" (both of which are nothing but thoughts you place in your own mind), why not reframe the experience in a way that inspires your creative juices instead of draining them? You might say to yourself, "This plot twist is a great one; let me save it for another character later in this book." Or you could think, "Wow, what a great idea for another story." Or perhaps you can tell yourself something as mild as, "Well, I guess I know my character better now. I'll rewrite this chapter and learn from the experience."

Reframing is an extremely valuable tool for artists who feel frustrated and stuck at the beginnings of projects. If you believe you are going nowhere, it often indicates that your inner critic is halting you from trying out ideas because you fear making a mistake. It can be useful to reframe your early work entirely, viewing whatever you do in the context of "This is a good start for my project and I can always come back and revisit it," rather than thinking, "I don't think this is the 'right' start for this book (painting, song, etc.) so I'm not going anywhere until I can get it right."

It is always useful to remember that you can alter your thoughts about many situations. You can feel angry, frustrated, tired, upset with yourself – or you can transform your feelings into patience, understanding, and self-respect for the efforts you make.

THE MARCEL PROUST APPROACH

The great French writer Marcel Proust (1871–1922) is known for a style of writing called stream of consciousness, in which he poured his feelings out onto the page like water over a dam. Proust's novels are long extensions of his thoughts and memories, with thousands of words devoted to the smallest of incidents. For example, in his famous novel *Remembrance of Things Past*, Proust devoted 30 pages to simply describing rolling over in bed at night.

For creators, the value of the Marcel Proust approach to stream of consciousness lies in the fact that when you are stuck, you need to release your mind from rules and formulae so you can open yourself up to fresh ideas. If you are at an impasse when writing your novel, stop thinking about writing your novel *per se*, and begin writing just about anything. If you are painting and don't know what color to use next, stop thinking about painting the piece in question and head for a new canvas where you release all preconceptions into a stream of consciousness of colors and shapes. If you are choreographing a dance, go off into a studio and simply dance your head off using whatever movements occur to you in the moment.

Stream of consciousness allows you to reconnect with your innermost feelings and thoughts, a veritable "brain dump" that lets your creativity hang out without regard to correctness, appropriateness, or brilliance. You simply lay all your thoughts bare – and in doing so, you let yourself tap into authentic feelings and ideas that arise from deep inside you. By relaxing yourself into stream of consciousness, your mind easily and quickly floats from one idea to another, surging in feelings and memories that often contain the seeds of the solution to your stuckness.

The Marcel Proust approach is similar to what you may already do in your journaling or in the "morning pages" associated with the book, *The Artist's Way*. All three methods are aimed at the same phenomenon: releasing your mind from your inner critic that halts your creative work – that little voice that claims a certain passage you are writing is "stupid" or that your painting is "ugly." As Proust taught us, it's very creative to simply let your mind spill out, and even your ramblings can turn into a world-renowned piece of literature.

THE POTTERY APPROACH

When I was 25 a few decades back, I decided to try pottery as a form of artistic expression. I signed up for a summer course at a small pottery studio in Cambridge, Massachusetts. Within months, I was sitting at the potter's wheel, throwing vases, sugar bowls, and pitchers. During this time, another student potter suggested that I read a book called *Centering in Pottery, Poetry and The Person*, by M.C. Richards, which has turned out to be one of my most inspiring reads.

In *Centering*, Richards uses the potter's wheel as a metaphor for life. When you try pottery, you quickly learn that if you do not center the clay on the wheel, it is nearly impossible to pull the clay up into a balanced object. For Richards though, centering clay means far more than simply plopping it down in the middle of the potter's wheel. Centering also must take place in your mind, in your feelings, in your entire physical being. In talking about knowing how to center, Richards wrote:

> Wisdom is not the product of mental effort.... it is a state of total being, in which capacities for knowledge and for love, for survival and for death, for imagination, inspiration, intuition, for all the fabulous functioning of this human being who we are, come into a center with their forces, come into an experience of meaning that can voice itself as wise action.

When you are stuck, it often means that you are not centered in your being. Your inner artist is at odds with something in your life that does not support your art. Something is awry that tilts your "clay" – that is, your ideas, your projects – and you will not be able to get unstuck in the same way that a potter is not able to fashion a nicely centered pot.

The Pottery Approach is thus oriented towards finding ways to center yourself. Perhaps you need to meditate, go for walks every day, or have a talk with someone who is causing you emotional pain. Perhaps you need to create a nice spot of color on the wall at which you can stare to re-center yourself. Whatever you do to get centered, your goal is to be able to approach your artistic endeavor by being fully there – mentally, emotionally, spiritually, sexually, physically – as one integrated, wise artist. When you are in this state, you will be capable of working with your creativity in the same truly blissful way that potters work, becoming one with their clay as it spins around on the wheel, their hands becoming the pot and the pot becoming their hands. In short, when you and your art merge into one "beingness," there is much less opportunity to get stuck because all of you, including your inner critic, becomes one with your art.

And if you cannot find an activity that centers you, I highly recommend taking a pottery course!

THE BUDDY APPROACH

Creativity-halting goo can sometimes be thick and viscous, and getting out of it on your own is just not possible. Your inner artist is going nowhere, spinning its wheels, like a car stuck in mud or snow. Sometimes you need a "buddy" to get unstuck, a colleague who can push or pull you out, by listening to you and perhaps by sharing some ideas. Simply talking about your creative block with another person is often enough to get you going again because in the process of articulating your ideas to someone else in a non-judgmental conversation, you can often stumble upon a fresh way to explain your concepts or an insight you didn't have before.

The Buddy Approach is best done with a partner who is, like you, a creator and thus can understand the artistic difficulties you may be going through. It is best not to choose a family member or spouse based simply on the fact that he or she knows you well. This can backfire, causing more problems than it solves if you do not like the advice the person gives you. Instead, select as your buddy an artistic peer, someone who does the same type of art as you or even someone who works in an entirely different art.

The Buddy Approach is useful for several reasons. First, your colleague's comments and listening provide an outside view of your work that can be beneficial when you are lost in your own ideas. The buddy may see the proverbial tree through the forest that has become your mind. Secondly, a buddy can help you silence your inner critic, by being more sympathetic, encouraging, or just plain honest in telling you that your ideas are fine, keep working. Finally, if you are willing to listen, a buddy may have suggestions to enhance your own ideas or that provide you with solutions to your creative problem.

Many artists are reluctant to share their work with others before it is completed, and that is understandable. However, there are times when there is nothing better than a colleague or friend whose shoulder you can lean on in a time of need. Artists who shy away from making community with others may be missing out on the valuable resources that other artists can provide. One way to combat a reluctance to talk to other artists is to take a class. Even if you decide not to share your ideas with others, you can listen to other people sharing ideas and vicariously partake in an extended buddy system that supports you in the background.

THE MATRIX APPROACH

When your getting stuck involves indecision or an inability to choose from among what seem to be too many good ideas, the best solution may be the Matrix Approach. This solution is based on resorting to logic to evaluate your ideas and choose the best one according to a set of criteria you develop. The name of the approach refers to the fact that you construct a "matrix" or grid, with rows and columns in table format. In each column, you write one of the ideas you have, and in each row, you list one of the criteria that will help you decide the best choice. For example, if you are writing a non-fiction book and you are trying to decide whether to write a book based on, for example, 7 steps to better health, 30 days to better health, or 10 secrets to better health, you would need a matrix consisting of 3 columns. Then in the rows, you would list criteria such as names of competing books in Row 1, spin-off opportunities for each title in Row 2, the editor's preference in Row 3, and so on.

The Matrix Approach, in theory, can help you get unstuck by simply checking off which column and row intersection makes the most logical sense. Then you can count up the X's and see which decision wins. However, given that art is not science, the Matrix Approach often requires a level of subjective analysis and feeling that might lead you back toward your quagmire. You could end up with a grid that has X's everywhere – and you're back at indecision.

Nevertheless, the Matrix Approach can prove useful when you have a large number of choices because, at the very least, it can help you eliminate a few lesser choices from the crowd so you can focus on just the one or two best ones. In this way, the Matrix Approach can help you get out of the quicksand a little faster and without as much pain as you might have experienced.

THE SPIRITUAL APPROACH

In the last decade, the role of spirit in creativity is resurging, as more artists are turning themselves over to a "higher" power to direct their work. For some people, the higher power is embedded in a religious tradition, while for others, their spiritual approach is rooted in a profound respect and appreciation for human creativity within a mystical cosmos. Whichever the case, a spiritual approach to overcoming stuckness suggests that you stop thinking about your creative problem and simply give yourself over to whatever higher power you believe in to provide you with the answer.

It is of course impossible to ascertain if the spiritual approach works because a higher power truly exists and answers the prayers of artists, or if there is something about releasing your worries into the cosmos that allows fresh ideas to come to you. Perhaps it is a combination of the two. What counts is that the spiritual approach seems to help many people feel that their creative work is linked to forces in the universe that guide us into a more harmonious, peaceful existence. By releasing their creative blocks into the ether or to their worshipped God, they lighten their own anxiety about creating, which may indeed be an opportunity for new creating to occur.

If you are not religious, or are agnostic, your spiritual approach need not be any more than going up to a mountain top and contemplating your creativity as you sit among the boulders that have been on this earth for millions of years. I often go camping at one location in the Sierra Mountains in California where, at 12,000 feet, I experience profound insights into my place in the cosmos, which reinforces my love for the creativity that I possess.

THE REWARD APPROACH

The Reward Approach can be an effective method to get out of stuckness when the creativity-halting goo is thin and leaves you with a sense of power over your situation. This approach requires you to be brutally honest with yourself in evaluating whether your stuckness reflects factors that you can control – if you truly wanted to. For example, we all experience times when we simply don't want to get to work; we would rather watch TV or go for a walk than feel the pain of writing, painting, or practicing our instrument.

But in these types of situations, if you are truthful with yourself and are able to admit that the problem has more to do with your own negative attitude or your laziness, you might realize that this is the right time to adopt the Reward Approach. As the name implies, you simply offer yourself a reward for committing to get your work done or for achieving certain milestones along the way to total completion.

For example, you might make a contract with yourself that for every chapter you complete on your novel, you will allow yourself a nice dinner at one of your favorite restaurants, and you won't go to that restaurant unless you do complete the chapter. Other rewards could be buying yourself a desired piece of clothing, or a night out, or that new electronic device you desire.

So many of us are not good at abiding by contracts we make with ourselves. It is easy to tell yourself, "I know I said I was going to work tonight, but I'm just too tired." The problem is, of course, if you let yourself off the hook day in and day out, you accomplish very little towards your creative goals. You thus must find a new way to abide by your self-made contract. That is where the rewards come in.

In general, the more meaningful the reward, the more success you will have in fulfilling your commitment.

THE HERO APPROACH

One of the most intriguing ways to learn how to get unstuck is to find yourself a hero, that is, a luminary in your field after whom you might model yourself. If you are a writer, pick a living or historic writer whose life or work you admire. Read everything you can find about the person, including his or her work habits, thoughts on the writing life, and problems with writing that may be similar to yours. Then, each time you sit down to write and especially each time you get stuck in the goo, ask yourself, "What would [insert name of your hero] have done about this situation?"

The value of the hero approach is that it spotlights for you a work ethic and commitment to quality that you will slowly internalize as your own. Finding a hero among the greats of the creative world – whether it be Michelangelo, Monet, Mamet, or Maroon Five – builds your self-esteem and your passion for art, both of which are instrumental in defeating your inner critic and helping you get unstuck.

In addition, as one of the other articles in this anthology points out (see Michael Mahoney's *The Hero Within: Using the Mythic Journey to Discover Meaning in Your Creative Work*), you are effectively a hero in your own creative journey, which requires you to survive many battles with the evil forces of non-creativity. In order to return victorious from your journey, you must think of yourself as a hero, with courage, ambition, and daring to get through the combat. But as your own hero, even you need allies, and the best ones are those who have made the journey before you. They know the danger zones, the pitfalls, and the secrets to coming out alive.

However, be careful about selecting a hero and turning him or her into an object of negative comparison for yourself. It is not productive to make an accomplished artist your hero if the person constantly reminds you of your lack of commercial success. Choose your heroes based on their human qualities and the values they bring to their craft, not based on how famous they are or how much money they made. Make them real heroes in your work, not celebrities you blindly worship.

THE HIRE-A-PROFESSIONAL APPROACH

The last approach to getting out of creativity-halting goo is, of course, to hire a creativity coach. Like hiring a doctor when you are sick, a lawyer when you need legal advice, or an accountant when you need your taxes done right, a creativity coach can fashion a comprehensive program for your specific stuckness – i.e., the nature of your goo, its thickness, stickiness, how deep in it you are, and so on. A creativity coach is trained to analyze your concerns and problems, and to work with you to devise solutions that get you out of the quagmire and back into happy, productive creating again. A coach can help you decide which of the approaches above – or many others they may have created themselves – might work in your situation. You can find creativity coaches at www.creativitycoachingassociation.com, which lists coaches available to artists and creators in many locations throughout the world. Coaches can also work with you by email and phone, so you are never far away from having professional assistance available to you to analyze your creative problems and propose solutions to get you unstuck.

❖ ❖ ❖

Rick Benzel is a creativity coach, writer, and editor in Los Angeles with a passion for helping all types of artists get unstuck. He enjoys brainstorming with creators to help them develop, articulate and organize their ideas. His coaching practice has helped writers, screenwriters, and visual artists. He offers various workshops in the Los Angeles area, a one-day brainstorming Inspiration Tour, and 7- or 10-day retreats in France. He is the creator of this Anthology and the founder and Publisher of Creativity Coaching Association Press, the publisher of this book. He can be contacted at creativitycoach@verizon.net or at his website, www.personalcreativity-coach.com.

SEEKING LIMINALITY

MAKING THE MOST OF THRESHOLD EXPERIENCES

❖

BY CHERRYL MOOTE

A frontier has two sides. It is an interface, a threshold, a liminal site, with all the danger and promise of liminality.... the side that calls itself the frontier, that's where you boldly go where no one has gone before, rushing forward like a stormfront, like a battlefront... Nothing before you is real...It does not exist, it is empty, and therefore full of dream and promise...and so you go there. Seeking gold, seeking land, annexing all before you, you expand your world.

- Ursula LeGuin -

Artists are seekers. We seek perfect technique, effortless execution, divine inspiration. We seek the liminal moments, the liminal experience.

A liminal experience? What is that? Is it safe? Will I need shots? A liminal experience is a time when you are in transition from one state of being to another state of being. The word liminal is derived from the word *limen*. A limen is a transverse beam in a door frame. During a liminal experience you are moving from a time when you know the rules and the expectations to a time when you must create new rules for yourself and expect the unexpected. You are crossing a threshold. Artists need liminal times when they retreat from the everyday world in order to clarify who they are, to have time to learn how to speak their own voice.

Visual artists today face a difficult challenge. In a time of plentiful tools and materials, our art world has been dragged into the swirling vortex of cookie cutter mediocrity. Art supplies have become big business. In order to sell more products, the manufacturers and the stores create projects that are foolproof, fast and efficient. You take a class, you mimic a style, you have instant success. Everyone creates with the same tools, the same supplies. There is no need for risk. Just do it like the teacher says. Read the product project guide or pick up any number of magazines that have been created for artists and crafters. And then you wake up one day and think, "I'd like to try...." You create something new, just for you. Is it safe? Will it fit in? Do you care? You are on the threshold of new territory. If you keep exploring, you might find yourself in the middle of a liminal experience.

When we start to see ourselves as artists rather than people who dabble in art, we move into our first liminal art experience. We feel unsure of ourselves, we miss the old rules that tell us how to do things right. We may step back and examine the way we have been creating. We become seekers, because artists are seekers. We begin to yearn for the times when we have sudden insights, intense bursts of inspiration; when we create art that glows and pulses with life and meaning. The quest for the 'aha' moments becomes everything.

The problem is that unless we examine the process of reaching a liminal experience and understand as much as we can about these experiences, we don't learn as much as we should. We are in fact cheating ourselves of the full lessons to be learned. We end up flitting from project to project, devouring books and articles, chasing after the perfect teacher, constantly looking for liminal insights, for the high that comes from these experiences. We get frustrated, and many artists lose hope. The solution is to look at the way we structure our artistic lives and to understand more completely the process we are undertaking.

I can be a slow learner. For several years I went to England for a week of study. I learned the same thing every year, in almost the same way. I would get frustrated on the second or third day of class because I couldn't make my paper and tools create just what I had in mind. I would go for a long walk on the beach. I realized that I was trying to make my tools and paper do something that they weren't meant to do for me. I'd go back to the classroom and allow my tools to make the marks they were meant to make on the paper they were meant to make them on. I would create something wonderful, something that looked like I made it. I would feel complete as an artist. A new artistic path seemed to be coming into focus through the doorway. I would fly home, and in the weeks and months that followed, I would slowly but surely forget to remember to let my tools make the marks that I was meant to make. For me, the trip to England was a liminal time. It was a place in between, a place I knew where and what I might be. It was a time set apart from the everyday world where I could glimpse a new world, new rules, new possibilities. I just wasn't making the most of it.

To be truthful, relearning the same thing several years in a row wasn't all bad. I loved the time away, the friends I made there, the energy of the place. In the midst of a bleak winter day when nothing seems to be going right, I often pick up a rock from that beach and remember what it feels like to have things go right after they have been going so terribly wrong. What I needed to realize was that there was more going on here than I originally saw. I was an even slower learner than I thought. I had been missing the even bigger lesson, the larger liminal experience. I had forgotten that the journey itself has lessons to teach.

Years ago I read a book by Benjamin Hoff called *The Tao of Pooh*. In the book he uses Winnie the Pooh and his adventures to illustrate some important life lessons. One of my favorite passages finds Pooh contemplating what his favorite thing is. He is about to answer "honey, of course," when he realizes that the anticipation of honey may be just as important. Hoff writes:

> "Well," said Pooh, "what I like best -" and then he had to stop and think. Because although Eating Honey was a very good thing to do, there was a moment just before you began to eat it which was better than when you were, but he didn't know what it was called.

> The honey doesn't taste so good once it is being eaten; the goal doesn't mean so much once it is reached; the reward is not so rewarding once it has been given. If we add up all the rewards in our lives, we won't have very much. But if we add up the spaces between the rewards, we'll come up with quite a bit. And if we add up the rewards and the spaces, then we'll have everything - every minute of the time that we spent. That doesn't mean that the goals we have don't count. They do, mostly because they cause us to go through the process, and it's the process that makes us wise, happy or whatever.

What I had unconsciously overlooked was the journeys between the liminal experiences, the ones I had in England, the ones I had in countless workshops, the ones I had in my own studio, and the ones I had while I was teaching. The paths that I took on the way to those doorways were part of what led to new frontiers for me. Perhaps what I had been doing wrong is also what you have been doing. So, here are some suggestions for ways to prepare for liminal times, how to get the most out of them when they happen, and how to incorporate their lessons into your daily life.

PREPARING FOR THE JOURNEY

1. Get rid of dead weight.

Anyone who has ever taken heavy suitcases on vacation will know that packing light is a better choice. For visual artists, I find that there are two kinds of dead weight that need to be dealt with before they can set out in a meaningful way: their physical workspace and their preconceived notions.

Creating a workspace that is conducive to productive work is important. I am not discussing the type of studio clean-up fueled by the need to avoid artistic work, but rather the considered organization of tools and materials in order to maximize working enjoyment. Take a few days and consider your stuff. What materials have no real meaning for you anymore and are just taking up space because you haven't taken the time to clear them out? Pack them up and give them to someone who is just starting out and wants to do some experimenting; take them to a school or an after school program; get them out of your space. I have a big studio area that constantly needs revision as I change who I am as an artist. If I don't take time to do this, it gets cluttered and claustropho-bic. I find myself avoiding it. I also find that when the creative urge strikes me I spend more time searching for things in my studio than I do creating. My studio is not the ideal space for me – I crave real windows, I hate the color of the floor, the dark paneling...but if it is at least some-what organized, and I have a few things in view that remind me of beauty and light and the joy of creating, I am more likely to feel more positive about going there to create. Don't take any physical junk on the journey.

Just as you don't want any unnecessary clutter in your studio, you should try to get rid of unnecessary clutter in your mind. Ogres, trolls and the ever-present critic on your shoulder should be eliminated. There are lots of wonderful books, tapes, and creativity coaches available to help with this process. One book that my students, my artist friends, and I have found particularly useful is *Fearless Creating* by Eric Maisel. Keeping unconstructive criticisms and attitudes at bay and being able to embrace a liminal experience without them is worth the work involved. Don't take any mental junk on the journey.

2. Choose your travel companion(s) wisely.

Go on the journey alone or pick your companions very wisely. Friendly competition can be invigorating at times, but it can also lead to feelings of inadequacy and even envy when your companions are reap-ing the rewards of their journey, and you are still lost in the wasteland. If you take this journey with companions, you may find you spend more time celebrating their successes and disparaging your own experiences than you do enjoying the journey. Conversely, it is very easy to be neg-atively affected by the struggles of others. Even if you are simply empathizing with them because they are disappointed by their own work, your work may be compromised. Choose your support system wisely. Keep from having your bliss sullied.

3. Plan a preliminary route.

Start mapping out a route. Listen to your inner voice. Where is it telling you to head? What is it interested in? What can you read about? Whose work should you look at? What teacher should you consider studying with? What practice do you need to do? Explorers embarking on a long physical journey begin to plan, assemble supplies, and train months before they leave. Artists need to do this too. What skills are rusty? What skills should you be learning? Make a plan for committing consistent, thoughtful time to the process.

4. Pack for the journey.

You have already uncluttered your work space but now you want to begin to pull out the tools and materials that you intuitively think you may want close at hand. When packing for a workshop away from home, I start by grouping together the things that are needed. Then I begin the process of weeding, compacting, miniaturizing. When taking a workshop or a course, there is usually a supply list provided, but I often get a feeling that there is a tool or a material that I should bring "just in case." If I follow this intuition, I am usually rewarded for carrying the extra weight at the other end.

5. Set aside the time.

Although liminal experiences can happen anywhere, at any time, they happen best when time is set aside for them. In most societies, liminal experiences are crafted so that a time apart from society is sought for deeply meaningful religious or cultural events. Young men are sent to the wilderness. Young couples get married and go on a honeymoon. Those about to be ordained go on a series of retreats before making the final commitment to the ministry. For me, I must find a way to take time apart from my day-to-day life, away from the normal rhythm of the world. If I organize my home life appropriately, I can take a course for several days while staying at home. It can be done by silencing the phones and TVs and retreating to the studio. However, I find that liminal experiences happen most often when I can remove myself from the realities and stresses of daily life and take a course or retreat time away from home.

6. Become committed and focused.

You need to commit to your art and the work that it requires in order to grow and develop as an artist. Reshape your schedule to make time for your artistic work. You need to learn to ignore the phone, forget about TV, limit your email, and carve out times without distractions. When you go away to take a course, stay focused on the purpose of the trip. It is easy enough to get drawn into the social life of a conference, as there are so many like-minded people to talk to, so much eye candy to see, and so many tempting tools and materials to buy that you completely miss the time when liminal experiences can happen. You need to pick a conference or retreat where the organizers are aware that too many distractions, although enjoyable, can seduce you away from the purpose of the trip. Be diligent about immersing yourself in the art experience. Time for camaraderie with other artists is important, but likely needs to be limited. Decide in advance how you want to spend your time. Then be disciplined.

7. Choose the right guides.

Choosing the right teacher is critical. Is she going to encourage you to create your own work or does he simply want to create clones. Is it cookie cutter art? Cookie cutter art is safe; liminal experiences and the art that comes out of them aren't safe because you are creating in a way that clearly expresses who you are and how you interact with the world artistically. The art world is full of cookie cutter art classes because people want the quick fix, the finished product at the end of the week, something to show for their time and money, something that family, friends and colleagues can understand and admire. If you are looking for a liminal experience, you need a teacher who understands that art is a journey. You need a mentor who encourages you along the path. You want a course that gives you some meat and even some bones to chew on during the months ahead. You want a class where you start to see patterns of thought and meaning emerging from your own work, where you can glimpse, even for a moment, a new world. Once you know the doorway is there, you can do the work to find it again, even if you lose it temporarily.

THE LIMINAL EXPERIENCE

Liminal experiences are not only difficult to explain to other people, they may be difficult to explain to ourselves. Often the insights we have are intuitive or fleeting images that aren't easy to interpret using standard forms of language. These times are different for everyone but there are some basic guidelines that apply.

1. Don't force it.

Liminal experiences can't be forced or even time managed. You may have done your best to plan for one to happen but it may elude you. Make the most of your work time anyway and don't get discouraged. Allowing time for your art, following your own intuitions and enjoying the act of creating are the best ways to entice a liminal experience into being, but they cannot be prescheduled. Remember that it is a journey, and, like Winnie the Pooh, discover that the anticipation of and preparation for a liminal experience can be rewarding in and of itself.

2. Don't spook it.

I often have the feeling that something magical is happening just outside my peripheral vision. If I turn suddenly and try to capture it, it skitters off and isn't seen again for days. If I am patient and wait for it to move into my field of vision, I am rewarded. Perhaps this is why artists who have been doing the preparatory work often dream great ideas. It may be why they occur when we are out walking, or letting our thoughts float within a great piece of music – the idea isn't scared off.

3. Contemplate afterwards.

Take time to be alone and relive the experience, savor it. Think about how it felt, what you saw in your work that you hadn't before, what form your work might begin to take now. Think about how true the experience felt, how right it was for you. Visualize the experience, anchor the feelings to a physical memento, lock the secret inside a piece of music, the smell of a flower... Make a marker that you can use to find your way back, a trigger or a key. Leave breadcrumbs for your creative self to follow back to the experience when life gets hectic or work gets discouraging.

4. Record the experience.

In addition to choosing a marker for yourself, find a way of recording what you have learned. Write it down, draw it, use hieroglyphics or expressive drawings. Make a physical record of the experience that you can refer to when you again find yourself in the wasteland. It is easy to begin to feel that the whole experience was simply a mirage. Write down every detail you can remember because you will forget. Keeping the record detailed makes it more real, more useful. You may want to have a special journal that is reserved for recording liminal experiences and insights.

REAPING THE REWARDS

You have had a great, mind-expanding, course-correcting liminal moment. Now what? By the time you have taken the plane or the train or the bus, or the car home, greeted your family, made up with your pet, and had a good night's sleep, it is easy to forget what you have learned. By the time you have been home for a week, done your laundry, unpacked your tools, and caught up on your email, the experience can seem like a dim memory or something that you read about that happened to someone else. How do you keep this from happening?

1. Schedule time for artistic exploration.

Formally scheduling time for art into your weekly activities is the best way to guarantee that you will indeed have time to explore your creativity and follow the path where it leads. If you are going away to study, assume that while you are away you will have had a great insight or at least that you will have learned some new skills that will need practicing to move those skills from short-term to long-term memory, to become part of your physical being. Before you leave, make sure that you will have time to take advantage of what you have learned when you get home. Something as simple as freezing a few meals ahead, keeping your social calendar clear, pre-booking play dates for your children, hiring a sitter, taking an extra week off...

2. Visualize how your work will change.

Take time to daydream, visualize and plan how you will begin to work your new insights into your art. Visualize yourself in the studio, what tools are out, what music is playing, etc.

3. Commit to change.

Develop a plan of action based on your visualization. Create specific goals that support your new vision for your work. By creating specific goals, the experience is made more real, more concrete. By creating specific goals with specific timelines, you commit to change.

Whatever you do from that time on, remember to ask yourself: does this reflect what I learned? If it doesn't, why not? Are you reverting to old, comfortable patterns? Are you afraid to continue exploring the new insight? If so, why? Has your old work been financially rewarding but not emotionally rewarding? Are you afraid that your new work won't be?

4. Commit to growth.

When you commit to change, you are also committing to growth. Growth means finding new insights and expecting new experiences. When should you begin to plan for growth, for a new journey? You likely already have and you don't even know it. If you aren't planning then you aren't growing and you aren't seeking. Artists seek.

❖ ❖ ❖

Living life as an artist is not easy. Living life as an artist who actively engages in the quest for liminal experiences is even more challenging. However, the rewards can be oh so sweet if, like Pooh, we remember to enjoy the anticipation of the honey, the eating of the honey, and the lovely lingering taste of honey in our mouths. Engage fully in all the myriad facets of the liminal journey. Remember that artists seek. Never forget to speak your own voice.

❖ ❖ ❖

Cherryl Moote is an accomplished calligrapher, bookbinder and paper artist. Her company, Moote Points, distributes a series of her bookbinding and paper crafting books and videos. Cherryl's natural teaching talent shines through in all her materials, allowing you to learn new techniques with maximum enjoyment and success. Grateful for the impact of many artistic mentors, she devotes a large part of her career to teaching, inspiring and connecting with other artists around the world. She actively mentors and coaches artists in Toronto and is also available for online or telephone coaching. Visit www.mootepoints.com to learn more about her publications and to see her artwork, and www.explorential.com to find out more about coaching, courses, weekend workshops and retreats planned for the future.

LIVE YOUR CREATIVITY EVERY DAY

BALANCING ACTS

WALKING
THE TIGHTROPE
BETWEEN YOUR
CREATIVE PATH
AND DAILY LIFE

BY LAURA CATER-WOODS, M.F.A.

Does this sound familiar? After what seems an endless time away from your creative passion, you finally have a full day to work in the studio – but your brain goes blank. You haven't a clue what you will do with the time you had slated for productive creating. Several hours later, you realize that all you have done is checked e-mail, played solitaire, moved various piles of stuff from location A to B, and answered unsolicited phone calls from fundraisers.

How about this scenario? Your brain is swimming with brilliant ideas and you can't wait to get to work. But once in the studio, you can't focus or find a place to start. Soon you are creating diversions and just making busy work for yourself. It occurs to you that those dishes really have to be washed, the trash needs to go out, and you should tidy up your workspace before you play with your paints. In short, you realize you have invented ways to avoid the solitude of the studio and ended up wasting your precious creative time.

What is going on here? Are you stuck? Blocked? Not really an artist?

Actually, none of these is necessarily true. It is simply easy to succumb to negative thinking and self-doubt when it seems that the creative time you get is being frittered away and nothing productive is happening. It is also common for creative people to feel guilty about taking time away from the responsibilities, obligations and distractions of their daily life. We all need relationships, we have jobs, and we are part of communities and families. We can end up feeling that the demands of "real life" are more important than our need to create. Or we may indeed be using our external commitments as an avoidance technique. Either way, we find ourselves resentful, frustrated and at odds with our sense of self. If we have people in our lives who do not understand or support our need for solitude, we can feel sabotaged.

The fact is, it is common for creative people to be overwhelmed by the blank page, the empty canvas, and the pressure of generating something from nothing. Wherever you are in your development as a "maker," you confront the need to generate ideas, and interpret and communicate those ideas in a unique way. Even students, working within a proscribed framework, must still find a personal response to their assignments.

So how do we take the tools and materials we love to use, combine them with our current skill levels and use it all to create an image uniquely our own? Where do we start? How do we start? And once we start, how do we keep going? How do we integrate our creative life with our daily life? What are the tricks, tools, ways of thinking that can help us live fully and wholly as artists in the world? In this article we will look at some ways to start, ways to keep going, and strategies for balancing the various parts of our lives.

TIME

First of all, nothing happens if we don't show up. How can we create that time, given our income producing jobs, our desire to be with those we love, our need for sleep, our wish to see the latest movie… ?

The first question is therefore, what are your priorities? If evening television or the morning paper is more important than working on your novel, okay, you've decided. Or have you? It's easy to fall into the avoidance tactics created by home workplace hazards: telephone, computer, email, television, and refrigerator. It is also easy to hold others responsible for your inability to go off alone to your studio. We say: "Oh, she doesn't understand, he doesn't support me, the kids need, I should, I must…"

Actually, we are most effective in all aspects of our lives when we can feel fulfilled. Everyone in a household benefits when each member of the household feels good about themselves. Very young children can learn that parents need quiet time too. In healthy relationships, spouses and partners want the best for the people they love. You can retrain family and friends to respect your time and your creative endeavors only when you first respect and protect them yourself.

Take an honest look at where your time really goes. For a week or ten days, keep track of time and how you spend it, just as you might keep track of money when preparing a budget. Be brutally honest with yourself. In addition to the obvious things (job, commute, meals, time with spouse, parents, children) track each errand, each moment you stop to check your email, each phone call and its real importance, each task. Write everything down.

After a week of tracking your time, set aside an hour and take a clear look at how you are spending this resource. What can be streamlined? Given up? Delegated? Can you group your errands and appointments?

Look for ways to trim out excess non-productive time to gain at least an hour a day for your creative work.

One uninterrupted hour can literally become the most productive use of your time each day. Protect it. Let the answering machine pick up or at least screen your calls. Close the real or metaphorical door to your studio to others. Practice your ritual of being in a "sacred space" where you cultivate your ability to get into the zone. When it's time to switch gears back to your normal life, be sure to leave things in process at a next obvious stage in order to eliminate back tracking.

The gift of having too many demands on your time is that you can learn how to use your time more effectively. When more becomes available to you, you won't flounder.

If, on the other hand, you have taken the step of leaving your day job and are supporting yourself (or hoping to support yourself) with your creative work, you may be overwhelmed by the variety of tasks in front of you. You are an artist, but you are also a small business. If you can keep this in mind, it is easier to deal with the endless demands on your time and energy that seem to have nothing to do with the creative income-producing work. Because not only do you have to make the stuff, you have to be able to handle the business aspect of getting your work into the world.

Some self-supporting artists make the mistake of thinking that they are creating only for themselves and have no need for marketing. They often believe that their audience will somehow find them. Yes, sometimes this happens, but often it doesn't, so how can the rest of us benefit from that creative work if we do not have access to it? Art communicates, illuminates, entertains and educates, but first it has to be seen. Try to remember that the audience completes the conversation of the work.

Submitting for exhibitions or publication, dealing with clients and publishers, handling the minutiae of paperwork and recordkeeping – wouldn't it be great to be able to delegate all that paperwork? Unfortunately, unless you have a really good patron, or an independent income, you must establish good work habits in the office as well as in the studio. Some people find that setting aside one or two days a week just for office work is most effective for them, while others find that they work most creatively in the morning, then switch to the office work later in the day. For others, getting the paperwork done and out of the way before going to the studio is essential. Regardless of which approach you take, remember that the creative work comes first and deserves your best attention. Try to structure your time accordingly.

SPACE

Many people debate the pros and cons of studio space in or near your house versus space away from home. Some feel that leaving home to go to a studio creates a necessary separation between the parts of one's life. Others hold that a studio in the home reinforces the idea of a holistic life, rather than an artificial division between creative life and domestic life. Still others insist that maintaining two separate spaces is a waste of resources.

My point of view is that no matter how large or well equipped a space, and regardless of where that space is located, if the artist cannot say yes to the work, it isn't a studio at all. Even a small desk top in a corner is enough if approached with the right attitude. What is essential, regardless of the amount of time and space you have, is to approach both as if they matter. In fact, your creative work absolutely relies on your attitude towards the use of both time and space. One artist I know calls this the "studio between the ears."

The important things are to:

- Dedicate and celebrate your available time.

- Dedicate a space just for your creative work.

- Say yes to the work.

Always approach being in your space at the time available to you as if it is important, even sacred. Perform a small ritual that tells your creative brain that its time has come. Some artists do this with small repetitive tasks, e.g. sharpening pencils, laying out paint on a palette just so, and others put on particular music. Some sit silently for a few minutes, meditating to center themselves. Whatever ritual you choose, make it a regular part of approaching your time and space. The repetition of a set of actions helps your brain to learn that when you do these certain things in this particular place, it is time to stop thinking about the mundane and not-so-mundane tasks of daily life in order to let those creative juices flow.

GETTING STARTED

You have now taken the biggest, most important step in your creative day. You are in your workspace and have carved out time. Now what? If you were in a workshop, the facilitator can talk with you, draw you out or give you an assignment. But here you are on your own – alone in the studio, alone with the empty sheet of paper. What will you do? You have time, want to work, feel compelled to work. Where should you start? Where do your ideas come from?

Questions to ask yourself as you start include:

- What fascinates you in the outside world/in your interior world?

- What shapes, colors, fragrances, sounds have meaning for you?

- What do you read about, where would you like to travel? Why?

- What have you been exploring in your ongoing studio work/ where do you want to take it? What forms repeat themselves in your doodles, in the objects you photograph, in previous artwork you have completed? Is it a geometric or organic shape, a particular texture? Perhaps it is an architectural motif?

- Is there a key element in all your interests?

These are good places to begin, such as with the one shape, color, movement that always speaks to you. Maybe this seems too simple. After all, isn't art supposed to have deep inner meaning? But consider this: Miro began with tree branches, Monet planted gardens so he could explore changing qualities of light and their impact on color, O'Keeffe is known for her oversized flower studies. These artists began with simple things that fascinated them. It was their repeated investigation and expression of that imagery that we now find compelling and which leads to the "big ideas" associated with their work.

For me, I am fascinated by a particular spiraling shape that I find everywhere. Sometimes it seems I could easily spend all my time exploring this one image, and never find the end of it.

You do not need a big idea; just one form, one shape, one line or color. Get out your sketchbook or visual journal and make notes to yourself focusing on an element you've identified. What colors, textures, sounds, and smells do you associate with the motif? Take notes using words, doodles, scraps of color or text pasted on paper, or collaged elements of any kind. Perhaps there has been a phrase haunting you... all this goes in the sketchbook/journal and becomes raw material for later. If you are the sort of person who needs a map, a plan, now is also the time to "design." But be careful that your design does not take the place of the complete work.

Next, make a preliminary sketch or two. How will you arrange the space? Diagram it out. Don't try to design the whole piece; just think visually at the macro level. If you plan your work too much in the preliminary sketches, you risk staleness in the finished piece. Conversely, if you don't plan enough, you risk slapdash work with no backbone. What you aim for is to find the balance between good design and freshness in the completed work. You don't need to know everything about the image ahead of time! *If you did, would there be any point in making the image?*

You have identified a place to begin; you have selected one element, thought about arrangement within space. You have a start, a simple direction that can lead you on an interesting journey. Now get your "stuff" together, your tools and materials, keeping in mind the sensory elements you identified to support the motif. If you usually go into neutral at this stage, don't get anxious. Your hands and eyes know what they are doing. Trust them. Trust yourself.

If you have a big idea and cannot start, perhaps you feel inadequate to express what is on your mind. There are so many complexities: where will it go, how will it get there? A good way to approach this challenge may be to break the idea down into its component parts.

Here the questions might be:

- What is the most important thing to me about this idea?
- How does it feel?
- What words, aromas, colors and textures do I associate with this element?

Find *one aspect* of your idea that you feel you have a handle on. Start there and let the image build itself.

As you begin to assemble your image or work, you may find yourself wandering in different places. There are moments of deliberation: what goes down first? Is it the focal point or the background? Often this decision is dependent on the materials you work with. For example, if you are a painter, there are "rules" based on the physical properties of your medium. If you are working with transparencies and glazes, ditto. Sometimes how the composition is built is determined by the temperament of the artist. There are people who always build their images from the center out, and others who start at the foreground.

Whatever your first step, take subsequent steps in "conversation" with the work. This is one reason I do not recommend too much advance planning. Once a color or texture is placed, the adjacent area must work in relationship to that first choice. Will it contrast in temperature, degree of intensity, texture, or size and scale, or will it be an area that blends? You may not know this ahead of time. Trust your eyes and your intuitive knowledge to guide you. As you make one decision at a time, you will let the creative part of you out to play.

KEEP GOING

At times, the conversation you have with your materials and the developing image may get uncomfortable. Don't fret. I consider this to be a valuable, albeit difficult; place to be, because it indicates deep work is taking place. Trust yourself to work through this sticky spot. Remember that intuition, representing what you know on a sub-conscious level, is working here. This is your deep and true understanding.

If or when you get stuck, it may be time for a break. Do this with deliberation and consciousness. (Knowing that a break is necessary is a positive thing. Castigating yourself for needing to stop is self-defeating.) Put the work on the wall, tidy up your tools and materials, leave the space so that your next step is obvious, and then go do something else. Repetitive tasks are a good choice for moments like these, such as folding towels, washing dishes, dusting a surface, deadheading flowers.

Some folks refer to this as mindless work, though I like to consider it as *mindful*. If you pay attention only to the task at hand, then your creative brain is free to play and solve problems. If you are always stewing about your work, bills, or career issues, you are not creating the calm clear place your creative brain requires. This can lead to anxiety, fatigue and feelings of stress, none of which are conducive to creativity. Find the activities that help you clear your head and later, go back to the work with clear eyes. You may be surprised.

Art, like any other worthwhile activity is much a matter of discipline, learned skills and having the correct tools. With regular positive habits, you can improve your odds of feeling good about yourself as an artist. Learning to set aside space and time, to respect them both and to take that important walk into your creative time with clarity allows you to work as a centered artist.

LIVING IN THE WORLD

So far we have discussed time, space, and business. What about health and love? We all know the myths about the tortured artist, the dysfunctional genius, alcoholic and nasty, who nevertheless creates the work of great genius. But what a narrow view of creativity. I hold the point of view that, in fact, the majority of creative people raise families, are neighbors, pay taxes and may be disguised as your attorney or the barista at your favorite coffee shop. The odds are that most of us play more than one role in our lives. Staying healthy and balanced improves our chances of making good work. We need to be secure on the basic level, have healthy relationships, and feel as though we make a difference in the world.

Keeping regular hours as an artist is as essential as keeping regular hours as an employee. Art is part of your life, not a substitute for your life. If you are disciplined with your time and space, you will know that your workday has both a beginning and an end. You structure in time with family, time for exercise and time to deal with chores. Of course, there are times when you may have external commitments that require more from you, such as a new relationship, young children, an aging or ill family member who represent more urgent concerns. This is normal and necessary. Recognizing that these aspects of adult life are phases can help you do what is required. While you are tending those needs, you can also still take a bit of time to nurture your creative self. Filling the well is just as important part of the creative process as making the work. Every day, ask yourself, what will I do today to feed my spirit? Taking even 10 minutes each day to watch the patterns of light can lead to interesting thoughts and observations. Later, when you are back in studio, your ideas will be richer for having filled the well.

Above all, knowing that your creative work matters may be the most challenging and critical aspect of your commitment. It may seem that your studio time comes at the cost of time with loved ones and you must then make available time with others richer. It may seem that there are not enough hours in the day, but you must learn to use your available time wisely. It might seem that there is no external validation for your art, but you must persist in presenting it to the world. Above all, you must know that it is your job to make the work. As a creative person, you must show up, focus, work, make more work, and present it to the world in order to be truly balanced and whole.

❖ ❖ ❖

Laura Cater-Woods, M.F.A. is a working studio artist with an extensive international exhibition record and numerous awards. She holds an MFA in Painting (Ohio University 1990). Her mixed media and fiber art is held in public, private and corporate collections. Her images explore the textures and rhythms of details from the landscape, often interwoven with eccentric grids. In 1998-1999, she was honored with a Montana Arts Council Fellowship in Visual Arts, Mixed Media. In addition to Public Art Projects, Percent for Art Commissions, and gallery exhibitions, Laura teaches nationally at conferences and for private groups. Known as a nurturing and inspiring facilitator who offers highly personalized instruction, she is also a creativity coach and works with private clients, including writers, musicians and visual artists. More information can be found on her website www.cater-woods.com.

WARTS AND ALL

A USER'S GUIDE TO LIVING A CREATIVE LIFE

BY CHRISTINE FRANCIS

You've heard the stories. One day a stressed-out, underappreciated software engineer has an awakening. She realizes her true calling is to spend her days as a sculptor. She parachutes out of her position as Vice-President of Pharmaceutical Sales and finds rapture and fame selling her masterpieces on the Internet.

Similar stories abound for established artists as well. You've no doubt heard of an artist who found that switching from carving wood to blowing glass, or changing technique from plein air to encaustic, brought about a major artistic transformation and subsequent career advancement. These are rare and happy occurrences.

It's true that there are individuals who chuck their day jobs, promptly unearth a passion for writing, filmmaking or music and achieve immediate success. There are also artists who switch genres and become wildly rich and famous. But you should not be dismayed if your own creative insights occur in a less spectacular fashion.

Oliver Cromwell said, "Remark all these roughnesses, pimples, warts, and everything as you see me; otherwise I will never pay a farthing for it." Cromwell was directing Lely, the painter of his portrait, to fashion an authentic likeness. He wanted the real thing. We can assume he didn't want a slick representation but one that showed him as he actually appeared in the world, warts and all.

As a creative individual, you can apply Cromwell's caution to mean that in order to shape a worthwhile and authentic creative life, one you can continue to live with, it's necessary to acknowledge its challenges and learn to embrace them. Of course you can relish the glorious moments of effortless creating when they come along, but to reach the goal of living a creative life in the long term, it's necessary to take into

109

account and accept the not-so-glamorous warts that are inherent in such a life. When you have creative goals, you are likely to have a life that is sometimes blemished by creative blocks, financial concerns, and distractions.

A creative life is also often full of these warts: all-or-nothing thinking, overwhelming demands on time, self-defeating negativity, and the paralyzing rejection that can prevent you from carrying out your plans. By facing these imperfections and employing strategies for dealing with them, you can live a creative life that's "worth a farthing." For most, finding the way to creative living is not the lightning bolt strike of instant transformation, but the glow of a flickering candle that illuminates the way a few steps at a time.

ELIMINATING ALL-OR-NOTHING THINKING

"I'll tell you right now, I'm not an artist," Mitchell declared at the first meeting of our creativity workshop. A speech therapist formerly employed by a large school district, Mitchell had come to loathe the bureaucratic nature of his workplace. When he noticed that his impatience was beginning to affect his students, he left. Since then, he'd taken on independent contract work. Conducting his business in varied settings eased the discomfort of employment in a big institution for a little while. Still he was restless and searching for a fulfilling way to spend his days.

"I'm not an artist," Mitchell went on, "I can't afford to be. Everything I've achieved in life I got through my own hard work. I picked my career because it was straightforward. Go to school. Get certified. Get a job. I can't just go off and become an artist."

Mitchell's impatience was not only with the institutional setting and nature of his former job. His frustration also came from a persistent desire to express himself creatively. His creative nature was not being fulfilled at home or at work. He had severed himself from that possibility with his narrow thinking. He'd recognized the need to change, but was limiting his search for satisfaction to the classifieds.

Mitchell was exhibiting "all or nothing" thinking. In saying he was not an artist, his thoughts led him to believe that an artist is defined only as someone who works full time in a studio making art and supporting themselves from their work in the medium of their choice.

Mitchell had taken a chance and acted on his intuition to come to my workshop and give "this creativity thing" a try. He participated in creative exercises like *Detective Work* in the *Recovering a Sense of Power* chapter of Julia Cameron's *The Artist's Way*. In this exercise, we are asked to "restore the persons we have abandoned" by free-associating with phrases like "My favorite childhood toy was"…and "If it weren't too late, I'd…". Mitchell received support and encouragement from other participants, and during the course of the workshop, he rediscovered his passion for music. He dusted off his old saxophone and got new reeds. He practiced.

Is Mitchell now happily playing on cruise ships while he tours the world? No, that's not the case. A complete transformation of the type "I once was a postal clerk and now I'm a world-renowned performance artist" almost never is. More often it's a matter of just taking a first small step toward shaping the separate parts of your life into a well-balanced whole.

Around the time he started to sound quite good playing "Sweet Georgia Brown" on his saxophone, Mitchell reconnected with something he'd really loved to study in college before he'd made a beeline for his straightforward career. He remembered he'd once had a deep love of history. He arranged to enroll in courses that would lead him to meet the requirements for teaching history. He also envisioned an outcome where he would teach in a local community college that boasted a jazz ensemble.

Mitchell's story is unique but contains elements shared by all those seeking to live a creative life. His particular "wart" was the all-or-nothing thinking that led him to exclude his love of music from his life. He spent years denying his artistic self, believing that to embrace it was frivolous and impractical. He had the habit of distancing himself from his creative needs, introducing himself to the world with, "I'm not an artist." He was convinced that it was necessary to abandon music and history.

He thought, as many all-or-nothing thinkers do, that a practical career and creativity are mutually exclusive, that one has to be abandoned in favor of the other. But the persistent creative urge that survived years of bureaucratic discontent guided Mitchell to my workshop. His willingness to explore the creativity he'd been denying led him to shape a more satisfying life true to his real self.

Your thoughts may echo Mitchell's original fears. You may think you dare not explore the territory that is your creativity because to do so would require abandoning all aspects of your present life. The truth is, by getting in touch with your creative desires and finding ways to manifest them you live more fully. By accepting and embracing your creativity, you integrate all the parts of yourself, insisting on a complete and authentic warts-and-all life.

FINDING TIME

Whether you are making a living as an artist or simply looking for ways to realize creative dreams, the challenges are the same. The most frequently cited difficulty from my creativity coaching clients and workshop and retreat participants, is that of the multiple pressures and demands made upon their time.

Jessica was a fiber artist and email creativity coaching client. One of her fiber art pieces had recently sold at an artists co-op exhibition and she'd received an excellent review of her work in a prestigious newspaper. She had a responsible position in a department store and an ongoing family commitment to help out her single-parent sister by caring for her sister's toddler on weekends. She was sewing costumes for her local community theatre in her "free time." Jessica rarely made it to her exercise class at the gym and thought her lack of exercise contributed to the numerous colds and flus she'd been experiencing.

Understandably, Jessica complained of a lack of energy and time. She needed to finish several of her fiber art pieces by the deadline for an upcoming show. Though she was an early riser, by the time she got to her studio late at the end of each day, she didn't have the energy or motivation to approach her work. She began to think she wasn't capable of finishing and had been fooling herself to think that she was cut out for a creative life.

Have you ever stood in front of a mall or subway map trying to find your way to a store or particular stop? On the most helpful of these maps, there's a little red dot next to an arrow labeled "You are here." Once you get your bearings and find out where you are in relationship to where you want to go, you can set off in the right direction.

It's just as important for you to get your bearings and find your way from your present circumstances to your creative goal. Do you find yourself saying you can't find the time to create? If so, you have designated time as the ugly "wart" that won't allow you to proceed in living a creative life. Demands on your time won't evaporate, but you can accept them as a fact of life and find ways to manage them to benefit and honor your creative self.

To help assess your present location on the map relative to your present way of living (to find the "You are here" of your creative life), I encourage you to make a schedule of the way you presently spend your time, filling in as many details as possible including commute time, television viewing, and newspaper reading. The more detailed the map, the more valuable it is in providing reliable information about where you are and where you want to go in your creative life.

Do I hear cursing and moaning about this assignment? If you have an enormous amount of resistance to this exercise, you are not alone. Creativity coaching clients regularly resist or downright refuse to approach this task at first. It's uncomfortable. It reveals what things aren't working out. It means making some changes. My conversations with clients about scheduling virtually follow this pattern:

"I'm too busy to get to my studio. I can't get my creative work done."

"Do you have a schedule?"

"Of course I have a schedule. I just told you how busy I am!"

"There's no doubt you are busy. What I mean by scheduling is writing down everything you're committed to during a typical week, along with corresponding times for each activity. That way you can see where there may be room for your art."

"Hey, I'm an artist! Creative with a capital C … a free sprit. I don't want to be tied down. I won't live my life tied to a schedule. I'll be trapped."

"On the contrary, a schedule has the liberating effect of opening your life to include your art."

"Okay. I'll try it but I don't know when I'll have time to make a schedule."

"Exactly!"

In his book *First Things First*, Stephen Covey asks, "What does it matter how much we do if what we're doing isn't what matters most?" Our lives are full of demands on our time and we must take care to spend some of it on what matters most. As adults with duties and responsibilities to families, to careers and communities, we often find our opportunities to create greatly diminished. We have car pools and dentist's appointments. We have volunteer work and social obligations.

But as creative people, we also recognize a persistent longing to bring creativity into our lives. With our plates so full of obligations to others, we can neglect the responsibility we have to ourselves to live a life that incorporates the whole and true self that we represent. Making a realistic schedule is a first step in ending that neglect.

Jessica decided to give the assignment a try and to shape a schedule that included her fiber art work. It takes some time to try out ways to keep a calendar. Some clients like to use a whiteboard for writing a day's or week's plans, others prefer a pocket day planner, while still others use a plain wall calendar. Planning in any way you prefer is an ongoing process that needs tweaking and adjusting to meet changing needs.

Once Jessica had wrestled her planning into something she could live with, it was time to look at which activities would lend themselves to modification or change. As you might expect, Jessica found that all her commitments wouldn't fit into a day. She had to make some tough decisions about how she could make room for the creative work she was aching to do.

She chiseled away at her schedule that had seemed so hopelessly set in stone. She decided she could afford to cut back her working hours at the department store and approached her manager with the modifications. They were accepted. She enlisted her mother in helping with the weekend babysitting.

She began a fitness program three days a week during her lunch break. She asked for an assistant seamstress to help with costuming. She decided to put off reading the newspaper until the weekend and listen to the news on the radio on the way to work instead of watching it on television.

Ultimately, she "found" time to finish her fiber pieces by working on them first thing in the morning and in the time vacated by moving some of her previous obligations. She was not only able to complete the required number of pieces, but ultimately entered twice the number of pieces as she'd originally planned. She incorporated time in her schedule to explore markets for exhibiting and selling her work.

Like Jessica, you can find time for achieving your goals by taking a thorough look at the way you spend your time, identifying what isn't working and making changes that will honor your creativity. You too can accept the wart of life's time demands and make it a part of living creatively.

NEUTRALIZING NEGATIVITY

There may be times when you find yourself thinking that you're lazy for not persevering, frivolous for pursuing art in the first place, or worse, untalented and unworthy of success. This thinking is a demonstration of another type of wart on the visage of a creative life. It's an example of the negativity wart. We can scare ourselves out of taking artistic risks and lose our motivation to create by listening to our own negative thoughts.

Carmen was a writer. She'd had several articles published and was working on a novel. She was stuck. She reported that she was constantly distracted and couldn't focus. She had too many ideas and then no ideas would come at all. In the course of working with Carmen to get her back to her desk and her fiction, I asked her to notice what sorts of things she was saying to herself. At first, she said that she wasn't aware of saying anything at all to herself, but over time, she "caught" herself thinking such things as, "I don't know what to do. I'm panicked. I should never have thought I could take this on. I can't finish because I don't know what I'm doing. It's too much. It's no good."

In her article "Self-Talk and Self-Health," Julia E. Wykle summarizes researcher D. McGonikle's three negative self-talk categories:

* *Awfulistic*: Everything is catastrophic.

* *Absolutistic*: Using "must," "always," and "never."

* *Should-Have*: I "should have" done x, y, or z.

Creative people display *Awfulistic* self-talk when they say, "I will be humiliated. I'll starve! No one ever helps me. No gallery will take my work. No one will buy my art. My manuscript will be rejected. Again! I'll starve."

Absolutistic self-talk manifests in phrases such as "I never finish what I start. I never have enough time. I always sabotage my creative efforts. I must have a proper studio and complete quiet before I can create. I can't write my novel until I retire."

The *Should-Have* self-talk of creative people sounds something like, "I should have majored in Creative Writing. I should have pursued a different career and now I've wasted all these years. I should have started dancing when I was three. Now there's no chance of becoming successful."

Carmen's self-talk was a sampler of McGonikle's categories and she may have created a few categories of her own. But she is not alone. If any of these phrases sound familiar, don't be discouraged. Engaging in these kinds of conversations is human. "Under the radar" thoughts are present for most of us, but if these thoughts are keeping you from getting on with your work, it's time to neutralize negativity.

Note that the aim here is not to eliminate negativity, but to neutralize its power to paralyze you and keep you from achieving your creative goals. You don't need to feel badly that you haven't accomplished wiping out your every negative thought! Rather than engaging in an exercise in such futility, it's better to simply start noticing what you're saying to yourself. When you practice the art of noticing self-talk, you are learning to manage it.

Last year, following a lifetime's fascination with drums and rhythms, I gathered the courage to take drum lessons. I was lucky enough to come across a teacher with a philosophy that doubles as an excellent strategy for managing self-talk. My drum teacher's philosophy has essentially two parts. Part one: Learn to hit the drum and play the rhythms. Part two: "Turn off" your Inner Critic! Part two of this drum philosophy is a principle that serves creative people well when they find themselves involved in a negative self-talk "conversation."

Ah, it's great to intend to turn off your Inner Critic, but how do you go about shushing it at crucial times? What about your thoughts when you're beginning your day or setting off to go to work? How do you go about neutralizing negativity when you're trying a new artistic technique or genre? I attended a writing workshop presented by psychotherapist, author and creativity coach Eric Maisel. He suggested the following "thought stopping" strategies for combating self-talk that inhibits the creative process: Notice it. Stop it. Replace it. Creativity coaching clients and participants in my own workshops talk about ways we can use these three steps to neutralize negativity.

Notice it. You can't change your thoughts if you're not aware of them. We humans talk to ourselves regularly. You can make it a habit to check-in periodically with yourself and notice what you're saying. A special time of day like the starting time for work or a habitual activity like brushing your teeth can become the trigger for checking in and "listening" to your self-talk. If you notice your thoughts are encouraging when you check in, congratulations! You are engaging in a beneficial practice and your creative work will be the healthier for it. If you notice your thoughts are negative, move to strategy two.

Stop it. Sounds simple. But just telling yourself to stop it or trying to will yourself to stop a behavior you were only mildly aware of until recently is a challenge. It helps to say the word out loud – "Stop!" Even after you've noticed your negative self-talk, it's possible to get caught up in an argument with yourself that generates more of the same! Saying "Stop" with authority really puts an end to it. In my workshops, participants practice saying "Stop!" with feeling. This exercise may result in noisy laughter, another sign you have broken the spell of negativity. Then it's time to move to strategy three.

Replace it. Create a positive, affirmative thought that acknowledges your talents and successes. I might notice myself thinking, "I've always been clumsy and there was that time I was the only one in the class who didn't learn how to make a ceramic ashtray!" I can now say, "Stop!" and replace those thoughts with, "I have many skills and talents. I've learned how to do thousands of new things. I'm a creative and capable being." To reinforce your habit of encouraging self-talk, it's a good idea to write some of these thoughts down and post them in a place where you will notice them. Negativity puts distance between you and your goals. Shifting your self-talk to affirmative talk shifts your thinking to expect the best and propels you toward your goals.

As Carmen practiced noticing, stopping, and then replacing her negative self-talk, her confidence grew. Her self-talk replacements included "I'm excited about this work. I accomplished a lot today. I know how to proceed. If I don't know, I can find the answer. I didn't write as much as I'd hoped, but I'm happy I got it done. I'm pleased with the way I handled distractions." She began to show up at her desk and make progress with her novel. She had faced the negativity "wart" and successfully employed strategies to allow her work to continue. Practicing affirmative self-talk comes in handy when dealing other creative life blemishes. It pays off in particular when we receive criticism or rejection from others.

REFLECTING ON REJECTION

Peggy was a photographer who had exhibited in mixed media shows with multiple artists. She'd made a few sales and had begun experimenting with new techniques and papers when she decided to enter a photography contest. Her entry didn't win. She then submitted some photos to a publisher. Months went by and she didn't hear back from them. She stopped working with the new techniques. When she began creativity coaching with me, she said she didn't know where to go next and was afraid she'd lost interest in photography. The rejection "wart" had stopped her creative momentum.

To combat the rejection blues, SARK, author of *The Bodacious Book of Succulence – Daring to Live Your Succulent Wild Life!* uses the term "The Glory of Rejection." She says, "If you're not getting rejected, it means you're not reaching far enough." She recalls some of her "favorite" rejections: from the London Times – "We don't do Inspiration" and from The New Yorker, "Your stuff is a bit too special for us."

Today SARK is a best-selling author. She suggests a remedy for rejection is to write your own rejection note to whoever rejected you. (I personally don't recommend you mail this letter. I think it's best to stay on good terms with potential publishers!) But the thought of rejecting the rejector is a way to find humor in the situation. For example, SARK writes:

"Dear _____. Your _____ is actually not right for MY work. Nice publishing try tho! Hope you can stay afloat. Good luck. _____

The Creator."

Just thinking about this exercise is enough to take some of the heaviness out of rejection. Lightening up is important. So is reflecting on the reasons for the rejection. Are you sufficiently market savvy? Is it an appropriate submission for the particular market? Did they already have sixteen floral themed pieces? Was your frame too big for the wall? If possible, it's best to get as much information about the reason for the rejection as you can. Try looking at the winning or accepted work. What can you deduce? Sometimes it's just a matter of a judge being tired at the end of a long day when your piece is considered. Sometimes you won't ever know the reason for the rejection.

Whether you are able to get feedback or not, it's important to "normalize" rejection as part and parcel of the creative life. You are a creative individual putting your work out in the world and you're going to experience rejection in various forms as part of your natural habitat. You can learn to take a deep breath and look at the rejection, assess it and keep going. Don't let it stop you in your tracks in an effort to avoid it. When you move through the rejection, you're giving yourself a chance for future success.

Anne Copeland, a creativity coach and quilt appraiser gave me some advice when I received a rejection letter for my poetry, "Every published writer has dealt with rejections. *The Mouse That Roared* was rejected some nine hundred plus times before being published. I guess if (the author) gave up on the first try or even the second, he would have never known what it was to become a best-selling author."

Anne's own research paper written with her appraisal partner was submitted to the American Quilt Study Group. They were asked to change the focus and resubmit. A different editor read it this time and asked them to change it back to the first way. Once that was accomplished, a different editor read it and asked for the first changes again. You get the idea. This went on through twenty-seven rejections! Through all these changes, they didn't give up and the paper was ultimately published in the *Quilt Study Group Annual Journal*. Anne says, "It would have been so easy to give up, but we would never have had that great experience!" Anne's attitude demonstrates that rejection can be seen as part of the creative process in the same way that doing market research and acquiring new skills add dimension to your work.

Peggy eventually contacted the publisher and received some helpful in-house reviews. She decided to take these comments under consideration and to continue with her new techniques. She planned to gather a sufficient body of work and submit slides for a university show. Still shy about selling, she challenged herself to make calls to contacts that had shown an interest in her work in the past. She had faced rejection, reflected on it and moved forward with her work.

You can live a rewarding creative life, fully accepting its difficulties and insisting on the "real thing" just as Cromwell did when he demanded an authentic portrait. By employing strategies for Eliminating All-or-Nothing Thinking, Finding Time, Neutralizing Negativity, and Reflecting on Rejection, the creative life you live will be sustainable and beautiful, warts and all!

❖ ❖ ❖

Resources

The Artist's Way by Julia Cameron

Bird by Bird by Anne Lamott

The Creativity Book by Eric Maisel

A Creative Companion by SARK

Finding Your Own North Star by Martha Beck

I Am an Artist by Pat Lowery Collins

One Day My Soul Just Opened Up by Iyanla Vanzant

❖ ❖ ❖

Christine Francis is a former full-time teacher turned creativity coach. She spent 19 years teaching in elementary, secondary and adult education. Now she combines her years of experience as a teacher with her passion for writing to help others create. Her articles and poetry have received recognition in *Byline* magazine and have been published in *Writing World, The Pink Chameleon,* and in Eric Maisel's *Creativity Newsletter.* She offers creativity workshops, retreats, and individual creativity coaching by email, telephone or in person. For her free online newsletter, send an email to: acreativecommunitynewsletter-subscribe@yahoogroups.com. "I accept clients where they ARE and provide a helping hand, supporting them in getting to where they WANT TO BE." See www.ACreativeCommunity.com or email her at coachcfrancis@aol.com.

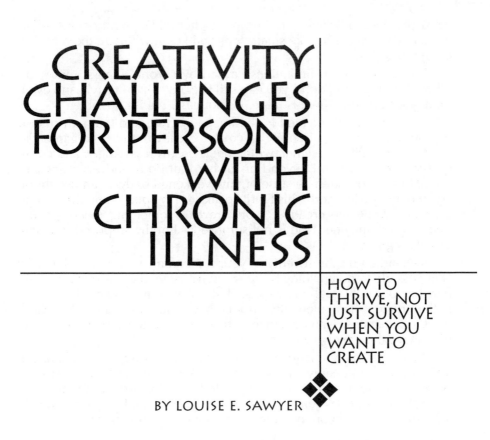

CREATIVITY CHALLENGES FOR PERSONS WITH CHRONIC ILLNESS

HOW TO THRIVE, NOT JUST SURVIVE WHEN YOU WANT TO CREATE

BY LOUISE E. SAWYER

The movie *Seabiscuit* touched my heart. I identified with the courage of the horse and his jockey, as they both struggled to get back into the race after suffering major injury. I was happy when they had such a wonderful comeback and won the Santa Anita Handicap in 1940. I could sense the feeling of victory hard won, as they flew past the finish line.

Laura Hillenbrand authored the book *Seabiscuit – An American Legend*, and was a consultant to the film created by Universal Pictures. In her book, she wrote:

> Man is preoccupied with freedom yet laden with handicaps. The breadth of his activity and experience is narrowed by the limitations of his relatively weak, sluggish body. The racehorse, by virtue of his awesome physical gifts, freed the jockey from himself. When a horse and a jockey flew over the track together, there were moments in which the man's mind wedded itself to the animal's body to form something greater than the sum of both parts.

Laura's own life exemplifies the wisdom of her words. For the past 17 years, she has suffered from severe Chronic Fatigue Syndrome, and yet she wrote a bestseller. I'm inspired by her dedication to harness her weak body in order to take small steps and keep writing in the midst of enormous odds.

If you suffer from limitations caused by chronic illness, injury, or other disabling conditions, you can still live a creative lifestyle and even fulfill your dreams. There is hope. It's not easy, but it's possible.

I believe we are created in the image of God, and that part of our humanity is our soulful ability to create. Creativity frees the gardener, artist, actor, quilter, designer, writer, cook, seamstress, singer, and composer to go above and beyond his or her frail body and even unclear mind. In spite of, often because of, my weakened body, I can delight in collaborating with God – his Spirit speaks to my spirit – and the two of us watch while the creative "work" reveals something much greater than I could imagine. God is not surprised – I'm the surprised one. He says, "It's good."

Depending on the severity of your limitations, you may feel as if it is impossible to do anything besides survive every day. Feeding yourself may be your only goal many days. That's okay. I understand. However, in this article I share a few ideas from others who have been able to find ways to integrate creativity into their lives, even when they feel as if they don't have the energy or the time.

There are many challenges to consider, including low self-image, lack of time and energy, and severe limitations. This article focuses on symbolizing your self-image as separate from illness or disability; pursuing the kind of passion that makes you smile; practicing your pacing for projects; and accommodating alternatives for limitations.

GOING ON A CREATIVE RETREAT

Let's begin. First, pretend that you're at a retreat center and you are relaxing, listening to a speaker, as others share their own experiences with creativity. Perhaps they hold up a greeting card, a bunch of basil, an ivory bracelet, or a book of haiku poetry. You admire their work as it is passed around from hand to hand. You are inspired by the colors, the uniqueness, and the simplicity.

What's going through your mind? Do you think, "I love this one." Or "I could do better." Or, "I sure would like to create something like this." Well, you can.

Now imagine that you will go to this retreat center for four weekends. After each session, you get to play with a simple "tortoise step" activity (one small step at a time). In other words, you come to the center to be inspired over four weekends, and you have weekdays to integrate creativity into your life. Here's a description of such a program that helps you easily imagine this plan.

WEEKEND ONE: SYMBOLIZE YOUR SELF-IMAGE

Welcome to the first session of this retreat on Creativity Challenges for Persons with Chronic Illness. Our topic today is "Self-Image."

A sense of identity is often based on occupational, spousal, parental, or sibling roles. People who have chronic illness and are unable to work or socialize tend to get confused about self-image. They may start basing their identity on their weak, painful bodies, and the resulting limitations. Many "natural" reasons explain why this may happen, including isolation, misunderstandings, lack of vocation, and society's negativity towards those who have chronic illnesses and do not "contribute" to the community. It's hard to feel unconditional love towards yourself when you feel lousy, invisible, and are considered "unproductive."

However, as the saying goes, "You are not the illness." Noted talk show host, Dr. Phil McGraw, reminds people, "Don't get confused between self-image and body image." It often happens that the person who is sick becomes "enmeshed" with the illness, so that it is hard to tell who the real person is apart from chronic illness.

Truly, if the illness continues for decades, then I think this is a normal response. It then becomes necessary to spend much energy and time working on the illness and learning how to accommodate limitations in order to survive. Daily activities might take a lot longer to do, or may be impossible. Extra activities might need to be fitted into a life with very low energy; such as health care, preparing foods from scratch, ordering special air filters, doing extra house cleaning, and finding alternative methods of communication. Significant others may start seeing only the illness and the restrictions and stop seeing the real person who is struggling to survive and needs empathy and practical help.

If a person is mostly isolated, but when in the community pretends to be 100% fit in order to fit in, even though she or he is in severe pain and feels utterly ghastly, the pretense may cause even more feelings of loneliness.

However, one thing that illness does for many people is to provide the incentive to dream, reflect, and discover a new self. Here is where creativity can play a role and be significant in helping a person express a sense of self.

At the back of the book *Seabiscuit* is an interview by William Nack with Laura Hillenbrand. She shared: "The illness has left me very few avenues for achievement, or for connecting with people....It [writing books] enables me to define myself as a writer instead of as a sick person. Because of this, I felt an immensely powerful motivation for writing this book, and writing it as well as I could."

Let's hear now from participant Robert, who shares his experiences with illness, creativity, and self-image with us.

> *Robert Neis:* I have Multiple Chemical Sensitivities and struggle with aloneness, lack of social interaction, and lack of understanding

from others about what I go through each day. I'm not able to go to the places, or do the things I used to do. I was a licensed aircraft maintenance technician with inspection authority. I often feel weak, and that makes me feel less of a man than I was before I got MCS. However, I feel that creativity keeps me busy and therefore, sane. Being able to create a unique piece of jewelry out of ivory restores my sense of self-worth. Also, knowing that some of the things I make are cherished and appreciated by complete strangers gives me a good feeling.

Thank you, Robert, for your honesty. Now Judi, please share your thoughts.

Judi R: I feel cheated out of doing the many things I could be doing if I didn't have MCS and kept reacting to toxins in the environment. I've even had to give up going to church. However, through my writing I am able to express some of the frustration I feel at not being able to be as active in society as I would like. Hopefully other people will learn about MCS, since the lead character in my science fiction novel is an MCSer – a few of the other characters are, too.

It's natural for us to have difficulty with our self-esteem and authentic self when we have severe limitations. We know they don't define our souls, but in this society we tend to have low tolerance for imperfections. Creativity can play a significant part in helping you cope, come to terms with illness and losses, as well as give you a sense of usefulness. We may not know who we might have been if we had not been ill for many years, but we still know who our real, authentic self is when we look at ourselves from God's perspective.

Frederick Buechner, a novelist and non-fiction author, wrote in *Telling Secrets:*

I believe that what Genesis suggests is that this original self, with the print of God's thumb still upon it, is the most essential part of who we are and is buried deep in all of us as a source of wisdom and strength and healing which we can draw upon as we choose. I think that among other things, all real art comes from that deepest self - painting, writing, music, dance, all of it that in some way nourishes the spirit and enriches the understanding.

I agree with Buechner and am aware of God's thumbprint upon my original self. Words can't describe what a difference this has meant to my well-being and to my release from creativity blocks. I became ill 32 years ago and the longer I was ill, the harder it was to think of myself as a worthwhile person. As a result, I pushed myself a lot to function, when I needed to rest. I also did everything I knew to do to get better and received much prayer for healing.

In 1989 I felt very challenged when I started going through a major relapse. I was exposed to an extra amount of formaldehyde in a new graduate college building, where the ventilation system was not working properly. As my ability to function decreased, I often visualized myself walking with Jesus on the seashore, and gradually my self-image changed:

The seagulls squawk and I feel a sense of peace watching the rhythm of the waves. Jesus picks up a shell and holds it open on his hand. I bend to look at it and don't see anything but seaweed, but he gently removes it. I see a precious pearl gleaming in the sunlight.

What a relief to know deep in my heart that God considers me precious and calls me his "Pearl." I call my inner child artist "Pearl Girl."

Tortoise Step Activity #1

Each day this week, take 10 minutes to look for an image which symbolizes your inner self, your authentic identity, or a positive self-image. Here are a few ideas: Take a tour of your home and notice the various images in the rooms. Look at pictures in magazines. Go for a walk in the woods. If you wish, take your camera and capture the image.

Each evening jot down a description of the image, or draw it, in your notebook or journal. List how you feel about this symbol or how it relates to your self-image.

> *What if we took more personally this capacity of things to be close to us, to reveal their beauty and expressive subjectivity?*
>
> Thomas Moore, *Care of the Soul*

WEEKEND TWO: PURSUE YOUR PASSION

Welcome back for another session. I hope that you found some images which made you feel good this past week. Today our theme is "Passion."

When we live in a chronic illness environment, it may be difficult to know what makes us smile. The pain and weakness may absorb all of our time and energy, and we may feel sad that we can't do the things we used to do.

In *Anatomy of an Illness*, Norman Cousins wrote about his experience of being poisoned by hydrocarbons from diesel exhaust and how becoming seriously ill changed the way he handled his life. He began a partnership with his doctor to use intravenous vitamin C, and lived in a hotel watching amusing films.

Cousins describes the psychological experiences of the seriously ill. He talks about these characteristics: helplessness; fear of never functioning normally again; reluctance to be thought a complainer; isolation; conflict between loneliness and the desire to be left alone; lack of self-esteem; and the void created by longing for the warmth of human contact.

In *The Transparent Self*, Sidney M. Jourard compares "inspiriting" types of activities with "dispiriting" ones. He says, "events, relationships, or transactions which give a person a sense of identity, of worth, of hope and of purpose in existence are 'inspiriting,' while those that make a person feel unimportant, worthless, low in self-esteem, isolated and frustrated, and those that make him feel that existence is absurd and meaningless are 'dispiriting.'"

One day I was talking to my art therapist, Carola Ackery, and we were discussing this topic of creativity and chronic illness. She mentioned several benefits of creating, including:

- A sense of achievement even if one is not satisfied with the end result – at least, you tried.

- A benefit for self-esteem

- An opportunity to take one's mind off problems

- A chance to "go" to another place – away from the stress of daily life

- Positive effects on your whole system – mentally, physically, and spiritually.

Carola told me, "It's important to assess what is stopping a person from creating if they say they want to, but don't. Do they really want to do it? Do they have a fear of failure, or even a fear of success? What helps me is to not push myself, but just to do whatever it is I want to do – that relieves the pressure."

Genovese, now please share your experience with us.

Genovese Basil: A clinical ecologist told me 20 years ago, "You have chemical sensitivities to petroleum-based petra-chemicals, which includes formaldehyde and gasoline fumes, as well as many other common everyday products."

I thought about how, years before, I was able to eat my mother's peppers from the garden, but I could not eat store-bought ones. I had always liked plants, but I found it difficult to use transplants because my hands reacted to the soil. Then I discovered that formaldehyde is used as the sterilization of potting soil. I have to use peat moss, because I don't react to it.

What saves me and my sanity is my gardening. I feel very poorly in the morning, as if I cannot do anything, but when I get out to my garden, I am fine. I get energy from the fresh air and from the "spirit" of the garden. My creativity blossoms in the garden. It's as if the garden talks to me. I feel what it needs. I also feel very close to God in the garden, as I listen to the birds sing. My love of gardening has developed into a lifelong vocation or ministry. The seed was planted when I needed to eat organically and my love of plants has developed into a passion of growing vegetables. The benefit is that I can sustain a living and share what I grow.

Thank you, Genovese, for sharing from your heart. I've been blessed by eating your organic produce, herbs, and garlic, for which you're well-known. What you say reminds me of Norman Cousins' comment about Dr. Albert Schweitzer in Africa. Cousins watched Schweitzer play the piano in the evening and wrote, "He felt restored, regenerated, enhanced. When he stood up, there was not a trace of a stoop. Music was his medicine."

Helene, I believe you have something to share with us.

> *Helene Dunlop:* I'm a retired legal secretary and have Myalgic Encephalomyelitis. I think that I would have become very involved in creative activities if I had not been ill when I retired. But I do little things to make my home look beautiful. I seem to be a "natural" interior designer. In fact, one day a workman came to do a job and he said, "What a beautiful living room. Who did the interior designing?"
>
> I naturally accommodate my limitations without giving it much thought, but I also naturally make my home beautiful because it provides serenity. I like things to be orderly and visually attractive. Sometimes family and friends consult with me about how to hang a painting or rearrange their furnishings.

Thank you, Helene, for giving us a glimpse of how you bring beauty into your life. I notice how you dress carefully and beautifully, and I also have thoroughly enjoyed the outings you've driven me to in the years since I lived near you. Your appreciation of details in nature and in housing helps me focus more on them than I used to. You live a creative lifestyle.

◆◆◆

Tortoise Step Activity #2

> This week, your activity is to track your smiles. What makes you smile when you're alone? If you're shopping, is there something you see that inspires your creative thinking? Would you like to make something similar? When you see a duck swimming in the pond or a flower in a garden, do you think, "I'd like to take a photo of that or make a sketch with colored pencils"? Does a news event give you an idea for writing an article?
>
> Each evening jot down in your notebook whatever made you smile that day. Add any ideas which you have for creativity projects.

> *When I create, God lights a fresh candle of joy for the world.*
>
> Thomas Kinkade, the "Light Artist"

◆◆◆

WEEKEND THREE: PRACTICE PACING

Welcome back for another session. Today we talk about "Pacing." This topic is very significant for people who wish to create, especially while struggling with chronic illness.

If you're like me, you have "on" days and "off" days, and sometimes feel as if you can't commit yourself to anything because you are too ill, need to rest, and just get through the day. You may not be able to count on several good days in a row. If the ups and downs go on for years, or even decades, then it is difficult to include structure in one's life.

How do we get to the place where we can find time, energy, and structure to create and even commit ourselves to a project?

One of the best ways for me has been to look at the basics that I need in my life and gradually work towards setting up "foundations" to provide for my survival needs, such as food preparation, household maintenance, health care, and advocacy support. In order to get the kinds of help I need, I've had to spend much of my time on advocating for food money, healthy housing, practical help, and health care. I even had to set up a non-profit "microboard" of directors to assist me with advocacy letters.

Without having done this foundational set-up, I couldn't go ahead and spend time and energy on creating, group facilitating, and coaching. Besides money, assistance, time, and energy, there have been other benefits to this foundation building. I've learned how to stand up for myself and I've learned patience, persistence, and pacing.

So how can you stop the severe ups and downs and pace your way to success? I don't have the answer for your life because only you know your situation, the level of illness, and whether you have a window of energy time which you are able to take advantage of. I have one or two hours each day in the afternoon when I feel better. I also have more energy in the summer and can take online writing classes.

I've learned about pacing, in general, from Frances Dodsworth, a registered counselor who specializes in Integrative Body Psychotherapy. She has experienced health challenges herself and has supported people with chronic illness. She is wise when it comes to the topic of pacing.

Frances, please share your suggestions with us.

> *Frances Dodsworth:* Pacing requires "tuning into" one's body/mind rhythm. This can be painful and difficult when there is illness or trauma in one's past or current life. Yet even when it is hard, tuning in is the basic gift we can give to ourselves. When doing that tuning in process, one discovers more than one voice that wants to be listened to. I will mention a few of them.

> There is the voice that pushes one to do more and to do it faster. That voice comes from many sources in the individual: eagerness to live life to the fullest and therefore to do and be all that is possible; a deep and old feeling of not being good enough unless always producing something; a dread of feeling too deeply the old and current emotional pains of one's life, pains that can be somewhat masked by busyness.

> There is the voice that coaches collapse and the giving up of all effort. It may come from a yearning for rest, a ceasing of the Herculean task of performing all of the necessary duties of life. It may also come from deep core exhaustion, especially in those who are sick.

Then there is a wiser voice. This voice is not overly reactive to the storms of emotion, yet open to the full range of input from the body, mind and soul of the individual. It weighs all of the input: physical abilities and limitations, emotional states, ambitions, yearnings, and necessary chores. Then it suggests, usually in a quiet voice, a suitable pace.

Tuning in to one's whole Self is the path toward authentic pacing.

Thank you, Frances. You've reminded us to listen to the various voices within us and to listen more deeply to the quiet, wise voice in order to follow a suitable pace. Now let's hear from two participants about how you find the time and energy to create, and to pace yourselves. Sr. Mary Joan wants to share.

Mary Joan Meyer: I'm a spiritual director and I've recently published a book of my haiku and photos. My biggest challenge in creating is to be able to focus and concentrate and get the clutter out of my mind. Fatigue is a part of Lupus, which I have. In the morning I have a lot of energy. At night I have time but my mind and body are too tired to create.

On my day off, I get my chores done early and I am more relaxed to be creative. I sometimes go to a park where I get inspired. It helps me to get away from my home. I also schedule weekend retreats where I can get out in nature and walk, contemplate, listen, be silent, and be aware. When I free myself from clutter, I open myself to hear that small, inner voice. My thoughts and feelings emerge in poetic expressions and images. I have also begun to take pictures to accompany the verse.

When I get back home and am stressed or become cluttered, I go back to these places in my mind and heart and find myself re-creating again.

Thank you, Mary Joan. I appreciate your sharing your own experience with us.

Monika also wishes to share.

Monika Quinlan: I was a science teacher before I got MCS and now I'm a lay minister in the Catholic Church. I'm writing a book about MCS and faith. Writing is something I do naturally and it gives me a great feeling of satisfaction. I tend to base my identity, unfortunately, on accomplishments, but I'm working on that issue. The illness has caused me to feel useless and so creativity gives me a feeling of being useful and helpful to others. In order to have the energy and time to create, I don't go out much or do a lot of housework or other activities. However, I try to incorporate my writing into daily life. I do "creative thinking" while walking, cooking, exercising, or when I can't sleep. I keep two note pads handy – one for reference/research/notes, and the other for creative writing.

Thanks for telling us about your writing activities, Monika. I like what you say about integrating creative thinking and writing into your daily routines.

Tortoise Step Activity #3

This week, think each day about what you might be able to structure into your life as a minimal creativity time or a "bottom line practice." In other words, what is the smallest activity or the shortest time in which you can do something creative?

Here are a few examples:

• take 10 photographs once a week

• write one page on my novel each day

• garden 10 minutes a day

• draw 10 minutes a day

If you have difficulty deciding what activity you want to do, review your lists of images and smiles. Write down in your notebook the shortest increment of time or the smallest creative activity that brings a smile to your lips and heart.

> The Inner Home demands that we rearrange our priorities
> to take care of it; the comfort it offers calls us to do that
> rearranging so we can enjoy our inner home.
>
> Betsy Caprio and Thomas M. Hedburg, *Coming Home*

◆◆◆

WEEKEND FOUR:
ACCOMMODATEALTERNATIVES

Welcome to our final session of this retreat. Today's theme is "Accommodation of Our Limitations" by using alternative tools, materials, and techniques while creating. You may naturally integrate alternative ways of doing things into your life in order to survive and make things easier for yourselves. I know I do.

Some are simple things like preparing the evening before whatever needs to be done the next morning, if you don't have much energy or clarity of thought until afternoon. Perhaps you make extra meals when you cook supper, so you'll have something to eat the next day instead of looking at the fridge and wondering, "What am I going to eat?" If your blood sugar dips without frequent snacks, then you're likely conscious of making sure there are meals and snacks ready.

Maybe there are disability accommodations you need to practice in your life, such as using a cane. Or perhaps you substitute rice or soy products instead of using dairy-based milk and cheese or gluten/wheat cereals and breads. In the same way, we can learn to accommodate limitations we have for creating, such as non-toxic products if we're sensitive to chemicals; disability aids if we have painful wrists and backs; or frequent rest breaks if we have overwhelming fatigue.

Laura Hillenbrand, in her interview with William Nack about the writing of *Seabiscuit*, discloses:

> For the four years that I researched and wrote this book, I did virtually nothing else. I devoted everything I had to it. I had my office set up so that there was a refrigerator, cereal boxes, bowls, spoons, and a giant jug of water right by my desk, allowing me to keep working without wasting energy on fixing meals. I stacked my research books in a semicircle on the floor around my chair so I wouldn't have to get up to get them. I couldn't travel to my sources, but found ways around that by making maximum use of the Library of Congress' inter- library loan service, the Internet, my fax machine, email, and, of course, my telephone.

> There were days when it was almost impossible to move, but I usually found something I still had the strength to do. If I was too dizzy to write, I did interviews. If I was too weak to sift through books, I sat still and wrote. Sometimes I worked while in bed, lying on my back and scribbling on a pad with my eyes closed.

As I shared in our first weekend session, I've been inspired by what Hillenbrand did to accommodate her limitations and write a best seller.

Karen, please share your experiences with us.

> *Karen Forbes:* I'm a holistic health practitioner with a background in the highly creative industry of hairstyling. Since acquiring MCS, I have had to tailor my work to fit my health needs and at the same time, I've been able to service those who are homebound by their sensitivities. I get to be creative styling hair as well as practicing health care. This kind of service blesses me personally.

> I had to come up with non-toxic solutions. Traditional hair color is very toxic and hennas do not cover gray and are limited in color range. I found a hair color through the health food store that lets me do what I want with minimal smell. I have to refer those who want perms to a salon. With some research I've come up with a small list of hair care and skin care products for people who need natural, unscented personal care.

> For fun, I like to create greeting cards with stamps, embossing, fabrics, and fabric paint. I've found a non-toxic, water-soluble fabric paint I can use. Buying a house this past year has given opportunity to more creative outlets such as choosing colors to paint and the challenge of finding a tolerated paint. I found a clay-based heritage color paint line from England that I can paint with myself.

Thank you, Karen. I've enjoyed your unique greeting cards and thrive on your hairstyling.

Thank you, everyone, for your participation in these four sessions on creativity challenges. There is another tortoise step activity, if you wish to do it this week. Discover ways to accommodate your limitations so that you can create well.

♦♦♦

Tortoise Step Activity #4

This week notice what accommodations you make for your physical limitations when doing daily tasks. Then think about how you can make a similar accommodating alternative in order to create a project you'd love to do.

Start putting into practice whatever you need to do to enable you to create without harming your health.

> What "acceptance" really means then is taking responsibility for constructing a life in the spaces between these moments of dysfunction, and adopting habits that will keep them to a minimum in intensity and frequency.
>
> Cheri Register, *Living with Chronic Illness*

♦♦♦

Even though we have limitations, we know that God's grace has no limits. He is the creator, and we mirror God as we create. He invites us to partnership with him in creativity, because we are created in his image. He considers us worthwhile and precious and helps us fulfill the desires of our hearts. So, let's pace ourselves and integrate creating into our daily life.

Bless you all.

❖ ❖ ❖

Louise E. Sawyer is a writer, artist, group facilitator and creatvity coach. Her background experience is in pastoral counseling, editing, research, and linguistics. She has pioneered several "real life" and email health, prayer, and creativity recovery groups. You are welcome to subscribe to "Creativity Challenges," a free monthly email newsletter accessed through Louise's website at http://coachlouise.tripod.com and to write her at coach_louise@yahoo.com.

PROFIT FROM YOUR CREATIVITY

TURNING YOUR PASSION INTO A PROFITABLE BUSINESS

BY DANNY N. MALLINDER, B.M.A.

If your happiness is defined as loving what you do – and getting paid for it – then this article is for you. I passionately believe in your ability to not only be creative but to make money from it and have fun while doing so. If you are an artist, entrepreneur, musician, writer, scientist, inventor or work in any other creative area, you can make your creativity pay.

Making money from creativity is a reality for thousands of creative people around the world today. If you examine the diversity of creative industries that have come onto the market in recent years, it is clear that the opportunity has never been better. We are in the right place at the right time. In America alone in 1997, the "creative economy" was estimated to be worth $414 billion. Today this market has grown even larger, the result of thousands of individuals exercising their creative imaginations.

It has been my passion since my youth to make money from my God-given talents. I am known as a highly creative thinker, artist, and entrepreneur. I have a marketing background with years of small and medium-sized business development experience. It has never made sense to me to work for someone else. I desired to create an abundant life of purpose from my own creativity as a successful entrepreneur and later as an artist, and now I seek to inspire others to do the same. My subject is how to make creativity pay. I am living and breathing what I teach because creativity matters.

Human creativity is all around us, in everyday life, in our homes, at work, at school, in our leisure and entertainment facilities and events. Creativity has transformed our cultures, our lifestyles, and our daily family life. Creativity creates meaning, not just for the billions of people who

131

get to enjoy it, but also for the creator – the inventor, artist, entrepreneur, musician, writer, and the many other creatives. Creativity transforms and gives meaning to our lives.

When an individual takes his or her passion and adds creativity, great things happen. We are blessed whenever we can find new solutions to old problems, create new opportunities, break down barriers, and open new choices.

Passion and creativity go hand-in-hand with productivity. This article is about how to take what you are passionate about and start becoming more productive. If you apply these practical steps, you will make your creativity pay, gain recognition, and develop a strong incentive to create more. By applying these simple steps, you can use your creativity to help make your world a better place – and your place a better world!

Of course, in this article, I am limited to cover each step only in brief, so I am including here just the basics, hoping you will take the necessary steps to learn as much as you can beyond this article.

Before we begin the journey, ask yourself how serious you are. Do you really want to take the steps required to make your creativity pay because it is not going to be easy. I understand if you might be feeling a little scared to take the journey. You are in the company of many others, including myself. It has only been a short time since I made my own transition to focus on my creative passions and organise my life and business to reflect my beliefs. If you are certain to have made this decision, let me show you what you need to do to make it happen. Are you set?

FIND YOUR PASSION TO IDENTIFY YOUR CREATIVE PRODUCT

When I refer to creativity, I am not referring to that which is private and personal. This form of creativity certainly can enrich your life and those around you. Not all creativity has an economic outcome.

The kind of creativity I am referring to is the kind that generates a product sold for profit. It might be a piece of art, a song, scientific formula, a new way to make life easier. You need a creative product, which will require a marketplace, is driven by economics, and plays by legal rules.

How do you identify the right creative product? Passion. It must be produced from your talents and your passions, not from what you think would be a great product. You need to stop thinking and start feeling. Find what you love doing, create something of value that you believe in. You need to be passionate about what you produce because this will drive you past the obstacles and give you reason to continue through difficult times.

How do you find out what you're gifted at? There are many different personality, behaviour, and thinking styles assessment tools available.

For example, one is called the HBDI thinking style assessment, which identifies your preferred approach to emotional, analytical, structural, and strategic thinking. There is the Myers Briggs Type Indicator and many other career profile assessments that match your abilities, intelligences, learning preference and skills to your preferred vocation. I offer my clients a very effective assessment tool, which can be accessed via my website.

Once you know what your passion is, you can begin to identify your creative product(s). To do this, ask yourself the question: *If I could create one creative product and be guaranteed that I would not fail, what would it be?* Look inside yourself – what do you want to make, what do you feel you were born to create?

SET YOUR GOALS HIGH: HOW MUCH DO YOU WANT TO MAKE?

Are you close to identifying your creative product? If yes, you are doing well Now is the time to begin setting your goals. You need to know where you are headed or your journey will become a pointless wandering in the wilderness. This simple principle is what distinguishes successful people from failures and frustration.

Begin by asking yourself: *How much money do I want to make from my creative product this year?* Clearly define your financial goals. If they are too general, you will accomplish little.

In setting your other goals, be sure you have made them clear and comprehensive. By defining and naming them clearly, this helps you determine what resources you may need, the people you will to need to talk to, and the training you might need to accomplish your goals. There are many goal-producing programs on the market you can use to help you, or you might consider finding a mentor, or hiring a life or creativity coach.

DON'T WAVER, BELIEVE IN YOURSELF 100%, AND STAY FOCUSED!

You should believe that your creativity is the most valuable asset in the universe if you truly want to make money from your creative talents. It all starts in your mind! Believe in yourself.

Succeeding as a creative person is first a state of mind. Anyone can be creative and do creative things. But there is a larger step that you must take in your beliefs – that your creativity is valuable. You must project this belief out into the world. Your positive beliefs about yourself need to come out in your conversations, your gestures, your emails, in the content on your website and most importantly in your creative work.

The reason you are reading this article is because you want to make your creativity pay off. It's not a question of determining what you want to do with your life, you already know that. You know what you are good at and you want to be paid for what you love doing: being creative. Sure, there will be times when you will want to give up and get a normal job, but you don't want to end up dreaming, like so many others, what it would have been like if you could have made your creativity pay off. You are prepared to take the risk to find the opportunities that make it happen. You have to get seriously focused and determined.

We have discussed how it starts with YOU making a decision to follow your dream and fulfil your destiny. You don't just wake up one day and arrive there; it is you who creates your destiny. Your destiny was determined the moment you set your goal a few minutes ago; you did write down your goals, didn't you?

This step is also about maintaining your ability to stay focused on your goals. We often give up because the mechanics of turning creativity into profit seem too hard. Merging creative work with business can seem difficult, boring, and technical – not for the creative mind. But while it is true that you may have some setbacks, you can master what it takes to succeed.

Highly successful people have an amazing trait; they stay focused on their goals. Your level of focus determines the level of your success. How do you stay focused? It is a skill you need to learn and apply. It takes discipline. If you are determined, you will not be diverted from your goal until it is achieved.

Here is what to do maintain your focus. First make sure you read your goals loud everyday. Write them down and stick them somewhere where you will see them everyday. In this way, they become embedded in your heart.

Next create a list of all the things you will not have if you don't accomplish your goals and a list of all the things you will have if you do. Then create another list of obstacles that you believe stand in your way, and a list of how you are going to eliminate them. Read these 4 lists every day. Do this and you will stay motivated and focused!

ARE WE IN BUSINESS OR ARE WE PLAYING A BOARD GAME?

Now you have a creative product, goals, and you are focused. What next? A product needs to be managed by a business. Making art with the intent to sell it for profit is engaging in the process of economics, the exchange of a product for profit.

In this sense, successful creativity needs to be seen as a business if you are going to make money from ideas. There are a number of business board games you can play now to learn more about business. But let's get serious – this is not a game if you are going to reach your goals.

This is where innovation comes in – the development and commercialisation of ideas. Creativity and innovation are critical for business effectiveness. Taking any idea and making it work financially requires an extreme amount of creative output. There is the production, marketing, distribution and consumption of goods and services, called the economics of business. Richard Florida said in his groundbreaking book, *The Rise of the Creative Class*, "Human creativity is the ultimate economic resource."

Is doing business easy? Think again. I had a meeting with my accountant a few months back during which he expressed his thoughts on making money and running a successful business. He had been an accountant for many years and seen businesses come and go. He told me that in all his years being involved in business, he could definitely say that making a business profitable is not easy. He had never seen someone make *easy* money.

The sooner you kill the idea that seems too easy – an idea that makes you think you are about to be super rich overnight – the better off you will be. Sure, you might become super rich but the real thing takes time and a lot of learning. There are no short cuts or special potions you can take. The reality of business is hard work. Learn the art of business –buy books, attend seminars, buy e-courses, and subscribe to business and marketing newsletters.

This short article doesn't allow enough space to discuss all the different aspects of business success, but let me point out one important issue. If you are not good at managing your time and money, you will most likely make similar mistakes in business. It is important you not only learn about how to run a successful business but also learn how to manage your money and your time.

Your ideas require you to act as a businessperson. You may need to employ the services of outside business people to advise you. You should have an accountant and a lawyer, and if your area of creativity merits it, you might employ the services of a manager or an agent.

My last point on business is to make sure to secure the rights to your ideas. Intellectual property provides economic rights to its creators that allow them to benefit financially from their work and provides them with recognition and incentives to create more. Study all you can about intellectual property and implement the development of new intellectual property into your business strategy.

LET THE WORLD KNOW, MARKET, FIND AND KEEP YOUR FANS

If creativity requires you to engage in the business process, then what is one of the most important components of successful business? Marketing.

Marketing is just one of the commercial processes of economics, but it is one of the most important. No exchange of goods for profit is completed without a form of marketing; without marketing there is no business, profit, or money generated. You need to understand and engage in marketing more than any other activity, especially marketing yourself as a brand.

It begins with asking yourself, *Who is my market?* Is it small to medium sized companies, over 45 age group, or taxi drivers? You need to identify who your market is before you decide how you are going to reach it.

Assume you are an artist selling paintings and you decide to sell to people who can afford to pay at least $1,000 per painting. That is one market. Now assume that your paintings' central themes are about saving the environment and you know people who buy environmental paintings are mostly in the 30 – 55 age range. They care about the world, attend or are associated with organizations that promote a safe environment.

Identifying your market is also known as identifying your customer profile. This helps you develop better relationships, provides sales opportunities, tells you where to advertise, and allows you to track what they are buying.

Take a piece of paper and write down in detail who your customers are. Think about what they do, where they go, and what they buy. Once you have compiled your list, you can begin to brainstorm about how to market to them. Before that you also should identify why they should buy from you? Is it because your creative product is unique or of greater quality? This is part of competitive advantage.

The key is that you need to get people's attention. Your product should stand out from the crowd and seem to say, "Pick me." Dare to be different.

This brings us to *branding*. I suggest that you aim to brand your entire world – yourself, your company and your creative products. There are so many things you can brand, from buildings to clothes to you. Branding is about letting people know you have arrived. Use your website, business cards, and brochures to do as much branding as you can and make sure they all share your distinctive logo.

How do you win over customers once you have their attention? By communicating with them as often as you can. I called this "relationship marketing" because in the long-term, profit doesn't come from sales but from customer relationships. Here are the components of a good relationship marketing strategy: 1) A marketing database; 2) Personalized, customized, updateable information; 3) Automated communications; 4) A way to target communications directly to your customers; 5) Any form of loyalty reward for buying more or referring others.

The more you direct personalized communications to your customers or potential customers, the more they open their mouths. Word of mouth is the most cost effective form of marketing there is. It is more credible than salespeople, reaches more people faster, and gets people to act. Build relationships with your key people who talk a lot and have influence over others. Communicate as often as you can with them. But don't ask them to buy constantly; instead, develop a relationship with them and see what happens. Ask them if you can place them on your mailing list. Send them updates about you, your company, and your creative product. The key is to stay active, talking to more people everyday.

If you would like to explore the power of effective relationship marketing program visit my website for more details of what I offer my clients.

WORK WITH PASSION AND PURPOSE WHILE CONSIDERING OTHER INCOME STREAMS!

You are almost there. You are passionate, have your creative product, goals, are focused, and have set up a company, secured intellectual property rights, designed your brand, identified your market and are beginning to communicate with customers. It is almost time to start producing with passion, but before this be sure you are satisfied with your product. Do you know how to make it better, faster, more attractive. Be prepared to do all it takes to make sure you are 100% happy with your product.

The reason for this is that you must be more excited about your product than anyone else. You must love your product to the point that you inspire others to love it.

When people pick up on your passion, they will want to know about your product, and they might buy it. My painting mentor says he sets a goal to paint for only 20 minutes a day. But when he paints, he does it to "set himself on fire," and his passion makes people come to watch him burn.

You are now producing your creative product with passion and purpose, and you have everything we have discussed so far. What next? Now it is time to consider other income streams, i.e., more ways to make money from your product. Income streams are the many ways in which money can flow into your business. Your opportunity to be financially successful is increased through multiple revenue streams. One new income stream can enhance and increase money from another.

Here is a list of ways to generate income streams that has been compiled by a New Zealand organization, ARMS, that supports artists.

1. Sales of primary products – selling your main artistic output, consisting of the creation you can sell.

2. Performance or installation – live shows, events or exhibitions based on your product.

3. Merchandising – creating products with your brand or other copyrighted material based on them.

4. Licensing – letting a third party use your art or brand to sell other products or merchandise.

5. Commissions – obtaining work for a fee.

6. Teaching, tutoring and mentoring – passing on your knowledge, wisdom and skills to others for a fee.

7. Sponsorship, advertising and endorsements – taking corporate or government dollars to support your artistic pursuits in return for helping promote their business.

8. Patronage – receiving help from a generous benefactor who wants little or nothing in return.

9. Grants and funding – competing for a share of a pool of (usually) government money.

10. Alternative sources of income – such as investments that let you keep pursuing your dream.

CONCLUSION

I hope you have absorbed all that is required to move from an idea to making money with your creativity. We all have creative talent, but it is a matter of identifying our passion to create with it, to make it work in the real world. This requires getting focused, setting goals, and setting up your business. My business is about how to help you do this. This is my passion to inspire, lead, and instruct creative people with dreams about taking their talent and making it work for the good of the global world.

Always remember that money itself is not the valuable piece in the equation; it is the idea itself, the intellectual property you create. Harness all you have and make your world a better place. I am more then happy to support you and would love to hear from you if you want more help realising your dreams. Visit my website and subscribe to my inspiring e-newsletter. I look forward to meeting you soon. Good luck

❖ ❖ ❖

Danny Mallinder, B.M.A., is a creative entrepreneur, international creativity coach, and personal transformation facilitator, having recently won his country's title in the International Body Transformation Challenge "Body-For-Life." With a background in business, personal and physical development, Danny has successfully established businesses and implemented marketing promotions over many years. He is also a successful mixed media artist, an active actor, and filmmaker. Danny has been described as an inspiring leader, willing to go the extra mile to help others, while teaching from his own personal failures and successes. He is a passionate advocate for transforming your world with the powerful force of creativity through his company, Gocreative. If you desire to become more creative, join Danny's inspiring newsletter or contact him to learn how he can help you find your passion, generate ideas, enhance your profitability, improve your image, grow your customer base, and maximize sales through effective, targeted marketing strategies. For more information, resources, coaching, community and results-oriented solutions go online to his website: www.gocreative.info or make contact via email at: danny@gocreative.info.

EXPRESS &
HONOR
YOURSELF

SELF-APPRECIATION

HOW TO STAR IN YOUR OWN LIFE

BY BEVERLY R. DOWN

You only live once- but if you work it right,
once is enough.
– Joe E. Lewis –

The tragedy of life is not that it ends so soon,
but that we wait so long to begin it.
– W.M. Lewis –

Several years ago, I learned something invaluable from Marianne Williamson, a spiritual teacher and author. Marianne was asked in an interview why our culture has such a fascination with "stars," be they film, literary, music or sports celebrities. She replied that the reason for the obsession was that most people were not yet "starring" in their own lives.

Wow! That simple statement had a profound effect on the way I perceived my entire career as a teacher, social worker, artist, activist, and business entrepreneur. It was one of those "light bulb moments" of understanding. Immediately, I started putting my new insight into action. I was already committed to being a "builder of people," but I began to subtly shift the focus of my work to helping others raise their level of self-appreciation so they could star in their own lives.

I have now seen that my new orientation truly helps people improve the quality of their lives. A few of the benefits brought about by having increased self-appreciation are enhanced creativity, deeper discovery of one's life purpose, and a shift in becoming more compassionate to others.

This has been true with all types of people I've worked with, regardless of age or socio-economic status. I've helped children in preschool, teenagers and their parents, and adults all the way up to the elderly. I've counseled mentally handicapped adults, multi-millionaire business associates, welfare clients, personal growth teachers, artists, stay-at-home moms, and prison inmates, to name a few. Whomever I worked with, I've noted that we are all the same when it comes to our yearning for more self-appreciation and self-love. As my son, Heath, said to me during an epiphany he had at the young age of eight years old, "You know mom, I've been thinking, people are really all the same, just in different ways."

My purpose in this article is to explore how increased self-appreciation can have you starring in your own life. In specific, I want to tell you about what I call my **S.T.A.R. program**, a compass for self-expansion to guide yourself in optimizing your creative potential. Along the way, I'll provide you with practical tips, exercises and examples to help you to shine even brighter as you become the person you were meant to be.

Before I begin, let me be honest with you. You know the saying, "We teach best what we need to learn." Well, it certainly applies to me and is why I'm passionate about this subject. Personally, the largest and most painful challenges in my life have been in the areas of my own self-worth and self-esteem. I used to laugh at myself, as I thought I was responsible for single-handedly keeping the self-help industry going. I cried the tears of a clown though. My husband, Rick, would find me reading a new book and say, "Another self-help book? You're going to drive yourself self-helpless!"

I had some major excavating to do in regards to false beliefs I held about myself and the nature of life before I was able to access my true self. Transformation is individual and genuine change does not happen overnight. For years, I read that low self-esteem was a psychological problem, but I now advocate that it is also a spiritual issue.

I want to know God's thoughts…the rest are details…
– Albert Einstein –

I am not bound to win, but I am bound to be true. I am not bound to succeed, but I am bound to live up to what light I have.
– Abraham Lincoln –

What I'm learning about myself and in working with others is that *self-appreciation is the most important ingredient in living a life of authenticity and joy*. It's what makes us feel happy living in our own skin. When we value ourselves, we can more fully develop our potential and genuinely feel good about sharing our unique gifts and talents with the world. As we grow in our ability to feel good about who we are and what we have to offer, even *more* is given to us! When self-appreciation grows, so does the ability to access your soul's wisdom and inspiration. Talk about a win/win situation! As Mae West used to point out, "Too much of a good thing is wonderful!"

REFLECTING ON YOUR STAR

So, how do *you* define being the "star" in your own life? Does your life excite you? What is your life's purpose? Are you living it? Can you appreciate your potential as a human being?

Being the *star* in my own life means to me that I am an authentic person. We want to be in integrity with who we are right now, as we continue to grow. It is essential to think for yourself and to let go of seeking external approval. Like many others, I grew up being a people-pleaser. It was hard for me to say no to someone in need. My husband called me *Mrs. Save the World*. When I finally got to the real reasons beneath my tendency to become over-involved in everyone else's life, I realized that my motivations weren't as altruistic as I thought; beneath it all, I really needed people to like me. And the reason that I needed people to like me was because "**I**" didn't like me enough.

To thine own self be true.
– Shakespeare

Make yourself happy and the world will follow suit!
–Beverly Down

Being the star in your life means being your own ultimate authority. Did you notice how I just quoted myself above, right next to Shakespeare? Why not? Why not feel confident enough to take risks, respect your own thinking, and put your creativity out into the world?

One day I was writing at my computer and a seemingly unrelated thought entered my mind; it had nothing to do with what I was writing about. The thought was, "Thou shalt have no other Gods before me." It sounded like Moses was talking in my head or something! It was kind of startling. I immediately stopped my writing. I then asked myself, "and what does *that* mean?" I became silent and waited for a reply. The answer I received was, "To put other Gods before me was to make *another* an authority over myself. We are not to do that because each one of us is God in our own life, each one of us has a *direct* pipeline to the Source of All That Is." (By the way, there is a useful lesson here: learn when to let your thoughts play out - your inner guidance is very responsive. Just keep gently asking yourself, "What did that mean?" until you get an answer that resonates as truth for you.)

I have loved this journey towards self-mastery, although I'll admit to feeling at times that I was a kindergartner (at best) on this path to becoming fully conscious. To live a conscious life requires courage, commitment, self-love and a sense of humor. Gratefully, I have come to know the presence of Spirit in my daily life.

While we may have a bit more self-appreciation in one area of our life than another, we need to know for certain that how we feel about ourselves will color every area of our life to some degree. The good news is that we can learn to appreciate ourselves more, as with any learned skill. It doesn't take long to put into practice new ideas, which in turn will bring new results! When we are centered in the truth of our beings, what we produce is authentic.

BECOMING A STAR IN YOUR OWN LIFE

I have created a system for practicing and expanding your self-appreciation based on the acronym "**S.T.A.R.**" Realizing that there are as many paths to God as there are people on this earth, I offer to you this system or method for use as a guide. Take only what resonates with you and let the rest go.

By **S.T.A.R.** I am referring to the following:

S – Source

T – Thankfulness

A – Asking

R –Receiving

Allow me to expound on how this system works and why I believe it can be a useful tool to assist you in realigning with your true essence. By keeping the elements of **STAR** in your life, you can experience the success that you desire! It is with my deepest love and respect that I share with you what I have found to be true. Enjoy!!!

S – SOURCE

There is One Source, One God, One Spirit, One Creator of All That Is. We are each a soul having a physical experience. We are a physical extension of a non-physical Source. We are creative, energetic beings and we co-create our world with this Universal Energy. We can never be separate from this Source, although we can create obstacles that block our awareness.

People in different spiritual traditions may call the Source by different names; what you call it doesn't really matter. What matters is that you acknowledge and *feel* your connection to this Divine Energy. Truly understanding that the One Power that created the universe is in you, as you, is an amazing realization.

When we allow this knowledge to sink deeply into our psyches, we begin to access God-like qualities. We do not have to do anything to prove ourselves worthy or to deserve these gifts. They are given freely. They are everyone's birthright.

> *You are a child of the universe, no less than the trees and the stars; you have a right to be here.*
> – Max Ehrmann

*Men live on the brink of mysteries and harmonies into
which they never enter, and with their hands on the door-
latch they die outside.*

–Ralph Waldo Emerson

I find the insights above from Ehrmann (found in the beautiful *Desiderata*) and Emerson to be very motivating messages. To enter into the mystery of life whole-heartedly and to connect with the abundance of the universe are worth our time and attention!

Ernest Holmes, a spiritual author and teacher, commented on the connection between creativity and spirituality, "Throughout recorded history, our great poets have revealed the presence of God through their poems. The greatest music ever composed was written by the hand of a mystic, and the best art has come from men and women of spiritual perception."

From my perspective, our purpose on Earth is to reconnect and to become one with the God Source within us. Every spiritual teaching that I am aware of states that we are here to learn the lessons of love. Our greatest journey is to go within ourselves and connect with this powerful, creative force.

Emma Curtis Hopkins, an 'early thought teacher,' said, "People can rebel against the word 'God,' but everyone can relate favorably to the word 'Good.'" She said that the world was hungry for satisfaction, and just in speaking the truth of our nature in seeking goodness brings satisfaction to the mind.

Our ego casts a veil of illusions to make us feel separate from God. The truth is that we are never separate from the Source – there is no spot where God is not. Each of us, at any moment, can access this Source of Infinite Intelligence, Infinite Creativity, Infinite Well-Being, Infinite Abundance, Infinite Goodness and Infinite Love.

An Exercise: I received this tool from my angel guides while meditating and use it frequently. My guides said, "Whenever you are feeling depleted of energy for any reason, know that you are completely surrounded by Love at all times – you need only reach out and take it! Just close your eyes, take in some deep breaths and imagine yourself breathing in Love. You will be replenished in minutes, for it is Love (the Source) that feeds your body and your soul."

T – THANKFULNESS

The state of gratitude is a perfect energetic match to connecting with the Source. There are Spiritual Laws that govern the Universe. The "Laws" do not govern us as do laws made by lawmakers—the "Laws" instead are a description of the nature of the Spiritual Universe. Spiritual Laws are terms universally used to describe divine creative principles.

When we feel grateful, we set into motion the powerful Law of Attraction (also called the Law of Resonance, Law of Increase, or Law of Vibration) which states, *That which is like unto itself will be drawn.* When we are in gratitude, we become magnets for our good – we attract love and move beyond our intellect. What is good for us will automatically be what is best for others as well.

Thankfulness becomes a way of life when we realize that the Source of All That Is, is not only in us, but is who we are. The world looks different through these eyes.

> *If the only prayer you say in your whole life is "thank you," that would suffice.*
> – Meister Eckhart

> *The primary purpose of all human life is to live a life that is full of joy and delight.*
> –Omni/John Payne

A therapist friend, Carlin, shared with me an insight that I've never forgotten. After spending over thirty years as a counselor for people with unhappy dysfunctional lives, Carlin sought to find a common denominator. She kept looking until one day she found it: it was a lack of gratitude! It wasn't that her clients were short on things to be grateful for, they just were unable to acknowledge their blessings and *feel* gratitude. We cannot be feeling gratitude and feeling unhappy at the same time.

An Exercise: I call this exercise *Five acknowledgements a day brings positive things my way!* It is very simple: just acknowledge five things that you felt good about each day before you go to bed. Keep a pen and paper by your bed and list them if you want, or just recount them in your mind before dozing off. I believe this is a wonderful way to grow our self-appreciation. Sometimes it seems that people are only too eager to point out what is "wrong" in life. They walk around grumbling with a dark cloud over their head like Eeyore, the pessimistic little donkey in the *Winnie the Pooh* series. We get what we think about. So start collecting evidence that your life works and acknowledge it each day.

A Tip: If you catch yourself walking around grumbling negative things out loud (or silently), switch over right away to saying GOOD things out loud (or silently) to yourself. Let's mind our minds (and our mouths).

A Tool: Another good idea is to *begin* your day with gratitude. It sure feels better than dragging your behind into the kitchen for coffee and immediately jumping right into your things-to-do list. I made up a laminated "shower card" that I hang in my shower to remind me to start my morning on a positive note. So instead of thinking about yesterday or what I've got to do today while I am beginning a fresh new day, I am intentionally programming myself with positive thoughts. I've actually made up hundreds of these shower cards through the years to give as gifts for friends and family members. Here's what I write on them:

> I am positive. I am confident. I radiate good things. I am magnetic to my highest good and it is magnetic to me. I am one with all that is. The power that created the universe is in me and I direct it. I like who I am. I am grateful for my wonderful life - for everyone and everything in it. And so it is!

A – ASKING

To activate the laws of creation, to become the co-creators that we came here to be, we must ask for what we want. Whether we are conscious of this or not, we are always creating. Thought creates and what we focus on expands.

Asking is not begging or pleading, but stating in a positive manner that which we desire to be, do, or have in our life. Since we are energetic beings surrounded by Universal Energy, our thoughts are electrical. We want to be sure to ask or state our intentions in a way that will activate the Universal Law of Attraction in our favor.

Here is the secret: We must become an energetic match for that which we ask for. It is important to ask from a place of love, not from lack or scarcity.

An Example: *Dear God, my life is your life. Please use my gifts and talents for the betterment of the world. May your will be done.*

It is not our job to create the outcome – the Source does that – it is our job to choose what we want and we do that by the thoughts that we give our attention to. The more we think a certain thought, the more powerful it becomes. This is why affirmations (positive statements made to ourselves declaring that something is already so) are so useful.

An Example: *I am a channel for God's creativity and goodness.*

When we lack self-appreciation, we can fall into the illusion that life is a struggle and that to get what we want in life is hard work. I *am* getting better at understanding that if I do what I *Love*, not only will it be for my highest good – it will also be the best thing that I can do for others, because in truth we are all one. If I am doing work that I love, then I am doing God's work because God is Love. We are to ask for what we want, listen for our guidance and then "move our feet." God is love in action. God Energy is a verb!

A Tip: Another reason to become proficient in asking for what we want is this: There are scores of "unseen helpers" ready, willing, and able to assist you in your journey on Earth. Picture that they are near-by, at all times, just on the other side of the door, but here's the catch: the door knob is on your side. It is up to you to open the door. Because of free will, they are not allowed to interfere. You have to invite them into your life if you want their assistance.

An Example: I was recently driving around in my car with a long list of errands to accomplish, without nearly enough time. As the stress mounted, I was not having fun or able to enjoy the sunshine of the day. I remember thinking, "This is not how I want my life to feel." Then I said a prayer: *"I want to change the way I am seeing things. I want to see what is real. Help me to see the love."* It took only a minute or two for new thoughts to enter my mind and my heart to bring tears to my eyes. As I looked around me, the world was expanded and transformed; time seemed to stand still, it was surreal. The sun got brighter, colors became more vivid, and I began looking at people along the streets with more compassion. There was beauty and love *everywhere* that I had missed just a few minutes before. My heart was filled with joy. Wow! Change your perception and you change your world. If we *ask* for something *with our hearts*, it will come to pass!

> *Always be a first-rate version of yourself, instead of a second-rate version of somebody else.*
> –Judy Garland

> *I have an everyday religion that works for me, Love yourself first and everything else falls into line. You really have to love yourself to get anything done in this world.*
> –Lucille Ball

R– RECEIVING

To receive that which we desire, we must remain open in order to allow what we want to reach us. We want to be in an energetic state of no resistance. Keeping our mind and heart focused on that which we want to create will bring it to us more quickly.

Keep in mind that there is also a period of gestation between the time we put forth a desire and its physical manifestation. Our task is to stay focused and follow our inner guidance until we have what we want. If something we have asked for is not for our highest good at the time, our soul may temporarily delay our receiving it until we are ready to have it in our life.

Just know for certain that we are infinitely and unconditionally loved by the Source. We have to believe that what we have asked for will come to pass, as long as we do not contradict ourselves by resisting, thus giving out mixed messages. This has taken lots of practice for me. I used to be very impatient. I've always been a high energy person – at times my energy felt like a tiger pacing around in a cage. Thankfully,

I've learned to relax, breathe deeply, focus and then let go. Our energy/vibration must match what it is that we want before we receive it. We cannot keep looking back at the absence of what we want to show up in our life. We have to stay focused on what it is that we want. Our focus determines our reality. Indeed!

> *The law of floatation was not discovered by contemplating*
> *the sinking of things.*
> –Thomas Troward

> *He does not look back who is bound to a star.*
> –Leonardo DaVinci

A Tip: I've learned that our feelings and emotions let us know if we are staying focused on what we want or not. How we are feeling about what we are asking for is like a great barometer measuring if we are attracting or repelling it. Our emotions are absolutely connected to the fulfillment of our desires. Our emotions are a wonderful gauge to show us how connected or aligned we are with the Source. We want to pay close attention to our feelings, as they represent our inner guidance system.

An Example: I love it when I get "goose bumps" about something. In my mind and heart, goose bumps are when my angel helpers brush their wings across my skin to tell me to pay attention. I can hear them saying, "Pay attention to that idea!" or "You want to do more of that!"

One of the commonalties that we all share is that we are growth-seeking beings. But one of the myths that many of us have bought into is the myth of "perfection," which often prevents us from growing. If we waited to share our gifts and talents until they are perfected or when we think that we know everything, none of us would ever get as far as even opening our mouth to speak. We are each an evolving being who can only share the best of what we know at any given moment.

Each of us receives guidance in our own unique ways. Sometimes I receive my inner guidance in the form of poetry. One time when I was asking for guidance after having experienced a business setback, I wrote the following poem, *Faith Is the Force*. It actually felt like I was taking dictation. It gave me inspiration and hope:

FAITH IS THE FORCE

It doesn't matter where you've come from,
Just know the truth of where you are.
What matters most is where you're going,
Whether your dream be near or far.
Don't give your life away for errors of your past,

Let your mind create an image of your heart's desire to last.
Hold tight to your future's vision,
Don't let your dreams delay,
Breathe in, breathe out,
Let your PURPOSE fan the fire today.
Trust and Hope will guide your speed,
And you'll choose the highest thought, word, and deed.
Let go, Let God, and soon you'll find,
That FAITH is the force, let your eyes be blind.
An eternity of happiness awaits you!

– Beverly Down –

My wish for each of us is to fully awaken and to embrace the elements of **S.T.A.R.**– Source, Thankfulness, Asking and Receiving – in our individual lives. May the Spirit within guide us, help us to follow our bliss, and live lives filled with joy and love! Let the veil be lifted so that our true identity, as co-creators is revealed. Let our creative expression soar! May self-appreciation grow within each of us so that we become whole, thus transforming the world with our Love…

Amen, and Awoman!

❖ ❖ ❖

Beverly R. Down has been a lifelong teacher and student of psychology, spirituality, and metaphysics. She is self-employed as a Health and Wellness Consultant, a Humorist, Motivational Keynote Speaker, and as a Creativity Coach. She has won awards in public speaking, and is known for her creative workshops in personal development where she incorporates her intuitive abilities, as well as her musical and theatrical talents. Her gift is "Illuminating the Extraordinary in the Ordinary." Beverly lives in upstate New York with her husband, Rick, and her son, Heath. She welcomes comments about this article and hearing about your experiences in becoming a "star" in your life. Feel free to email her at BeverlyDown@aol.com or visit her website www.star-creativitycoaching.com. Please put "STAR Program" in the subject line of your email so she won't delete it as spam.

WRITING YOUR OWN PAGES

THE ART OF LIVING CREATIVELY

BY PRASHANT ZISKIND

When I was ten years old, I surprised my mother by informing her that I wanted to be a trucker, then a cowboy, waitress, carpenter, secretary, logger, and a fisherman for starters. Having been born into an upwardly-mobile middle class family, education was everything and college, a foregone conclusion. Yet drawn irresistibly to the opposite of my own experience and insatiably curious about people's lives, I sensed at that young age something that would later guide my life as an adult…that if I really wanted to know something, I had to live it.

My mother, a former librarian, had other plans for me. Concerned that such a vision would lead me into a life of insecurity and poverty, frustrated by the limitations imposed upon her own life by her generation and culture, she encouraged me to enter a profession that would allow me to experience the freedom and opportunity to lead the independent life that she had not been able to attain for herself. "You can go to the library and read about all those lives," she told me, "but you have to choose only one for yourself."

THE BLANK PAGE

Childhood is the formative time for us all. We begin with a clean sheet, a blank page upon which to write our lives. Deepak Chopra describes this blank page as "the field of all possibilities" and some cultures honor that mystery by remaining open to witnessing the life unfolding there. Ours is not one of those.

Unaware as children of the great gift of this field of all possibilities and unable to protect it, the blank pages of our lives become circumscribed by the parameters and influences of our world. The voices of family, teachers, religious figures, friends and society at large begin to write upon those pages, shaping our beliefs, attitudes and the direction our lives will take. So, as with all children, the page that was my life began to be filled with my own tentative but excited scribbling, which was then heavily overlaid by my parent's hopes and dreams for me.

By the age of ten, I had already been working for two years as an actress and dancer in Hollywood. This was the page my mother had written out for me and I went along with it, happily enough, as this world provided me with the infinite variety that I thrived upon. My father's scribbling on the page was different. His was a message of support that came with the caveat that I would go to college, no matter what. His dreams for me were more modest than my mother's...that I marry, have children and somehow make the world a better place than I found it.

LIVING TWO LIVES

As a child, I lived two lives simultaneously. One looked like every other kid's life. I went to public school, struggled with my studies and homework, hung out with friends, tested myself through sports, and entered the ambivalent but exciting arena of dating.

The other had no relation to "the real world" at all. I was living the life of what most people see as a fairy tale: living in Hollywood, working with movie and TV "stars," watching myself on TV, being asked for my autograph, receiving lots of money. This was the opportunity my mother hoped to give me.

As with all experiences, being a child actress had both its challenges and its gifts. Its gifts were many...getting to work with extremely talented people, being able to develop and express my own abilities and creativity, developing the self-confidence that comes from accomplishment, living within a varied and interesting environment, and learning about people by being exposed to the best and the worst in them.

At the time, perhaps the greatest gift that I thought I had was being able to reinvent myself on a daily basis. In those days, I was always changing who I was. I altered my persona on a regular basis from the age of eight until my early twenties. On a typical day I would arrive home from school to discover if I had an audition scheduled for that afternoon. If I did, I would ask my mother, "Who am I today?" and she would tell me what character was wanted. We would then search through my rather extensive wardrobe trying to find the clothes most likely to suggest that character and I would begin to slip myself into her mind-set and personality.

In a world where we appear to be slotted into a strict definition of who we might be from birth, through our social and economic status, our education, our race, our religion, and our parents' dreams for us, my childhood experience opened me to a very different possibility. I saw that my life did not have to fit the mold I had been born into. My mother had had the courage to venture outside the definition of what children were supposed to be doing at my age. From that I learned that I could step outside the world of my culture's expectations and actually flourish from doing so. This was the seed bed of my discovery that I could change that definition as often as I wanted, and that the world would accept me as however I saw myself.

In fact, my success in Hollywood was totally dependent on my ability to submerge my innate self and to replicate accurately what others wanted me to be. Such are the requirements of the acting world. In that world, the producer, the director, the screenwriter and the studio were major players in filling up the blank page of my life. They dictated who I was and my success depended on how convincingly I could become that person, which was both understandable to me but also vaguely disconcerting.

SELF-DEFINITION FROM OUTSIDE IN

It is now in hindsight that I realize that what I considered the greatest gift of being a child actress, that of realizing that "who I was" could be re-defined at will, was actually something profoundly disturbing to me. I lived with that paradox for many years.

Through my experiences in Hollywood I became very sensitive to the misuse of the act of self-definition. This industry, not unlike our culture at large, is based largely upon image, not truth. Many within it make their livelihoods from re-inventing actors, giving them a new persona and selling that persona to the public. Such self-definition comes from the actor's desire to manipulate the material world and also, often, from an apology for, or dissatisfaction with, who they are. Actors are not alone in this apology. Many people wish they were someone other than who they are. However, for many actors, this act of submersion and then re-invention of themselves on the altar of fame is a rite of passage eagerly sought. I did not seek it, but it came anyway.

Eventually I came to see my relationship with continual self-definition as the proverbial cloud with a silver lining. That I learned to think outside the box, that I could be whatever I wanted to be (or so I thought), was the silver lining. That all the definitions of myself came from other people, I began to recognize as the cloud.

My recognition of this paradox occurred slowly as my career in Hollywood stretched across almost twenty years. There were periods within it when I was famous for a time. Fame can be a very mixed blessing. It has an underbelly that is not visible to the casual observer. As wonderful as it was to be acknowledged for my work, a pattern occurred with this recognition that I began to find greatly upsetting. It repeated itself hundreds of times until, as an adult, I would often hide the fact that I had been an actress.

I became most conscious of this underbelly from the reaction of my "fans." It happened in their eyes. At first there would be puzzlement as they tried to place who I was. The moment they realized they had seen me on television or in a film, I could see myself vanishing, to be replaced by their vision, their definition of "movie star" and whatever that definition entailed. "I" was no longer there. Only "star" remained and their behavior, as well as their expectations of me, changed accordingly. Many actors savor this disappearing act. I found it profoundly upsetting. One moment "I" was there, the next, "I" disappeared to be replaced in their eyes by the fans' conception of who I must be.

It was precisely this intense experience of seeing my "Self" being erased that served as the catalyst for my life-long journey of self-definition. I grew increasingly aware on a subconscious level that the blank page of my life was being heavily influenced by those around me and that I was losing a sense of who I really was.

That left me, after graduation from U.C.L.A. with a bachelor's degree in English Literature and a secondary teaching credential, with a tremendous thirst to discover what had been covered over by others' definitions of me. I did have some idea of who I was but I wasn't sure how much of "who I was" was real and how much had been developed in response to Hollywood's demands. Finding out what was real became an imperative. It triggered a spiritual and creative journey that has ever since been the focal point of my life.

SELF-DEFINITION FROM INSIDE OUT

In my early twenties, I decided to review the pages of my life to see what had been written there while simultaneously trying to ascertain who I was underneath all the scribbling. I took a rather extreme path to discover this but felt it necessary under the circumstances. I left the world as I knew it. I quit Hollywood. I divorced my husband (a good man whom I loved but in many ways had outgrown) and began to explore my sexuality. I moved from Los Angeles to Cambria, a small town of 3,000 on the coast of California. I simplified my life, subconsciously trying to re-create yet a new blank page and to begin again.

At the center of this period was the spiritual search for my "true self." Knowing from my Hollywood experience that what I did was not who I was, I allowed myself to work at whatever I could to support myself on the outside while engaging on this inner journey. I learned that to discover who I was, I needed to go inside myself, not outside myself, for the answer.

I began to read spiritual books and to meditate so I could explore my inner landscape. At the same time I worked as a waitress, a Tai Chi instructor, a dance instructor, a housepainter (after apprenticing with a friend), a polisher of belly-dancers' finger symbols... whatever work I could get. On some level I was aware that trying out all these various occupations was perhaps nothing other than my "living out" the vision I had of myself from when I was ten – in addition to being a way to financially sustain myself.

Ironically, learning to think outside the box combined with much inner inquiry subsequently led me to be true to my youthful prediction and my relish for variety. In Cambria I began to write poetry, explore my spirituality and sexuality. Drawn by the physicality and adventure of it, I hired on to Southern Pacific Railroad first as a brakeman, then an engineer. I literally worked the train lines between San Francisco and San Luis Obispo for the next five years, a far cry from my years of fame as an actress.

My spiritual exploration continued simultaneously and eventually led me to live in a spiritual community in Oregon, where for two years I widened my experience of meditation and brought my spirituality to the center of my life. At the commune I experienced the second environment in my life that encouraged me to redefine myself at will. There I worked as a mechanic, a sheet metal worker, a cook, a dishwasher, a warehouse foreman, and a bus driver.

Later journeying took me to Hawaii, New Mexico, Nelson and Vancouver, British Columbia, and into the worlds of massage therapy, hospice, video production and journalism. It also brought other spiritual explorations, into Buddhism, Sufism and Jewish Renewal.

Not exactly what I envisioned when I was ten, but not so different either.

GIVING YOURSELF THE FREEDOM TO CREATE

Now, enough of my life… and let me talk about yours. My question is, who gets to define who YOU are? The power to define is the power to create…or to destroy. To whom are you giving that power? The act of defining yourself is the act of taking your life back from whomever or whatever is holding you hostage. It is the very essence of freedom.

It is relatively simple to allow someone else to define you. You know what is expected, you have some idea of the way to get there. Others most likely will have gone before you so there will be signposts along the way. If you reach your goal, there will be someone handing you a diploma or applauding you at the end. And best of all, if you don't, there's always someone else to blame.

Defining yourself and living your own life means taking responsibility for whatever you create for yourself. There are no guarantees you will reach your goals. Your dreams may never be realized. You may have to move through uncharted terrain filled with your own doubts and misgivings as well as the ridicule and disbelief of others. Why would anyone choose a path filled with such uncertainty and challenge?

- Because writing our own pages is what makes us fully alive.

- Because following the voice of our creative longing is the answer to our soul's calling.

- Because creating a life that has meaning for us and sharing that meaning with others is our soul's gift to us and our gift to the world.

WRITING YOUR OWN PAGES:
THE INNER JOURNEY

When we begin to craft our life for ourselves, we have the opportunity to write our own pages. Writing these ourselves invites a response not manufactured from our minds but from our very beings. It asks that we develop the capacity for deep listening, the capacity to distinguish our own voice above the clamor of so many others, a sensitivity to and the honoring of the guidance we receive through both our own intuition and our creative urges. It requires also, at times, moving against the flow of the world around us, being willing to risk upsetting those we love for a vision that they might not share or even be able to understand. It requires the courage to not settle for less than one's own truth and the expression of that truth through the creation of meaning in our daily work, our artistic efforts, our relationships and our lives.

This is the essence of living a creative and authentic life. The path offers a deep, often challenging, yet richly rewarding journey. It is a journey that requires courage, for it is a journey into ourselves, into the unknown. It is the courage to move into that void, consciously, by choice, even if that means submerging into that place of not-knowing again and again. It is being willing to be at times uncomfortable, confused and frightened, without apology to a culture that pretends to know what life is about. It takes courage to remain there until one can see more clearly the path, whether that clarity takes a moment or years to reach.

Only then can our "doing" in the world come from the right source. Once we have arrived at the definition of ourselves in this moment, even in the midst of realizing that who we are is changing constantly, we can act. We can put the results of our visions into the world, thereby enriching it immensely. It is not enough to simply define ourselves. We must write our own book and be willing to read it aloud to others.

To live a life of authenticity involves choosing to live with integrity, to integrate what we do with who we are. This creative process involves both conscious and intuitive facets, both an outer and inner journey. It is a two-fold path that involves both the act of self-definition and the act of self-expression. With the first we discover who we are and what has meaning for us. With the second, we put who we are and what we value out into the world at large.

Painters, sculptors, musicians, writers, dancers, and other artists are intimately familiar with the process of drawing on the creative impulse within themselves and bringing their creations out into the world. Like artists, any of us can start the process of going inside ourselves to discover who we are and to bring that out into the world. With every choice we make, every action we take, we define and create ourselves. At that point we too become artists. We become the artists of our lives.

Writing your own pages can be risky business. But as the spiritual teacher Osho has said, "You can't be safe and alive at the same time. You have to choose." What will YOU choose?

TACKLING FEAR

Becoming the writers of our own pages also means having the courage to step into our fears. Not all the time. Not consistently. There have been many times in my life I have been too afraid to move forward. There have been times of pulling the covers over my head and wanting the world to go away. I try to be gentle with myself at those times, do what I can to create comfort rather than challenge, remind myself that I'm human, that progress is not a straight line but one with many hitches in it. But ultimately, one must be willing to look directly at one's life periodically and do what is necessary to bring it into integrity.

As for me, my greatest fear in life is not that I will die old and penniless, although I might. It is not that I will be alone for the rest of my life, although it's possible. My greatest fear is that on my deathbed, I will look back over my life and feel regret that I didn't do the things I knew were in me to do because I had been too afraid to do them or that I had failed to find out what they were.

It is this fear, plus my insatiable curiosity about life in general, that keeps me evaluating my life, not only at midlife, menopause, or the times designated by sociologists as the "culturally-appropriate moments" but daily, through the mirror of this anxiety. To me this fear is my friend, an important motivator, like the positive level of stress in our lives that keeps us alert.

I don't know if we live one life or re-incarnate endlessly, although I have my leanings. All I know is that each moment we are given is precious, whether they are few or whether they stretch endlessly in front of us. Very few of us live each day with this awareness in front of our eyes. We lose sight of it as we face the challenges of our unique situations, as we settle into the often hard-won comforts we have earned or are dulled by the sometimes repetitive but necessary tasks of daily living. Perhaps only the enlightened feel inspired in every moment. I wouldn't know about that.

What I know is that it's important that I remember often enough to keep asking myself about what I am doing with my possibly one and precious life and if it is something that will keep me from that deathbed angst, should it happen tomorrow. Surely it is the young who are blessed by having their lives stretching out before them, but so are those in the ripening years of life equally blessed, for the shrinking of time brings with it the awareness of its great gift, that of having another day yet to live, to shape as we might, with no time to waste.

❖ ❖ ❖

Prashant Ziskind (née Trudi Ziskind) worked for twenty years in Los Angeles as the actress and dancer Trudi Ames in film, television, theater, and radio productions such as *Bye Bye Birdie*, *Gidget Goes to Rome*, *Dobie Gillis* and *My Three Sons*. She left Hollywood and received her bachelor's degree and secondary teaching credential from U.C.L.A in English Literature and Public Speaking. After teaching in the Beverly Hills and Los Angeles City school districts, she began a spiritual journey of self-discovery and has re-invented herself repeatedly, working in occupations as diverse as waitress, housepainter, Tai Chi instructor, Southern Pacific Railroad engineer, cook, mechanic, sheet-metal worker, massage therapist, journalist, and hospice worker. She is presently a coach for creative people in general and performing and visual artists in particular. Prashant is currently developing a workshop and book about life transitions and lives between British Columbia and New Mexico. She may be reached at deepcoaching@earthlink.net.

WRITING THE MEMOIR

A CREATIVE OPPORTUNITY FOR SELF-EXPRESSION

BY NANCY MANOCHERIAN

Have you ever considered writing a memoir as a creative opportunity for your self-expression? The memoir is not just for writers; it is a tool for all artists who are seeking ways to enhance or augment their process of creating.

The thought of writing about your own life may feel egocentric, embarrassing or too challenging to take on as a creative project. But allowing fear to thwart your natural impulse to explore that most unfathomable territory – your own essence – is like allowing fear to prevent you from acting on any creative impulse. Just as fiction is the writer's metaphoric interpretation of the inner self, the memoir is the written expression of the individual's essence. In deciding to write your memoir, what it all comes down to is a belief that your life is worth writing about. The thought "To write or not to write a memoir; that is the question" is truly a moment of creative opportunity.

How does one begin to write a memoir? Are there any rules to follow? How do you know what to write? I offer the following guidelines.

WRITE WHAT YOU KNOW

The first truth about the memoir is to write what you know. As with other truths I've gleaned, my own experience was the best teacher.

Every creative person understands the decision to take on creative work is a loaded moment. Inspiration is the motivation, but discipline is the reality. My experience as a writer and creativity coach is: When the muse calls, you better be ready, but even when she doesn't, you better be ready, too!

159

In my case, the inspiration was loud and clear. I started rather spontaneously writing poems and melodies. Characters appeared out of thin air, then a story along with a cast and crew. Before I knew it, I was in over my head. I was producing a show, MY show. It was exhilarating and terrifying. It was a clear case of "Be careful what you wish for." I had been wishing and hoping, praying for a gift – and got an obsession.

Then as suddenly as it arrived, it was all over; my muse went out to lunch. But my urge for greater self-expression nagged and tugged at me like an impatient child anxious for a hidden gift. I kept spinning words, but where was the prize? Write, write, write…but who would read it? Isn't that the plight of every creative soul? We are drawn into writing, but without an audience, it feels like such a lonely existence.

Then in a flash, I heard the sage advice, "Write what you know." And what did I know best? It was my life. I embarked on the long journey of the memoirist. It felt like the right direction, but I did not know what I was getting myself into.

Most writing is a revealing activity, but for me it is the most profound exposure. Almost more than sex, so to speak, the act of writing requires complete and total abandon to another. In this case, the other is the "voice" that directs the hand to perform the grueling task of getting its word on paper. As much as marriage, the act of writing demands a commitment to believe in the serious permanence of wedding the word to paper.

But even more than the "disguised" writing of the novel, the memoirist must be willing to go where no one else has ever gone, where no one else could ever go – putting one's own life on the page. To write about one's life or even a small piece of one's life is like looking in a fun-house mirror with the world watching your reflection. Every action of your life takes on a surprising distortion. The sense of being "naked before the world" takes on a new meaning, but at the same time, this is precisely the value of looking at your reflection.

STARTING OUT AND FINDING YOUR FOCUS

Starting your personal story can announce itself in a blaze that keeps on burning, or it can start as a small spark that requires your constant fanning into flames. If your narrative does not impose itself on you or become clear to you, you do not have to decide up front what form your life-story will take; just think about giving it some type of defining shape.

A most natural route to the memoir is through a burning desire to revisit one of your life's defining moments or events. It might be a trauma or a shining success story propelling you into action. Try compiling a list of outstanding memories, funny stories, or unbelievable "this-could-never-happen-in-real-life" scenes to help organize your ideas and suggest your working title. A great title can be an excellent jumping off point, but give yourself permission to allow it to change as you develop your story. A theme or title often helps to provide a focus and direction as you write.

Consider, for example, the following memoirs by various celebrities; notice how their titles give a sense of focus about the authors' lives:

- Renée Fleming, The Inner Voice: The Making of a Singer
- Jenna Jameson, *How to Make Love Like a Porn Star*
- Tommy Lee, *The Dirt: Confessions of the World's Most Notorious Rock Band*
- Nelson Mandela, *Long Walk to Freedom*
- Queen Noor, *Leap of Faith: Memoir of an Unexpected Life*
- Sting, *Broken Music: A Memoir*
- William Styron, *Darkness Visible: A Memoir of Madness*
- Elie Weisel, *Night*

Focusing your theme is vital in selecting what and how much to write. For example, you may feel that from the moment you were born, your life has been a series of amazing sideshows beyond belief. You've had experiences that would make no mother proud, let alone your own mother, and you could fill volumes. But you must not. It is best to concentrate your writing on a specific time period or set of events, or perhaps some anecdotal excerpts from your whole life tied to a theme.

This is not to say that you can't be creative in the telling of your life, but a detailed blow-by-blow version of your entire life (unless you are very young) will tire you out and run out of steam! Getting bogged down in never-ending tedious details of your entire life can lead to a creative crisis. "Who will read this? What is this about? Why am I doing this?" All these doubts will rise up at 3:00 a.m. and keep you from sleeping. Then you'll be too tired to wake up in the morning and write, which is actually the time when your ideas are freshest from sound REM sleep.

This kind of self-sabotage is the familiar enemy of the creative. It leads to self-doubt, which then leads to idleness, and further leads to self-flagellation. Once you reach the lowest place, it is difficult to pick yourself up and proceed. It is better to take precaution than to allow the abyss to grab you.

So, my advice is: pick one or perhaps a few moments of pain or pleasure in your life and milk them for all they are worth. If an event or time in your life had a profound effect on you, it will have an impact on a reader. If, in fact, your whole long life (so far) has been an endless spectacle, you will want to play it up so that it reads like the life of Forrest Gump (the movie); episodic and fancy-free.

ADMIT YOUR WEAKNESSES AND FOIBLES

Reveal your strengths, but revel in your vulnerability. When it comes to human relationships, your strength is your vulnerability. Everyone has an Achilles heel, which is why it is so refreshing, even life affirming, to read about others.

Truth be told, when we read a success story, we look for the weakness in the writer. We find gossip irresistible because it discloses foibles. We seek to understand how individuals overcome obstacles to find their inner strength or overt power. The German word *schadenfreude* is appropriate here. It captures the feeling that we can laugh at our own malicious satisfaction at the misfortunes of others. It is not so much that we take pleasure in another's pain as it is that we reassure ourselves that everyone suffers as we do; imperfection is the human condition. What can we do but laugh at our predicament? Bottom line: the ideal memoir allows for both empathy and entertainment.

If you were a victim of unusually tragic circumstance, you might endow your personal story or the character you create in your memoir with the ability to elicit empathy without pity. Contemporary writers such as Lucy Grealy (*Autobiography of a Face*), Augustus Burrows (*Running with Scissors*), and Anne LaMott (*Operating Instructions*), achieved bestseller status with their memoirs written with seemingly effortless humor and pathos. Kay Redfield Jamison, through personal revelation and professional analysis, charted new territory with an informative yet unsympathetic account of her own bipolar disorder. Each of these writers successfully portrayed themselves as victorious victims rather than helpless, pitiful losers. If you choose to portray a loser, humor is the best bet for winning an audience.

If you have kept a diary or journal in your life, peruse it as if you are a detective looking for clues to someone's defining characteristics. It may serve you to observe the tone of your writing in order to identify the overriding personality that becomes your main character. As an observer, you may see yourself as strange, funny, morose, happy, introspective, neurotic, observant, serious, or some other characteristic, which may surprise you.

Giving yourself a third person identity, even if you write in the first person, can be a means to creating your signature "voice." By becoming an observer of your life, you may feel embarrassed, disgusted, impressed or otherwise startled by yourself. But don't judge yourself! You may never have realized how serious, funny, or sarcastic you are. Just allow it to be what it is. Forcing a desired quality on the protagonist of your life story is just an attempt to make yourself look good and will most likely alienate readers who want to read a real character. It is your authenticity that is the key to your success as the writer of your life.

FEAR NOT CLICHÉOPHOBIA

Earlier, I used what some might consider a cliché, "Naked before the world." The use of clichés can be an obstacle, but clichés also can provide an opportunity for the writer to find his unabashed voice. The memoirist's quest is fraught with such challenges, large and small, to be tackled and conquered if she is to be a success. The greatest challenge you face as a memoirist is seeing each obstacle not as a threat, but as a challenge and opportunity. You will find that anticipating hurdles can render obstacles less formidable and make you a stronger memoirist.

Not only are hackneyed phrases hard to avoid, but finding a way to write your story in a new way is a challenge. Though everyone's story is obviously one-of-a-kind, unless you are a celebrity, you may think that no one is particularly interested in your "ordinary" story. If it is not in some manner "strange," you may feel that you need an angle, something to make you stand out from the crowd. Right?

No. Strange or not, you have a right to write. Fear is the great crippler. If you allow it, what I call "clichéophobia" will stop you before you even start. Instead, feel the fear and start writing – clichés and all. Your life IS unique, as you will see.

In fact, in the telling of your story, you may surprise yourself by discovering an angle that elevates you to celebrity status, if only in your own mind. Even if you've lived a model "unstrange" life, you can delight in the accolades of your own shining report.

Know also that readers are intrigued by success stories. If you are creative, chances are you can make your life interesting or exemplary in some capacity. Look for your quirks. It is your idiosyncrasies that make your story worth writing...and reading.

FOR WHOM DO YOU WRITE?

The first way to consider this question is to be aware that the word "memoir" implies remembrance. Humans have innumerable ways to remember life's events. Aside from mentally recalling and recounting situations, we are collectors of stories; we all enjoy the nostalgia of our letters, diaries, and photographs. Many writers use poetry to capture and record observations and emotions. These items are tangible evidence of memories, which may comfortably fit into your book of life.

Although some writers hope for a broad audience, you may be content to compile your own memories as a legacy for your family, children or friends. The source of every memoir is the self, regardless of who may eventually read it. Bearing this in mind will help keep you true to yourself and consequently more readable by others. Remember: Authenticity is the key to your soul and to the hearts of others.

DISCIPLINE IN WRITING

Understanding the logistics of revelatory writing is a good start towards understanding the self and the nature of self-expression and self-discovery. One way to ensure that you accomplish the task of creating a memoir is setting a regular schedule for writing. Surprise, surprise! A memoir, as with any other writing project, requires concentrated mental energy as differentiated from random stream of consciousness or free flowing writing. Setting up a regular time and a goal to write is the best way to establish discipline and kick off your project.

Unless you are a seasoned writer, begin with small quantities of time to devote to writing. It is easier to build up your writing time than to start with impossibly high expectations. For instance, you may start with one hour a week and aim for a goal of just one page of memories. Setting a goal of a page at a time can help the process. As you feel more comfortable with your output, you will be surprised at how quickly an hour passes. You will add hours and pages in increments until you may have to revise your schedule around your writing!

I recommend you choose a time when you have no other responsibilities, if that is possible. Interruptions are annoying and, if you are in a flow, will frustrate your progress. Many writers feel that writing first thing in the morning works best. Fresh from dreams, ideas have a way of moving from thoughts into words. If nothing useful presents itself, let your thoughts run wild and write whatever comes up.

Once you develop a level of discipline, you will find yourself moving deeply towards your core. As the creator, unraveling the mystery of your inner being becomes not a choice, but rather a necessity. Whether pen or chisel, brush, body or whatever medium, the imperative of the artist is towards absolute self-abandon – and spontaneity.

How do we train ourselves to be spontaneous? Ironically, it takes discipline to become spontaneous! Like inspiration, losing oneself to the point of spontaneous writing is elusive. The mind has a way of interfering with the artist's best intentions to create. The creative person is inventive with excuses; he is as adept at creating excuses as he is at creating the life worth writing about. Unfortunately, one's creative avoidance can work against one's best intentions. When ideas are in short supply, he may find himself engaging in all kinds of mindless tasks to avoid the real work. Emptying the trash, cleaning the fridge, folding laundry suddenly demand his immediate energy. Certainly you need to do your chores, but you can adjust your priorities. The dirty dishes will be there after you have cleansed your soul through your creative work. (On the other hand, if you think about mindless work as a way to access the unconscious, go ahead and make use of washing dishes as a relaxation exercise.)

In short, discipline begets spontaneous writing. Spontaneous writing begets a disciplined writer.

Setting a schedule to sit and write is just one kind of discipline. But learning to sit and meditate is another kind of discipline that I recommend for memoir writers. I would venture to say that the inaction of meditation is as vital to the process of memoir writing as the physical act of sitting. An important aspect of remembering is the "freedom" you need to achieve through the discipline of the mind.

What do I mean by freedom through discipline? A common problem, or obstacle, for the writer is the imagined critic. While our own scrutiny of our work is essential, it is often dangerous to our freedom. It is easy for the creative writer to slip, indeed fall off the deep end of self-criticism and into the realm of crippling self-doubt. Every word, phrase, space, and punctuation mark becomes magnified into a surrealistic object of questionable value. Revising a bland sentence structure can become an obsessive nightmare.

For most of us, the inner critical judge is a constant companion who must be silenced. When the judge feels more like an overwhelming jury of peers, jeers and leers, we get locked up and blocked. We need to regroup. If you catch yourself overworking a thought, this is a good moment to take a breather and apply a relaxation technique. In order to access our intuitive self, we need to carve out an inner space into which our ideas can collect. Meditation is an excellent time-efficient, effective tool. It is always available and costs nothing. It is the perfect remedy for the distressful feeling of "Stop the world, I want to get off!" Quiet sitting is easy to learn and its method can even be acquired via the Internet.

In addition to meditation, many other ways exist for creative people to "get clear" when feeling blocked. You may find exercise, jogging, swimming, or yoga a means to mental relaxation. I find that many fresh ideas emerge towards the end of a vigorous walk. Still, as my most sage counsel, I recommend meditation as the primary, indispensable key to the creative kingdom.

THE POWER OF AFFIRMATIONS

I like to help my clients see obstacles as a challenging opportunity for creative growth. Unfortunately, there is one obstacle that must be seen for what it is. Fear. It is the dirtiest word in the creativity coach's language! Fear is the basis for every excuse we make not to write.

But when we understand the source of our fear, we can work to out-smart it. We, as human beings, are invested in looking good. Everyone has dreams of success in one form or another. Whether in business or love, art or craft, we search for ways to look good to ourselves and to each other. One of our biggest fears is embarrassment. The artist, like the lover, must reveal himself in order to experience the results for which he yearns. But if we are afraid, we shut down, and no revealing can be done.

It is important to recognize the iron jaws of the "fear-trap" when you see it. When you can feel the fear and can't proceed, it is time to use conscious affirmations to help stare down the dirty interloper. I say, learn to identify the enemy, then turn it into an ally. Take your worst thoughts and make them your best ideas. For every negative thought, there is a positive corollary.

1. If you are afraid or ashamed of your own narcissism, remind yourself that Narcissus bloomed into a beautiful flower. It is a good thing to see your own beauty. Reframe your shame with an affirmation. Say: *My life is worthy of a book.*

2. If you are afraid of exposing an embarrassing behavior, remind yourself that everyone has embarrassing moments. No one is per-

fect. That is what it means to be human. Say: *I am perfectly human.*

3. If you are afraid your work is inferior, remind yourself that not every Picasso painting was a masterpiece. We all have good and bad creative days. Say: *I am creating from the heart.*

4. If you are afraid you lack talent, remind yourself that even great performers have stage fright. Everyone has gifts and talents to be shared. Say: *I have a right to create.*

5. If you are afraid of failure, remind yourself that everyone (even the coach) has fear. Taking a chance is the only road to success (clichéophobes take note). Say: *Feel the fear and do it anyway* and *Nothing ventured, nothing gained.*

Remember that creativity comes with a price: taking a chance with your ideas. The reward is in the finished product. As with creating a new life, we hope for a perfect product. Each child is wonderful, unique and perfectly human. We love our child, but not everyone else will. We know this going in, but take the chance anyway. We do our best to have the world see our child or product as we do, and to accept it as something special. Time after time we hear the successful individual is the one who believes in her talents, despite fears of failure. There is no reward without risk.

We are most productive when we feel good about ourselves. Belief in yourself and faith in the process are the essential elements required for your project to thrive. Thus, use affirmations liberally. They may not guarantee fame and fortune, but they will help provide you with a sense of self-worth. Once affirmed, you'll be armed with a feeling of satisfaction and the success you will need to take the next step in promoting your memoir.

PUBLISHING YOUR MEMOIR

As stated above, writing can be a lonely enterprise. You inevitably wonder, "Who will read my work?"

Yes, we all write first for ourselves. But, clearly, unless we are writing a private diary, we usually write with the intention of being read by others, and to be honest, with the hope of also being appreciated by them. When you've managed to get a substantial piece of your memoir written, it is time to work towards getting it read.

You do not have to have a complete manuscript to solicit for publication. There are a variety of ways to go about getting published. Finding an agent or a publisher can be the most challenging aspect of your project. You may need to remind yourself that rejections are a part of the process, not a personal indictment. Your affirmations can come in real handy right about now!

"My work is valuable."

Word of mouth is a good way to start the process of finding an agent or publisher. A woman I know managed to get the attention of a friend's agent through sheer persistence. Her relentless letters, e-mails and personal encounters finally persuaded the agent to look at her work. Her book was published and sold quite well. Had she taken the first rejection as an absolute "no," she might not have accomplished her goal. A foot in the door is a good starting place, but without confidence, you can get stuck in a rut.

If you do not have any connections to the publishing world, do some research about publishers, agents and the kinds of work they represent. Many books and web sites will help you determine the appropriate outlets for your work and instruct you in the protocol and process of getting an agent or publishing house. You must remind yourself that there are countless authors competing for a finite number of reps. To get no response is not a rejection, and to get a rejection is not a judgment of your ability or talent. Many, if not most, famous authors received rejections before getting published. Even James Joyce had trouble attracting a publisher! Remind yourself:

"A rejection of my work is not a reflection of my self-worth."

You may also want to consider self-publishing. Because markets are ultra-competitive in today's world, there is no longer any shame in a "vanity" production. Many self-published works now make it into the mainstream by selling enough copies to attract the attention of mainstream publishing houses. The Internet is an excellent source for exploring this option.

I'd like to offer one more word of sage counsel. Your memoir, like my own, may have sprung from a place of catharsis. The confessional memoir may include embarrassing revelations you may or may not want to share as your own. Most publishers want a writer who will take an active part in self-promotion. You might want to consider a pseudonym or anonymous authorship, though this will impact your ability to find a publisher.

Similarly, if your work is embarrassing to others, it is incumbent on you to protect others from slander at any cost. Writing your story is not about shaming others, even if you have been abused or hurt by them. You can purge and tell your story while carefully disguising perpetrators or using a pseudonym, even if it diminishes your chances of getting published. Your story can serve as a model for others who have been through tough times. Spiritual growth demands forgiveness, not blame.

ACHIEVING CONNECTION FROM WRITING

One of my strong motivations for writing my memoir grew out of my own spiritual quest. My experience with meditation has been the source of many surprises. Not only has it cleared a creative path, but it has also opened me up to a deeper understanding of humanity. As I sought the Self, I discovered others.

The rewards of deep connection are what compel me to follow my calling and honor my purpose as a writer and a coach. To excavate the Self is, at times, excruciating work, laden with the blood, sweat and tears of any physical labor. I tend towards seeing the world as inhabited by the proverbial two kinds of people. In my mind, life is a game of Hide and Seek. I see the Hiders as those who stand in the shadow waiting to be discovered. I believe the Seekers are those who are either consigned to or choose conscious living, and once on that path there is no turning back.

Humans are by nature curious. We want to explain our existence both to ourselves and to one another. Some are satisfied just to be on life's mysterious path, while others are mystified explorers on a search for hidden treasure. A memoir can simply result from the desire to recount or reflect upon one's successes, accomplishments, and gifts. Or it can grow out of the magnificent magnetic energy of our own mystery. Whatever its source, the challenge of the memoir is your unique creative opportunity. Blessings.

Nancy Manocherian is a multi-media artist who has written and produced for the theatre in New York City. With degrees in art and psychology, she is a life-long learner with interests as varied as her talents. She is active on the boards of several arts and charity organizations such as Juvenile Diabetes Research Foundation and The New Group, a Broadway production team. Committed to education and mental health, she practices creativity coaching in New York City and Westchester where she resides with her husband, teenage children, and dogs.

DRINKING AT THE WELL OF CREATIVITY

THE CASE FOR COLLAGE AS A PERSONAL PRACTICE

BY DRU SIMMS

Wouldn't it be nice if we had a special creative well we could drink from when our creative energies dwindle or become completely blocked? Wouldn't it be nice to just have fun with art sometimes, without being concerned about how the work would be evaluated? Wouldn't it be nice to have a creative practice that would serve as a kind of meditation – helpful and inspiring when life is going well, but also therapeutic and steadying when we're in a crisis?

I've found one such "creative well" in the ongoing, gentle practice of personal collage – putting together simple, easy, non-demanding composite images "for my eyes only." I've developed an appreciation for this personal rejuvenative practice by turning to it on a fairly regular basis over a period of some thirteen years. Let me tell you how it all started.

A FIERY BEGINNING

In October of 1991, I lost my home, my possessions, and my neighborhood in the Oakland Firestorm, in which some 3,000 homes were destroyed and, most tragic of all, twenty-six people died. In response to the disaster, many wonderful service organizations set up various kinds of support to help the process of recovery, one of which was small weekly therapy groups led by professional therapists.

I attended one of these groups, which started with maybe eight people but eventually dwindled down to four women; two of us single, two married, all at different ages, and all in vastly different places when it came to things like insurance coverage, support from friends and family, health, and our ability to handle this overwhelming crisis. We met in a huge old estate home in Oakland that had once been quite a showplace but was now used for various social services and had become shabby and run-down. Everything seemed to be kind of a monochromatic gray, which struck me as appropriate. It reminded me of ashes.

The meetings were highly emotional – lots of tears, lots of anger, lots of pain, despair, and not a little profanity. I'm sure none of us, not even the competent, sensitive young therapist who was leading the group, could have anticipated the intensity of feelings that poured out in those dingy, but somehow reassuring, rooms. Before long, our facilitator invited another therapist to co-lead the group with her.

We had been meeting for a few weeks when our leaders gently suggested we might get some comfort from making collages.

Collages?!

What the bleep could they be thinking? How could that help people who had just lost their homes? Our reaction was uniformly hostile. One of us raged at the leaders for several minutes. I was more subdued but I felt betrayed. Couldn't they see we were in NO state to be cutting out stupid pictures and pasting them together! We had lost everything! We were depleted. Empty. Bereft. Overwhelmed with meetings, decisions, and grieving. The intensity of our negative response came out of the intensity of our loss. The four of us railed at the therapists for the remainder of that session.

The next meeting, they had the nerve – or courage – to bring up the topic of collage again, albeit with some trepidation. Again, we poured out resistance but with less hostility than the prior week. But then, it may have been this session or the next, somehow we reluctantly agreed to give it a try.

They laid out large 18-by-24-inch sheets of paper, a stack of magazines, scissors and glue sticks, and encouraged us to "let the images choose you" rather than having any preconceived idea of what to select. That was hardly a necessary instruction. Our brains and bodies were too exhausted to make conscious choices.

SCISSORS, PAPER, PORCELAIN

We sprawled around on the floor and began ruffling through the magazines, sometimes silent and at other times commenting about what we were finding. Gradually we began to tear and cut and shuffle our images, and slowly we began to assemble and arrange and paste them onto the large sheets of paper. We talked and cried. We reminisced over things that had passed from our lives forever. We shared images and nodded in empathetic understanding. We raged and grieved. We laughed hard over dark fire-related jokes that I'm sure only we could have thought funny.

The images I chose allowed me to visually express many feelings about the fire, including a perception which had haunted me for weeks. I had had an almost palpable sense of some kind of strange reality, somehow off to the left of my vision. When I held my awareness in some indefinable way, I could almost "see" it. I experienced myself there as a nondescript non-human "thing," the shape of an old-fashioned wooden clothespin, standing completely still in a bleak landscape, with indefinable bits and pieces of the material world blowing by me, some of it sticking, some not.

It surprised me to find this scene appearing in the upper left-hand corner of my collage as an old, faceless wooden statue, similar to one of the Easter Island monoliths, surrounded by a gray ashen landscape. Around and onto the figure, I had pasted torn bits of paper. Next to that scene was a contrasting one, which I realized was how the un-burned-out world seemed to me at the time. A porcelain figurine dressed in a beautiful long pink and white gown stood elegantly at the top of a set of marble steps, poised to descend gracefully into a lush formal garden. I imagined her saying, "Would you like a cup of tea?" and offering plates of perfectly iced *petit-fours*.

The rest of the collage was full of dark and chaotic imagery, and phrases such as, "When can memories be trusted?," "Truth in the Ruins," "There is a limit to what we can absorb," and "California, the Endangered Dream." Somewhere near the center, a woman with a "the-hell-with-it" look on her face throws up her arms, and above her, I had pasted, "Send for your passport to Polynesia." I had stood in the ashes of the burned-out house site with just such a look on my face and a similar desire in my heart.

When we finished our collages, we passed them around and each of us talked about what our own collage meant. By the time we were done with the session, we were won over. The process had been deeply moving. Having so many elements of our personal truths reflected back to us in images we had chosen was strangely satisfying and, indeed, as our leaders had suggested, comforting. It felt as if a little bit of healing had taken place. We agreed to repeat the process at subsequent group meetings. I put this first collage up on my wall in my temporary living quarters, where it continued to give me solace daily.

My second collage, completed at the next session, included darker, more chaotic imagery, but way up in the right hand corner was a small area of golden, sun-lit sky with the words, "A thin ray of Hope" pasted over it. Although it was early in my recovery process, I could see – and feel – a movement toward a more positive future.

I still have the collages I made in that group. I don't look at them often, but when I do, these many years later, they still move me deeply. I didn't realize it then, but those first collage-making sessions contained the seeds of what has become for me an on-going personal creative practice. I had already learned that, even in times of extreme crisis, personal collage can provide comfort and insight.

TWO BASIC GUIDELINES

You may be wondering how this personal creative practice differs from doing art qua art? The major underlying difference is in the intention behind it. In my personal collage practice, my intention is to open up to receiving information, inspiration, and rejuvenation from my Self – and for myself.

There are two basic guidelines I follow. First and most importantly, the critical voices, internal and external, must be firmly dismissed. As a creative person, you know you may be one of the worst "offenders" here as, understandably, your artistic standards are high and difficult to turn off.

Over time, my dreaded inner critic would say things like, "Oh that's too ugly visually," or "Oh, that's too ugly psychologically," or "This is a waste of time." Sometimes it would say, "Why would you want to go to that dark place? It will just perpetuate the darkness." But mostly I let these voices speak and let the image be expressed anyway. Even if the feelings were unhappy, angry or troubling, even if the resulting collage didn't seem significant or esthetically pleasing, it felt so satisfying to see the images emerge that I eventually found it easy to push the cautionary voices aside.

As for external critics, I am committed to protecting my work from them. Most friends with whom I have shared my personal collages have themselves been tuned in to the process and have refrained from evaluations, "positive" or "negative." In the rare instances where someone has made critical remarks, I have frankly just stopped showing them these personal collages. They mean well, but they're missing the point.

The more I dismiss my judgmental self, the more I can step outside my normal life routine, often suspending concern for whatever else may be going on for me then. Time spent this way develops a meditative quality in and of itself, and regardless of what I produce, I can return to the rest of my life with a new perspective. I may become refreshed, amused, inspired, puzzled, even disturbed – but I have new life material with which to work.

Once the critic is effectively banished, it's easier to follow the second basic guideline, which is to avoid having any preconceived ideas about what the collage should be. It's helpful to put aside notions of how you think the final collage should look, or even what images you think you should look for, or what issues you might be hoping the collage will clarify. Leaving the selection of images to a "random" process has the effect of allowing you to bypass your rational mind and open up to whatever presents itself in the moment.

While I am tearing out images, I let myself choose anything that captures my attention or causes an emotional reaction for any reason whatsoever, even something that makes me feel uncomfortable. The key is to let emotion or sensation take precedence over thought, whether it's because I'm responding to a specific image or part of one, or to its color, texture, lightness or darkness, mood, style, or something evocative of my past, or, perhaps most magical of all, some draw to the image that I don't understand. All images that appeal to me for the reasons above simply go, unevaluated, into a pile for possible use.

As I shuffle the images around in relationship to each other, my next step is to cut (or tear) away the background, so that new combinations can emerge. This is always a fascinating process. Images I would never have thought of putting together now combine to provide some entirely new and surprising perspective or insight.

In the middle of writing this article, I hit a slump and decided to take my own advice and put together a collage. I set a one-hour time limit, suspecting that I just needed to avoid the demands of writing more than anything else. I tore out some images and, more quickly than usual, began shuffling them around to see what I had. Two captured my attention, and I pulled them out of the pile. The first was a photograph of a porcelain Disney figurine of Snow White, her long yellow skirt flowing, in a dancing pose. The second, much smaller sepia-toned image was of a Native American woman dressed in beaded buckskin with fringes flying, also in a dancing pose.

As I moved the two images around to see how they would fit together, I tried them side by side and was surprised and delighted to see something that had escaped my notice when I had chosen them. Both dancers were facing forward and slightly to the left. Both dancers' right legs were extended gracefully out over their left, with one dancer's foot in a black pump and the other's in a buckskin boot turned out to the front of the picture in exactly the same way. Both dancers' right arms were down and out to the side, one holding her flowing, yellow skirt and the other allowing the long buckskin fringe to fly out. Both dancer's left arms were raised gracefully up and out to the left. In short, both dancers were in exactly the same position, a kind of a standing curtsy or bow. Maybe it doesn't take much to make me happy, but I get a kick out of that kind of coincidence. The images seemed to cry out to be placed together, and I ended up juxtaposing them by putting the smaller image of the Native American woman under the raised left arm of Snow White, almost as if the Disney figurine were holding open a sepia-toned cape and joyfully "presenting" the other dancer to the world. I added images – ocean water across the bottom under Snow's feet, and a magenta-colored sky over all – and let the emerging collage begin to "talk" to me.

LETTING THE COLLAGE SPEAK TO YOU

Although I had used many word cutouts in my earliest collages, I've come to prefer to leave words out now. This allows for a larger range of interpretation, especially if I return to the collage at some later time when I may bring completely new insights to the process.

However, I've found that, some time during the assembling process, a phrase begins to repeat itself in my mind, and I realize that the collage is "dictating" a title to me. The meaning may be subtle and complex, it may be descriptive, it may be a play on words, a pun, or a little joke, but whatever it is, giving my collage a title has become an integral part of the process. (The title of this article is from a title for one of my collages.)

In the collage of Snow White, it seemed as if she were dancing right on the ocean water under her feet. At that point, the title, "Dances with Waves," began to run through my mind. I could see that it applied to the relationship between Snow White and the water, but also to the fact that both figures were dancing and, in a sense, "waving" with their left hands. For some reason, that made me smile. The title also seemed to be a kind of Native American name, which felt appropriate. As is usually the case, even though I would try out other possibilities, such as "Walks on Water" or even "Dancing with Waves," the original precise title phrase continued to insinuate itself back to the top of the list, and there it remained. This collage is now officially called "Dances with Waves."

WRITING ABOUT THE COLLAGE

I also like to write about the collage in order to understand its messages more directly. This invites an integration of the visual, emotional and intellectual aspects of the process. (Some would say this brings the right and left sides of the brain together.) Although words can never substitute for images (as I've found in trying to describe the collages here) they can "mine" the collage for hidden treasure that might otherwise be only sensed rather than more viscerally understood.

A favorite writing exercise for me is one often used with dreams: to take each image in the collage, or at least the major ones, and write in first person, as if you were that image talking. You can then write out dialogues among the various images and see what they have to say to each other. Often, this will lead to a discovery of fresh metaphors.

A friend and long-time collage maker recently showed me one of her latest pieces, in which an older woman with a worried expression is looking toward the left of the picture while a younger woman, rather ghost-like and ethereal, is leaving out a back door. Off to the right side, a skittish looking rabbit is cowering against a wall. In dialoguing with the collage, the rabbit told her he was frightened because the two women were not speaking to each other. He would feel much better, he informed her, if they would talk. Being "of a certain age," my friend recognized this as an invitation to find out what her "youth" might have to say to her as it was "going out the back door" at this stage of her life. Her next step was to write the dialogue between the two figures.

This unique juxtaposition of images in fresh, unexpected ways often seems to free my imagination to question, explore, and imagine new meanings for issues I'm dealing with at the time. The new composite image mirrors back to me inner truths, and I can get to insights and understandings via a direct, nonverbal path. I can take a sounding on my present state, and learn something about my inner self. The images are consistently of value to me, giving me information about myself that I truly wonder if I would have been able to access otherwise. It's not a substitute for a therapist, but it can certainly be used as an adjunct to formal therapy.

For example, in "Dances with Waves," I speculated that Snow White could be the part of me that wants to be the "Fairest One of All," and to "dance on water," the part of me that aspires to an unrealistic standard of perfection. But Snow is also showing me the authentic Native American dancer, who is in exactly the same pose. Could it be that even the external, unreal, perfectionistic part of me is connected to my authentic real live Self? The relationship of the two figures to each other in the collage seems to be inviting me to relax about my outer, seemingly superficial form (a Disney figurine) and to trust that it is in harmonious synchronization with my inner, more authentic form (a Native American woman.) Perhaps it is saying, "Hey, lighten up! Have fun! We're dancing here!"

THE VALUE OF PRACTICE OVER TIME

One value of doing collage as a regular practice over time is that it forms a retrospective look at your inner journey. Over the years I have learned that I can return to it again and again as a way of reflecting "Me-Over-Time" back to "Me-Now." For this reason, I've learned to date each collage as I finish it. It may not seem important at the time, but it can be helpful later. I have also assembled my collages into a large portfolio, so that they will all be in once place in chronological order. Sometimes collages I do now hearken back to earlier work, and I can see connections, threads, progress made (or not).

As I looked at the figurine of Snow White in my current collage, I remembered that my first fire-related collage also contained a porcelain figurine. Hmmm, interesting. I looked again at the old collage. There was that elegantly dressed woman descending the steps into the beautiful garden. I was surprised to see that, except for fact that her left arm is holding a feather fan in front of her, this figurine is even in the same pose as the two figures in my current collage.

I don't yet know exactly what to make of the similarities, but it seems as if it might be more than coincidence. I did see that the earlier figurine, which represented the "normal" world to me then – so different from the fire-devastated reality in which I felt trapped at the time – was actually unreal. It occurred to me that I had, of course, been holding the rest of the world to some standard of "perfection," impossible for it to attain, just as now in the current collage, Snow White seemed to represent a desire for unrealistic perfection in myself.

I took heart from one difference. In the earlier collage, "I" was represented by the non-human form, completely out of touch with "the rest of the world," the pink and white gowned figurine. But now the relationship between Snow White (unrealistic perfection) and the Native American woman (the authentic dancer) was one of connection. Hopefully, this is telling me that, while I may be caught up in an unrealistic standard of perfection even now, I seem to be more in touch with an inner authenticity than I was at that stressful past time.

Of course, collages cannot substitute for accomplishing the tasks of the outer world (my collages did not rebuild my house for me), but they can serve as inspiration for a task at hand, creative or otherwise. Recently, a musician/composer client with whom I share the process completed a collage featuring a rather wild-looking young girl with unkempt reddish hair, who looked as if she had been running. Wearing a brown tunic dress, a bit muddy, and holding some flowers, she was looking straight forward with a direct, earnest gaze. As a background, my client added an actual photograph of an emerging star, full of gold, red and green tones, and gave the girl a small gold crown and a palm leaf scepter. She titled the resulting spirited collage, "Gypsy Queen," and kept it on her dresser where she could look at it every day. She said it seemed to affect her personality, bringing out her child-self, allowing her to be more joyful, a little more "brash" in a good way. Weeks later, as she faced the daunting task of composing her first string trio, she reported feeling the young, wild Gypsy Queen coming through. The collage helped her be less afraid of the creative challenges, more playful and less perfectionistic in responding to them. Not surprisingly, subtle strains of vibrant gypsy music are discernible in her final composition.

ALONE OR IN GROUPS

Another advantage of collage as a personal practice is that it can be done both alone and with others. It may be easier to get in touch with your true self, and the meditative benefits may be greater, when doing collage alone. Still, some of the most powerful, fun and moving times can be found doing collage in a group of non-judgmental, accepting friends. Sharing collages can provide the opportunity to learn intimate truths about each other and, just as we did in that original fire recovery group, support each other in facing life's challenges.

If you do participate in a group, it's a good idea to protect the process by avoiding evaluative comments about each other's work, even ones so innocent as, "I wonder what it would be like if you put this image there, and that image here..." Each person needs to speak to and for his or her own collage. Once you loosen this rule, you invite the critic, however innocently, back into the circle and weaken the process. If this seems too limiting, you can give the collage maker the option of specifically requesting feedback, but only after first presenting his or her own understanding of what has been made.

PRACTICAL ADVANTAGES OF COLLAGE

There are also practical advantages to using collage as your personal creative practice.

It doesn't require a lot of special conditions, so you can get to it easily and quickly, even when you're feeling resistant. As we all know, setting up special conditions for our creative work can contribute to stalling or procrastinating, so it's good to avoid a similar temptation with our private creative practice, if possible. Collage requires no special space – the dining room table will do – and both set-up and clean-up are relatively uncomplicated and easily accomplished.

It is not overly time-consuming. You can browse through magazines and tear out images any time, even when watching TV. You can collect images to use later, although there is some advantage to making the collage soon after you choose the images. A simple collage of, say, three or four images, can take as little as an hour.

It requires no special talent or skill. If you can cut and paste, you can make a collage. You don't have to be a visual artist. (It can even be more difficult for the visual artist than any others to put aside creative standards in order to surrender to the process.) For other artistic disciplines, perhaps especially those in the performing arts such as theatre, music and dance, it can be thought of as a form of "cross-training" in creativity.

It is inexpensive, even cheap. Collage doesn't require any expensive materials. Old magazines can often be obtained free. In fact, once your friends know you are doing it, they may be happy to inundate you with their discards. Magazines of all kinds can be used, but National Geographic and magazines about space or nature have proven especially evocative and useful sources for me. Any kind of paper can be used for backings and any kind of glue can be used to paste images down. So the expense of creating a collage is virtually nil.

You can expand beyond the basics. Of course, if you really get into it, you may find yourself casting about for the right weight and size of paper that seems to work best for you. You may find yourself wanting to buy a pair of small curved scissors, which works well for cutting around small, detailed images. You might like to use double-sided tape to stick your images down, or you might find it handy to use a kind of tape that doesn't stick firmly so you can pull it up and rearrange images without damaging them. And you might want to graduate from glue sticks to more expensive art glue which can be more reliable in securing the images over time. (The *Yes* brand glue, applied with a plastic spatula from the hardware store, is a favorite for me. It seems expensive but a little goes a very long way.)

You might even find yourself making your collages into greeting cards or matting and framing them. If that is the case, you will probably want to make color copies, sometimes enlarging or reducing individual images or the entire collage itself. Color copy machines have become relatively inexpensive, although color cartridges for them can add up. Otherwise, copies can be made at copy shops. One caveat, again: if you do prepare cards for public view or to give to others, be extremely wary of the inner critic's tendency to sneak back into the process.

A SPECIAL APPROACH: SOULCOLLAGE™

I could not write about collage without recommending a very special way to expand your personal practice, based on the book, SoulCollage™: An Intuitive Collage Process for Individuals and Groups, by Seena B. Frost. Seena is a therapist who has been using collage personally and professionally for over 20 years. The SoulCollage process involves creating multiple collages on card stock in a 5 by 8-inch format. The uniform size results in a set of collage cards that are easy to handle and to which you can refer back over time.

Once a card is complete, Seena recommends a basic speaking or writing practice for all your cards, one which has the advantage of shifting your perspective from yourself to the "self" in the card. This is accomplished by prefacing whatever you say with, "I am one who..." (For example, Snow White might say, "I am one who aspires to walk on water, but I am also one who shows you your authentic self.")

Seena's book teaches you how to organize the cards into four basic "suits," and how to use them for "readings" in much the same way as a tarot deck, only in this case, using a deck with images having special personal meaning for you. It can be done alone or in a group, and is a wonderful experience.

GIVE IT A TRY

If you do nothing more, I hope you'll try making a collage just as I did while writing this article. Maybe you will try it now, or maybe it will come to mind when you are in the middle of a creative project and your inspiration dries up. In any case, if it appeals to you, give yourself an hour or so. Go find any magazines you have around the house, thumb through one or two or them, and tear out a few images that appeal to you for whatever reason. Cut away the background material and lay two or three images down on a new background, even if it's only a plain piece of paper. Move them around and see if there isn't some way they fit together that feels more "right" to you than any other. If you have some tape or a glue stick, tack them down lightly.

Sit with your newly created collage for a few minutes. What does it say to you? If it could have a title, what would it be? Often it will offer up some phrase that seems to stick. Then take a piece of paper, and try a writing exercise, perhaps the one that Seena Frost recommends in her book. Write "I am one who..." and finish the sentence, speaking as if you were the card's imagery itself talking.

Then just let the collage hang around in your line of vision over a period of days or weeks, and maybe now and then read over what you have written. You may find that the process yields pleasure, information, or even inspiration, and you may want to try making another collage another day, eventually letting the process of personal collage become a regular part of your life.

❖ ❖ ❖

Resources

SoulCollage: ™ An Intuitive Collage Process for Individuals and Groups, by Seena B. Frost, Hanford Mead Publishers, Inc. See the author's web site at www.soulcollage.com.

Dru Simms has over twenty years experience as an intuitive counselor. She is a Certified Creativity Coach, SoulCollage™ Facilitator, and Emotional Clearing Counselor, and holds a California Lifetime Teaching Credential. She conducts her practice, "Creating for Your Self," in Sonoma, offering workshops, small groups, and individual coaching sessions. She utilizes the expressive arts, including collage, role-playing, improvisation, and visualization to support the individual's quest for authenticity and personal truth. Dru performs in and directs community theater, and recently stage-directed the premiere of a short opera. Her essay, "Living an Authentic Life" was included in Eric Maisel's *Van Gogh Blues,* and she is currently writing a book, *How to Survive a Personal Crisis,* based on her experience with the 1991 Oakland Firestorm. Dru is developing a website, www.CreatingForYourSelf.com and can also be reached by email at drus@vom.com or by phone at (707) 939-8047.

CHALLENGE
YOURSELF
TO HIGHER
CREATIVITY

THE HERO WITHIN

USING THE MYTHIC JOURNEY TO DISCOVER MEANING IN YOUR CREATIVE WORK

BY MICHAEL MAHONEY ❖

Every one of us is a hero.

You don't have to leap tall buildings or slay the proverbial dragon in order to perform a heroic feat. You have only to listen to your own true inner voice, the voice that speaks for the heroic creative potential waiting inside you, and inside all of us, ready to take shape in the world at a moment's notice.

Webster's dictionary defines hero as:

a: exhibiting or marked by courage and daring;

b: supremely noble or self-sacrificing.

These qualities are indispensable for any creative endeavor, to be certain, but they lack a fundamental truth necessary if we are to pursue our creative projects in a way that leaves us fulfilled and happy: the need for personal meaning in everything we do.

You can have all the courage in the world to tackle an immensely complex subject matter or idea. You can take huge creative risks, requiring daringness. You can create while being noble. But a hero does not search for the Holy Grail because he is brave; he seeks it because he desires the universal answers it provides. And of what use is self-sacrifice, if in the end it means nothing?

If we are to discover the creative hero that lies inside each and every one of us, then we need a deeper framework for understanding what heroes actually do and what they really stand for. Heroism, especially of the inner and personal nature, is given little importance in today's world. Our culture has replaced the ideas and values of heroism with that of celebrity. Instead of a model we can turn to in our own lives for support and guidance, celebrity leaves us with pure image, a projection of a fantasy life we can neither relate to, nor follow when it comes to our own creativity. Is it any wonder our society treats celebrities like the gods and heroes of myths, when we are unable to find a cultural mythology that shows us how to discover the gods and heroes within us?

So where can we turn in order to find such a model? We need only to look to history to find the right map, for the hero archetype is as old as humanity itself.

Originally published in 1949, Joseph Campbell's *The Hero With a Thousand Faces* traces the story of the hero's journey and transformation through virtually all the mythologies of the world. The very conceptualization of the hero myth spans across all cultures and myths. Like the creative source, it is universal.

Campbell discovered that all hero mythologies share the same basic stages. No matter the story or the part of the world from which the story originated, he found that the steps of the hero's journey are always identical. The steps are the same across all cultures because they are embedded in us, a universal roadmap to the soul's quest for meaning; manifested in cultural form. In *The Hero With a Thousand Faces*, Campbell provides this brief summary of the hero's adventure:

> A hero ventures forth from the world of common day into a region
> of supernatural wonder: fabulous forces are there encountered and
> a decisive victory is won: the hero comes back from this mysterious
> adventure with the power to bestow boons on his fellow man.

Like the hero's journey, our creative efforts strive to make meaning from a chaotic world. What is creativity if not a mysterious adventure? Is it not our task as creators to overcome the inner blocks and fears (fabulous forces) we find along the way? Could the boon that Campbell speaks of be a product of our creativity, a piece of creative work we want to share with others in the hope it will inspire new meaning? Is there a better place to find a map to our own creative journey than from within ourselves?

Campbell breaks down the hero's journey into several distinct stages. In the context of our creativity, each stage of the hero's journey can be seen as an integral step to finding our creative selves and completing a creative project. From Hearing the Call to Adventure in the Ordinary World and then Answering that Call, to finding a Mentor, discovering Tests, Allies & Enemies, facing the Supreme Ordeal, and finally taking the Road Back, we can learn a great deal about what we can expect from the creative process by following the lead of the archetypal hero. The lessons we learn in each stage can have lasting value not only in helping us to complete a creative project, but perhaps more importantly, in discovering our true selves as creative heroes.

THE ORDINARY WORLD

It's Monday morning. The alarm rings. Time to go to work. Again.

It seems like the more items you cross off your to do list, the longer the list becomes. You still have to pay the bills. Little Johnny has a cold. And don't forget to pick up the milk.

For most of us, just finding a single moment to eek out a small creative endeavor can seem like a Herculean task. Just like the heroes of myth, we begin our creative journey in the world we already know and understand all too well: our ordinary daily life.

This is where we learn about the hero and the world he lives in. We learn what makes the hero tick, what he desires, and most importantly what prevents him from accomplishing his dreams. The hero is faced with a problem and approaches it, often unknowingly, with a tragic flaw. The hero has limited awareness that he needs to change this flaw in order to reach his goal. He is too wrapped up in his daily endeavors to tackle his own limitations. He doesn't even know that he's a hero – yet. *[For purposes of this article, the hero is referred to as "he" to reflect Campbell's analysis. Clearly, heroes can be "she" as well.]*

All of us enter the present moment with fears, anxieties, guilt, negative self-talk, or past patterns that prevent us from creating. There may be specific events from our lives that wounded our creative selves, but like the hero, we are not yet aware of what they are. We sense that something is missing in this ordinary world, but we can't quite put our fingers on it. We may even know what we want to create, but we simply can't find the time or the energy.

If we are to move forward like the hero, we must be aware of how we live and act in this ordinary world, but not let it dictate to us who we are. We must acknowledge the past, but not live in it. Our focus must be on the present, on whatever actions will move us towards creation, instead of worrying about the issues that prevented us from creating the day before.

There will never be a perfect time in one's life to create. There will always be worries, doubts, responsibilities, duties, stress from relationships and work, and just plain life getting in the way. But if we listen closely enough as we move through our busy lives, we can hear something faintly calling to us. It's not like the other voices, the ones that tell us we "can't" or "should." This voice is different. It asks us to listen carefully to its message, a message of hope and change. *Things can be different if we learn how to create right now in the middle of it all.* Perhaps if we take the time to hear it, we can take the next step on the hero's journey.

Hero's Task: What prevents you from creating right now? Is it a thought, an event from your past, a specific anxiety? Write it down. Then tear it up and start creating.

HEARING THE CALL TO ADVENTURE

The hero sits, safe and comfortable in the ordinary world. He thinks he knows who he is, and he has no real desire to stir up the pot. But then he hears it.

It's just a whisper at first. A glimmering. A promise.

An *opportunity*.

What form this opportunity takes can be as varied as the stars. For Odysseus, the journey began when the vengeful winds of the God Poseidon blew his ship off course. In the movie Star Wars, the adventure begins when Luke discovers a plea for help sent by Princess Leia to Jedi Knight Obi-Wan (Ben) Kenobi on the planet of Tatooine.

A challenge or quest is presented, disrupting the hero from his toils in the ordinary world. Suddenly the world seems a lot larger, the possibilities infinite.

But the call does not come without risks. There will be grave consequences if our hero decides not to take up arms.

In mythology, the call can arrive in the form of a message, a herald, a gift, the arrival of the villain, even a death. In our own personal creative lives, the call may be much more subtle.

It could be a phone call, offering you the chance to write a screenplay. Maybe it's an article in a magazine, one that inspires you to finally write that poem. A dream that awakens you in the middle of the night. Or maybe it's as simple as a few thoughtful words from a friend.

Whatever its source, the call to create cannot be heard if your ears are turned. We must be open to receiving any inspiration our muse may throw our way. A fleeting idea that passes quickly as a whim could be a novel or a symphony for the right listener. But for one who lets the idea pass without a second notice, it remains simply a passing thought. The key is being open to whatever comes your way.

It's in this stage that we decide whether we have the capability to work on our creative projects no matter what else is going on around us. We understand that to answer this call, sacrifices will have to be made. After all, life as you know it is about to change forever. The call asks of you to embrace that change, without becoming attached to its outcome. When the hero begins his quest, he knows there are no guarantees that he will return successful. Yet he sets out nonetheless.

The call does not care what mood you are in, or what external roadblocks are tossed at you on any given day. It cares only that you heed it.

Do we have it in us to answer the call? We may not yet know how we're going to find the time to create, or what it is we will create, but we can at least envision the possibility. We can see it before us like a candle in the dark. And we trust that it is there for a reason.

Hero's Task: What is your call to creative adventure? List three different sources or events that have either inspired you to create or generated an idea for a creative project. If you struggle with this exercise, list three places you can turn to for creative inspiration. Once you list these places, choose one and seek it out.

ANSWERING THE CALL TO ADVENTURE

If just hearing the call to adventure were enough, the hero would never leave the safety of his known surroundings to venture forth and slay the dragon. The call must be answered if the village is to be saved.

This is the crucial moment of choice that separates those who create from those who don't. For creation, like the hero's task, is action. How many of us have had a fantastic idea for a book, movie, or product that we've carried around inside us for years, only to see it show up one day at the theater or bookstore? If creativity was a matter of simply coming up with a new or innovative idea, we might not have the telephone, Romeo and Juliet, or the Mona Lisa. Imagine if Michelangelo had walked away from the pillar of marble content with the vision of David he held in his head.

Unfortunately, for many of us, the creative journey ends with the call to adventure. Along with the hopes and desires for meaning that arise as the call finds our heart, so too do the fears and insecurities that plague our minds. The hero may not be willing to continue, for he knows that once he sets foot outside the ordinary world, he will never be the same. He is afraid of change.

This is the stage where the risks involved in the journey ahead become all too clear. In the heroic sagas of myth, these risks are tangible: the hero knows that all who have seen Medusa before him have been turned to stone. In the creative journey, these risks are self-conceived.

Oftentimes this refusal comes in the form of competing thoughts. The call to create is one voice trying to be heard among the din of many. Your mind may also be shouting at you that, "I am not talented," "I don't know how," "I don't have the time."

Whatever the source of the refusal to create, whether it be perfectionism, fear of failure, or the sting from previous criticism, the hero cannot proceed without facing his reluctance to commit to the adventure. Deciding to do our creative work, enacting a plan to make sure it gets done, is a commitment. And making a commitment, especially to the unknown, is ripe with anxiety.

This anxiety is the root of all our creative doubts. Whatever form it may take, it is anxiety that the creative hero must come to terms with. He must learn to accept that it is a natural part of the creative process. It is not something to try to defeat or conquer. Try to imagine anxiety as your uninvited travel partner. You did not ask it to come along with you on your creative quest, yet it has come nonetheless. But if you can place your anxiety walking beside you on each step of your journey instead of blocking your path in the road ahead, you can continue to move forward through action.

In addition to the internal struggle to heed the call, artists are also faced with external pressures to turn their backs on the creative journey. Like the call of the Sirens that tempted Odysseus' men away from their path into dangerous waters, so too will numerous worldly distractions attempt to pull the creative hero off course. It is the choice between the call of the world and that of creative expression. While the artist can certainly seek inspiration in the world at large, at some point they must return back to themselves in isolation in order for the creative process to take place. Yet everywhere we turn, the sirens are calling: television, phone calls, housework. We need not be tied to the mast of our ship like Odysseus in order to resist these distractions, but we must be aware of them and consciously limit their influence if we are to take the next step in the creative journey.

Hero's Task: Make a list of the negative or self-critical thoughts that rise inside you when you think about creating. Now turn each one around into something positive. Aim to make yourself matter. For example, instead of thinking "How can I ever manage to get any writing done when I have so little time," think "I'm certain I can find 30 minutes each day to do some writing." Get in the practice of catching these negative thoughts when they occur and reframing them with an opposite, positive idea.

MEETING THE MENTOR

Where would Frodo have been without Gandalf, or King Arthur without Merlin? In the next stage of the journey, the hero receives the guidance he needs in order to succeed in his quest. Many times it is the mentor who convinces the hero to answer the call to adventure.

The gifts bestowed upon heroes from their mentor come in many forms. These include protection, wisdom, training, and magical gifts. The mentor will often place the hero through several challenging tests, tests through which the hero becomes aware of the true nature of his enemy, which is often himself. These tests also teach the hero the knowledge he needs if he is to succeed.

The word mentor comes from the Greek word for mind, *menos*, one meaning of which is intention, force or purpose. It can also stand for "courage." A mentor does more than just provide advice. They alter the very nature of the hero's consciousness in order to steer them towards their true creative purpose.

The most important gift a mentor can bestow on the path of the creative hero is support. As creators, we often feel alone on our own island. We crave constant feedback, yet most times it is not possible to receive it because of the isolation we experience in order to be creative. We often have no outlet for the inevitable fears and worries that come along with the creative process. When faced with the blank page or canvas, the need to create even when we don't feel like it, the constant quest for meaning … what we crave perhaps more than anything during these times is simply for someone to say to us: "Yes, I understand." It is this support that enables the hero to continue on despite his own inner doubts.

Your mentor need not appear in the form of an actual person. Any source of wisdom that helps guide you through the creative process can serve as your mentor. It could be a form of communication such as a book, magazine article, or movie. It could be a tradition or ritual. It could be a code of ethics or honor. It could even be a deep part of yourself long forgotten or buried, a knowing that already lies within you, ready to help you whenever you need it if only you would ask.

Hero's Task: One place to find support and guidance is through a creativity coach. Can you think of other people or places you could turn to for creative support?

CROSSING THE THRESHOLD

Once the hero has accepted the Call to Adventure and heeded the sage wisdom of the Mentor, he or she moves out of the conscious Ordinary World into the regions of the unknown. But before he can make that final transition from the world he knows to the Special World where the source of creativity lies, there is one more test to pass.

Though our creative self comes from the deepest parts of our being, it is accessible to us at any time. However, most of us can't just snap our fingers to make it appear. That's because our creative selves are often protected by what Campbell called the threshold guardian. One such Classical guardian from mythology is the trickster Pan, described here in *A Hero With a Thousand Faces*:

> The emotion that he instilled in human beings who by accident adventured into his domain was "panic" fear: a sudden, groundless flight. Any trifling cause then – the break of a twig, the flutter of a leaf – would flood the mind with imagined danger, and in the frantic effort to escape from his own unconscious the victim expired in a flight of dread. Yet Pan was benign to those who paid him worship, yielding the boons of the divine hygiene of nature, bounty to the farmers, herders and fisherfolk who dedicated their first fruits to him, and health to all who properly approached his shrines of healing.

Even when we have taken that first step towards creating, we face a new challenge as soon as we approach the blank page or canvas. We are on the border between worlds, and standing between us is the sum of all our fears about creating.

Because we stand on the verge of the creative act, yet haven't taken that last leap of faith to embrace the act itself, it is here that we are most vulnerable to one last panic attack. Just what do I think I'm doing? I don't even know where to begin. And even if I manage to get started, no one will want what I make anyway!

Like the fear inspired in Pan's victims, our own fear-based thoughts are trivial and groundless, born of a false desire to escape our own unconscious. The more we try to run from the threshold guardian, the more likely he is to catch us in his grasp. By pretending these fearful thoughts don't exist, we either make up an excuse that keeps us from creating, or we repress the thoughts entirely, leaving us depressed or anxious without knowing why.

We must learn to face our own guardian like the farmers who honor Pan with gifts. By recognizing beforehand that it is perfectly natural to encounter anxiety at the first moment of creation, we can face the guardian head on, diminishing his power. It is only by naming that which we fear that we can gain control over it. Simply take this fear for what it is: a natural part of the creative process that everyone, from the amateur photographer to the famous author, experiences. When you begin to understand that having this fear doesn't mean there is anything wrong with you, when you see it as having its own separate existence, then you've paid homage to the guardian, who will now let you pass.

Hero's Task: Practice taking the first creative step despite any anxiety you may feel. If you are a writer frozen by the blank page, stop thinking and simply write down a word, any word. You can even write down how your anxiety makes you feel. The key is to get something down on the page. Once you do that, more words will follow, and you'll soon be writing despite yourself. This technique works with any art form, whether it's a blank canvas or a lump of clay.

TESTS, ALLIES, AND ENEMIES

Congratulations! By this point in the creative journey, you're actually starting to do the work. You've managed to overcome your initial doubts and self-critical thinking. You've entered the process of discovery.

Just like the hero must learn the differences between the new world he has entered and the world he left behind if he is to get through it successfully, creators must learn how to navigate the new creative waters they find themselves in once they begin a new project.

Along the way, you are certain to encounter various tests that will challenge both your fortitude and creative vision. There will be difficult creative choices to make, problems to solve. You might run out of steam, find yourself unable to complete what you started, or even discover that the project you are working on has lost its meaning for you and your true creative heart lies elsewhere.

The ability of the hero to pass these tests and continue moving forward depends on his ability to quickly learn the new rules of the Special World he has entered, and his ability to listen to his inner wisdom and intuition.

A common test for creators at this stage is perfectionism. As we are working, we may be tempted to stop our progress in the middle in order to fixate on getting things "just right." Or we may simply become blocked because we feel the work we are doing "isn't good enough." We go back over and over the work we haven't yet completed instead of continuing onward. It's a test of our resolve and our ability to finish what we started.

In order to pass the test of perfectionism, we must first realize that perfectionism is simply another form of the same anxiety we already defeated earlier in our journey. We find our way out through awareness. Each time you have a perfectionist thought, remember that this is all it is: a thought. It is simply one perspective out of many. It is possible to have an anxious thought without experiencing anxiety, but it takes practice. Simply observe the thought as it occurs and then let it go by as if you were watching a sailboat on a river.

Another risk at this stage is getting hung up by too many creative choices. What will happen if I make the wrong choice? We are frozen with indecision. In some cases, we may drop the project altogether to start something new. But chances are good that if you do this once, you'll do it again with the next creative endeavor, and the one after that. Because it's not the actual choice that leads one to indecision, it's the anxiety surrounding the possibility of making a *wrong* choice.

Once again, the solution to this test is awareness. We must realize that in the Special World, unlike the Ordinary World from which we came, there are no wrong choices. Without experimentation and risk, creativity is just cliché. We must remember that our goal is to complete the hero's quest. We can always go back later and make changes or revisions. For now, we simply want to keep moving. Whatever may be stopping you, you must make the conscious decision to proceed regardless.

Along this road of trials, the hero also learns who to trust, as well as who is trying to block their path. Allies and enemies to the creative journey may come from inside you, or you might find them in the people or situations you encounter each day. An ally could be a supportive spouse who helps you find the time to create, or your favorite book on creativity. Your enemies could be the influence of a friend who constantly wants you to go out drinking, or the amount of time you spend watching TV each day. The important thing is to recognize each for what they are and adjust your creative plans and strategies accordingly. Pay attention to those people and things that feed your creative energy and those that take away from it.

Hero's Task: List the things or people in your life that breathe positive energy into your creative efforts. You may be surprised at the allies you find. Are there ways your allies can help you that you haven't yet considered or tried? Do the same for your creative enemies. Are there people or things in your life that hamper your ability to create? What steps can you take right now to reduce their influence?

THE SUPREME ORDEAL

At some point in every creative journey, we must come face to face with our greatest challenge: to believe in the meaning of that which we are struggling to create.

It is here, in the final confrontation with his nemesis, that the hero must die in order to be reborn. This death need not be literal, although in many stories it can be. It is the transformation of an old way of being into the new, possible only when the hero confronts his greatest fear. This is the phoenix; bursting into flame in order to be reborn from its own ashes.

For the creator, this is the stage of the creative process where we must endure the ultimate surrender: giving ourselves completely to our work, no matter where it takes us. It is where we let go of our attempts to control the work's outcome. If we are to find true meaning in our creative efforts, then at some point we must let our ego go.

Like Darth Vader to Luke Skywalker, however, the ego is guaranteed to put up one hell of a fight. But in order to move past the old, limited notions and perspectives that prevent real creativity, we must be willing to open ourselves to the connections that transcend our individual selves and touch every corner of the universe like branches from the same tree. It is this broader view that enables creators to see the commonalities amongst all things in a new and different light. It's also the same place from which others who see the creator's work can see themselves reflected in it.

This is where the creative hero finally discovers an inner balance he never knew he was capable of. He is able to simultaneously surrender to the direction his work takes him, yet maintain control of his craft. He is both restrained by logic and free from it. Allow the process of discovery to take hold of you and carry you away while you watch carefully from above. It's a bit like riding a plane. You select the plane that will take you to the final destination you choose. You pick the airline, the flight time, whether or not a meal will be served. But once your initial plan is in place, once you're on board and in the air, there's nothing to do but sit back, relax and enjoy the ride. Of course, if you find out you're on the wrong plane or the airline has lost your luggage, then it's time to reestablish control.

So how does one reach this kind of creative balance? Unlike in fairy tales and myths, there's no magic elixir to imbibe or wand to wave. There is only practice through action. The way through the supreme ordeal is routine. By creating every day, day-in and day-out, whether or not you feel like creating or whether the day's events conspire against you, you set in motion a powerful remedy to any meaning crisis that facing the hidden depths of your work may bring about. You will be much less prone to creative despair on any given day or place in your work if you have come to realize through direct experience the true meaning you find inherent in anything you create is *that which you give it.*

By approaching your creative work everyday *no matter what*, you accomplish several things at once. You find meaning in the process of discovery rather than the outcome of what you produce. And you give yourself an important shield with which to defend yourself from any meaning crisis that may occur: the knowledge that you are creating your own meaning through your dedication to create each day, and that the meaning crisis facing you today could be the solution to your creative problem tomorrow.

Hero's Task: In what ways can you surrender to your creative work? What holds you back from enjoying the act of discovery, instead of worrying about the final product?

THE ROAD BACK

Once the hero has completed his quest by vanquishing his opponent and retrieving his reward, he returns to the Ordinary World to bestow his newfound wisdom on those he once left behind. If he does not share his boons with others, then his change is merely personal, instead of epic and universal.

Although the act of creation is primarily an isolated act, we want others to see our work and praise us for it. We crave feedback and we are motivated by the potential impact and meaning our work can inspire in others.

Many creators overcome the supreme ordeal but stop there. Still afraid of what others will think of their work, they tuck it away in a drawer or basement. Imagine if most of our great artists never shared their work with the public. If you do not share your act of creation however, you risk performing a grave disservice to yourself and others. First, you never know what you have. Just because *you* don't think it's marketable, or important enough, or good enough, doesn't mean the public will view it the same way. You may have tapped into something residing in the collective unconscious that was just waiting for you to bring it to light. Second, you cannot learn to master your craft without feedback. Third, the universe has provided the world with a creative gift, a gift that was made through you. It exists for a purpose, even if that purpose is still unknown to you.

Like the act of creating itself, where you simultaneously had to hold on and let go, the same is required here. After you've done all you can to market your work, you must extend your creative gift outward to the world, holding your gift proudly for all to see, while at the same time leaving it to find its own path as soon as it leaves your hands.

Once you have experienced the entire journey of the creative hero, it will become easier to separate yourself from your work at this stage. As you to start to fall in love with the journey itself, which continues anew with each new creative project, there will be less need to take any criticism of your work personally. The work itself is simply the hero's reward for completing the journey.

❖ ❖ ❖

Each time you venture forth on a new creative quest, you have a choice. You can focus on the journey's outcome, which leads to anxiety and doubts about whether the final creative project will be good or meaningful enough. Or, like a true creative hero, you can opt to be transformed by the very paths you take, finding meaning in the process itself. It's time to take the first step.

❖ ❖ ❖

Michael Mahoney is a published fiction writer, poet, and creativity coach with a background in Jungian and mythological studies. A former journalist and graduate of the University of Wisconsin, he currently resides in Boston, MA. He is currently working on several screenplays, a novel, and learning how to play the Celtic fiddle. Michael specializes in creativity coaching for writers and dealing with writer's block, as well as personal growth through creativity for all artistic mediums. He can be reached at mdmahone123@yahoo.com.

CREATIVITY AND YOUR INNER GUIDE

CONNECTING TO YOUR POWER WITHIN

❖

BY BRIANA RISKIN

Whatever creative type you are, be it a musician, a painter, an actor, a carpenter, a dancer, or a writer, accessing and listening to your "inner guide" is a powerful experience.

You might be wondering what an inner guide is or if you even have one. In this article, I will explore the nature and value of an inner guide, which all beings have. By learning to access your inner guide in numerous ways, you can get in touch with your creative core or essence. Your inner guide is not your ego, but rather your authentic voice or spirit. This article will show you how to tap into the resources your inner guide provides for you.

WHAT IS YOUR INNER GUIDE?

The concept of an inner guide is foreign to most modern 21st century people, but nearly all ancient peoples believed in the existence of the mind and spirit along with the body, and viewed them as completely interconnected. When a person had an ailment of the body, a healer would look at that person's spirit and mind as well. For example, a shaman working with an ill person would take a journey into the spirit world and ask the spirits to release the illness from the person's body. The shaman would come out of the trance and tell the story of talking with the spirits. This sharing of the story helped not only the ill person's thinking about their health, but also that of the community.

Around the 1600's, however, advances in science and philosophy caused a mind-body split to occur. Medicine in particular viewed the body as completely separate from the mind and spirit. In fact, the body began to be viewed as a machine with parts that could be replaced, similar to that of a clock. Then the French philosopher, René Descartes, made a lasting divide between the mind and the body when he said, "I think, therefore I am." This statement shows the value of the intellect over the body and the spirit. Some call this "mind over matter." Mind, body and spirit have been completely separated.

Today, this mind/body/spirit split continues to impact how we think and feel about ourselves and influences our overall health. Most people are disconnected from their bodies and often from their spirit. We are bombarded by messages in the media about making physical changes to our bodies, without even considering how those changes affect our mind and spirit. On the flip side, we are just learning that our thoughts have an effect on our bodies. In fact people have changed their bodies on a cellular level just by changing their thinking, and as a result, have improved their health. That is amazing!

Accessing your inner guide allows you to reconnect the mind, body and spirit, enhancing your creative power. Due to the focus in western society on the mind, your inner guide usually remains under layers of hidden possibilities. It often takes time to connect with it.

Your inner guide is something you are born with. Some people may call it by other names at different times and for different purposes. Some refer to your inner guide as your intuition. At other times, they might call it your inner artist or your inner healer. Whatever name you use, your inner guide is housed deep inside of your whole being.

Some believe that the inner guide is influenced by a higher power. Others, such as those who adhere to a Buddhist philosophy, believe it is solely a power within. In either belief though, the inner guide comes from your center.

THE SCIENCE OF YOUR INNER GUIDE

Ironically, modern science indirectly points to the concept of an inner guide that leads us to wellness and health in the very workings of the human brain. As research about the brain in the past decades has uncovered new discoveries, researchers have found evidence that a mind-body connection really exists. One of the most noted examples is the work of Dr. Herbert Benson, author of *Timeless Healing*. Benson did numerous studies over the past twenty-five years on patients who suffered from medical problems and found that affirming beliefs, such as a belief in a higher power, actually improved a patient's state of wellness.

Dr. Benson used what he called the relaxation response with patients in order to help them calm their mind and their body. His quieting technique often involved a spiritually-oriented ritual, such as focusing on a word like peace, to elicit the relaxation response. Essentially he taught patients to go "within" themselves, which seemed to cause decreases in breathing and heart rates, blood pressure, and muscle tension, while increasing the beneficial "slow" brain waves.

The science of brain waves is actually quite fascinating and worth understanding in order to recognize the significance of the slow brain waves. Throughout the day, the human body generates a variety of brain rhythms and patterns, depending on our activities. Beta rhythms, which are the fastest, occur when the mind is awake, alert, and actively thinking about our many tasks to complete. Alpha rhythms occur when we are at rest, or a quiet wakefulness. Theta rhythms occur when a person is in meditation or in the first stages of sleep. Delta rhythms occur when a person is in a deep sleep; their awareness is detached and the person is in a healing state.

When you seek to calm and heal yourself – the state needed to become creative – you want to move out of your regular *Beta* rhythm and move into slow rhythms, such as *Alpha* and *Theta*. In this sense, connecting with your inner guide means you must learn to quiet yourself and listen.

ACCESSING YOUR INNER GUIDE

We now know that there are many methods to quiet yourself and connect with your inner guide. Several methods use a form of meditation. Given the growing popularity of meditation in Western culture, it is now easy to find information on the variety of meditative styles and techniques that exist. I will discuss only a handful of the techniques, including visualization, guided imagery, body awareness, walking a labyrinth, and making mandalas.

Visualization

Visualization is the process of creating a picture or image in your mind. The picture can be something pleasing, soothing, or calming. Think of this process as similar to creating your own film and playing it in your mind. Perhaps you pause on one scene that you enjoy. Maybe you play and rewind a series of frames over and over. You might play the same film each time you do a visualization exercise, or you might create a new one.

Another way of looking at visualization is in relation to goal setting. The power of visualization is known in many creative settings, as it often can make a difference in achieving or not achieving a particular goal. If you visualize what you would like to be doing, it is more likely to happen.

Guided Imagery

Guided imagery is similar to visualization, except that you use someone or something (like an audio CD) to guide you through the images. There are many books, tapes, and CDs on the market that have guided imagery exercises fully ready to use or listen to. If you happen to prefer a certain book of imagery exercises, ask a friend to read a particular exercise aloud, or pre-record yourself reading the exercise onto a tape.

Body Awareness Exercises

Body awareness exercises can either be led by another person or done alone with a little practice. This method of going inward encourages you to relax by focusing on different body parts, one by one, eventually relaxing the entire body.

Walking a Labyrinth

Walking a labyrinth can be quite a powerful experience. Many labyrinths are found outdoors or indoors, and there are even small ones that you do with one finger. You can quiet your mind in a variety of ways while utilizing labyrinths. One idea is to enter with a specific question, then as you walk through the labyrinth, let your thoughts move freely around it. When you reach the center of the labyrinth, take some time to pause and reflect on how you've felt and what you've thought about the question. Wait for an answer that feels right. If one hasn't come yet, proceed to walk out of the labyrinth, reflecting again as you exit on the answer to your question.

Mandalas

Mandalas are used in spiritual traditions around the world and are circular 2-D or 3-D works of art that the creator makes in order to work through a particular issue or question. In the making of the mandala, the creator seeks to uncover his or her deepest, otherwise unconscious thoughts. Mandala making is a way of opening to your spiritual and psychological self.

According to Judith Cornell, Ph.D., author of *Mandala: Luminous Symbols for Healing*, one reason for creating a mandala is "because it can make the invisible visible – expressing paradoxical situations or patterns of ultimate reality that can be expressed in no other way." She adds that you "give form and expression to an intuitive insight into spiritual truth by releasing the inner light of the soul."

To make your own mandala, first gather some basic supplies, such as paper, pencil, and inspirational music. Then begin with a meditation exercise to quiet your mind. When ready, begin drawing a large circle on your paper, then proceed to draw a symbol within it that you either saw in your meditation or one that represents a feeling you experienced during the meditation. From there, use your mandala and its symbolic representation to help transform your creative power and gifts.

Inner Listening

Once you have chosen a method for quieting yourself, truly listen to what your inner guide says to you. While you may not feel it, your body / mind / spirit will tell you what a wise, creative being you are, with solutions and answers that can lead you to wholeness and success. If you are able to discipline yourself to access your inner guide on a regular basis, you will feel and see positive changes in your creative life and beyond.

Working with a Holistic Practitioner or Creativity Coach

As many of you may find, it can be difficult to get into a relaxed state on your own. It can also be challenging to discipline yourself to access your inner guide on a regular basis. If either of these statements is true for you, consider seeking the help of a holistic practitioner, or a creativity coach who works with clients in this way. If the term holistic practitioner is unfamiliar to you, here is a simple definition: someone who works with a particular body system to help create balance and wholeness within the person. For example, a Rubenfeld Synergist listens to the client's body with their hands, while also talking to the client in an open and compassionate way.

To find out which type of holistic practitioner is right for you, I recommend the book *Discovering the Body's Wisdom* by Mirka Knaster. Also, interview some practitioners over the phone before using their services.

If you are looking for a creativity coach who does guided imagery or some form of energy healing, simply ask them before working with them which techniques they use.

DISTINGUISHING EGO FROM YOUR TRUE INNER GUIDE

When first attempting to access your inner guide, you will hear many voices emanating from inside you and it might be difficult to discern which to trust. Beware that the "inner critics" are often the first to speak up. These negative, chastising voices are there because your ego feels threatened by your looking inward. The ego wants to be sure that you don't forget about it. It wants to be the center of your attention, or your consciousness.

The ego identity – the "I" inside you – is formed by your family and your culture. It is the person that people, including you, see you as most of the time. However, you are much more than your ego says you are. You have a larger self, sometimes called your True Self, or Essence, or Higher Self. Accessing your inner guide is about transcending beyond your ego center to engage the center of your True Self.

In order to reach that center, you must learn self-trust. You have to trust that you are able to have a deep mind, body, and spirit connection. You have to open yourself up to the experience. You have to trust that you are safe. You must let go of your ego's desires and allow yourself to enter into the mystery of your inner world – where you will meet your inner guide.

Beware that your ego has a lot to say, but so does your inner guide. In order to know which voice is speaking, listen and experience what feels right, empowering, good, and true. Your inner guide shares the truth with you. It is not always easy to accept the truth, but trust your inner guide. It is the wise part of you that speaks from the heart of knowing and understanding.

THANKING YOUR INNER GUIDE

After you have connected with your inner guide, be sure to express your gratitude for its wisdom. Naturally, there is a great power in gratefulness. I am sure that if you have ever taken a moment to look at your life and acknowledge what is good, even the smallest thing, you have felt your heart open up and warmth fill your body.

Expressing gratitude is also a great way to summarize what you just experienced. By saying, "Thank you for the wisdom to . . . keep my day job, while I pursue my dream of being a writer," you are acknowledging what you are to do.

There are a variety of ways to express gratitude. One way is to verbally state what you are grateful for. Another is to write down what you experienced and are grateful for. A third is to create a ritual that you do each time you access your inner guide. It might involve lighting a candle, saying a few words, making a physical movement of the body like bowing, then extinguishing the candle. Your ritual need not be complex, but you'll find the act of performing a grateful ritual will add a lot of feelings and thus meaning to your experience.

Finally, you might consider making a work of art as an expression of gratitude to your inner guide. This could be a piece that you continue to add on to each time you meet with your inner guide. The options are endless.

TAKING CREATIVE ACTION

We are all creative beings. Each of us has a gift to share with the world. It is important that we share these gifts, so that others are inspired and confident enough to share theirs, too. Connecting to your inner guide in the ways described above actually helps you feel the creative power you have within yourself. You have the ability to create work that will make a difference to someone else. Use your gifts. Take creative action.

I recommend that you record your meetings with your inner guide in a journal. Keep a record of your insights. Use these experiences to help you form a body of work. These records are your first step to taking creative action. Your actual creative work is the second step.

In taking creative action, it is fine to start small. Just as an infant learns to walk, you will experience some wobbling and some falling down. Only through your continued efforts will you eventually stand, and then take your first step, then another step, until you are finally walking. Walking is the gift of your creative work.

Whatever creative action you take, be sure that it contributes toward something you believe in. Remain true to your larger self.

❖ ❖ ❖

Briana Riskin is a teacher, writer and artist. She is currently working on her Masters in Human Development, which she'll complete in the spring of 2006. Briana loves being in connection with others, making art, writing, and reading. Her mission in life is to help others express their inner creativity. She lives in the Twin Cities with her fiancé, Tom and their cat, Tiger. She can be reached at brianacoach@aol.com. Visit her Yahoo Group called Creative Intentions at www.groups.yahoo.com/group/creativeintentions.

LIFE AROUND US, LIFE WITHIN US

FINDING OUR CREATIVE SELVES IN NATURE

BY PAMELA BURKE, PH.D.

Is your creativity a "wild child?" The thorns on a rose? A rampant flowering weed gleefully overrunning an English garden? A spider's gossamer web? The sap of a sturdy maple tree? A coral reef that feeds the quick and colorful fishes of your mind?

Consider the possibility that your creative self is as much an incarnation of nature as a blooming tulip tree or a granite rock weathered by the rain. Your creative self has its own simple beauty and a unique place in the complex natural systems of the planet. If you can see your creativity as an essential part of nature, you can grow and change. You can move and be moved. You can flourish and give life to the creativity of others as you express your self, naturally so.

This article invites you to envision your creativity as a natural phenomenon. The exercises ask you to release that vague, throbbing blob from deep inside your chest and toss it out into the world. You may be surprised by where it lands and by what shapes it takes on. It is eager to go and excited to show you where it thrives. Trust it.

These exercises are intended to give you a clearer sense of the *you* who is walking your creative path and how this you shows up in the world in everything you create.

SELF-GUIDED MEDITATION

Make yourself comfortable by sitting on the floor or in a chair. You are about to go on a mental journey. Close your eyes for a few minutes and clear your mind. Pay attention to your breathing. When you feel calm and ready to begin, open your eyes and read on, taking whatever time you need to do and experience the meditation.

Be prepared with a pencil and some unlined paper or your journal to draw or write down your thoughts and feelings as you do the meditation. There are specific prompts for writing along the way. You will use these notes later to formulate your creative essence.

Part I

You are on a journey. It is your own special journey. The "you" who is traveling is the "you" who is unique, the creative "you," the one filled with knowing and curiosity.

There is a path on your creative journey.

Visualize yourself moving on this path.

See your body on the path.

What is the texture of the path?

What is it made of? Sand? Water? Air? Pine needles?

How does it feel on your feet?

Is it wide or narrow?

What is to the right of the path?

What is to the left of the path?

Pause for a moment and sit on the path facing either left or right.

What do you see?

Draw or describe each detail.

What is near you on the ground?

What is within your reach?

What is at the horizon?

Add more detail on the parts of the scene that intrigue you.

In your mind, go to and touch the element in the scene that is calling for your touch.

Describe the call.

Describe how you touch it.

Describe its response.

Gently put it back in its natural place.

Write about the significance of this object.

Write words, phrases, sentences that come into your mind as you gaze on the scene.

Why is this place on your creative path?

What gives the creative "you" a sense of belonging in this place?

What about this place attracts the creative "you"?

What about this place excites or scares the creative "you"?

And again, why is this place on your creative path?

Part II

When you are ready, stand up and move forward on your path.

Walk at the pace your creative self needs to move right now.

Feel yourself in motion.

Describe your motion.

Are you walking? Crawling? Running? Dancing? Swimming? Flying?

Where are your eyes focused as you move?

Forward? To the side? Near your feet? On the horizon? On the middle ground?

Notice your breathing. Is it quick? Slow? Deep? Shallow?

What does your body feel as you move on your path?

Hold this image of your creative self, body and spirit together, moving on your path.

Describe this image in rich detail.

Describe it from the outside looking in. Then from the inside looking out.

Take a deep breathe in.

Slowly exhale.

Breathe in.

Exhale.

Begin to notice the land or water or sky on the left or right of the path.

As this new segment of your path comes into focus, choose a place to pause.

Describe the landscape or the waterscape or the sky.

What do you see?

What do you smell?

What do you hear?

Describe the physical attributes of this place.

Describe the things that are growing in this place.

Describe the creatures around you.

What else do you see?

Draw or describe each detail.

What is near you on the ground?

What is within your reach?

What is at the horizon?

Add more detail on the parts of the scene that intrigue you.

Go to and touch the element in the scene that is calling for your touch.

Describe the call.

Describe how you touch it.

Describe its response.

Gently put it back in its natural place.

Write about the significance of this object.

Write words, phrases, sentences that come into your mind as you gaze on the scene.

Why is this place on your creative path?

What gives the creative "you" a sense of belonging in this place?

What about this place attracts the creative "you"?

What about this place excites or scares the creative "you"?

And again, why is this place on your creative path?

Part III

Imagine now that there is a great wind.

This wind swirls around you and embraces you, obliterating your sight momentarily.

This great supportive wind lifts you off the path.

You feel it moving and you allow it to take you in its cradling cocoon.

It carries you across the land, to another land, to a new place, to a place you don't know.

The wind slows down. It unwraps its embrace. It gently puts your feet on the ground.

You open your eyes.

Where are you?

Describe what you see.

Become something that you see.

Imagine being this unique element of nature at its creation.

Imagine being this element of nature as it changes through time.

Imagine being this element of nature as it connects to every other element in this place.

Describe how this unique element of nature is essential to this place.

What exists in the world because of this element?

Describe your self, the creative "you," as this element of nature you have become.

What attributes of this element of nature are true about you?

What knowledge about nature and creativity do you share with this element?

Why did this place offer this special element of nature to you?

What exists in this world because of your unique creative self?

Why did the supportive wind bring you to this place?

Thank the wind.

Thank the place.

Thank the element.

Thank yourself.

RETURNING FROM THE MEDITATION

Welcome back! Did your mental excursion feel like a mini-vacation? Some people report feeling relaxed when mentally following their creative selves in these exercises and others report feeling exhilarated, surprised, frightened or upset. Notice what you were feeling. Notice where your logical mind was trying to nudge you into a "more reasonable" place or thought.

As you give your creative self more time in the natural settings where it thrives, it will become more assertive when logic intrudes. Try these meditations every few days and see how quickly and happily your creative self expands its freedom.

YOUR MEDITATION JOURNAL

Each time you do a meditation, reflect on what surfaced through your writing. The meditation prompts will guide you to return, repeatedly and more deeply, to how this natural place expresses your creativity. Notice how your answers to the prompts begin to form an impression of your creativity.

Here is a sample from one of my meditations. Note that, because I am a writer, my journal often takes the form of prose, but you can feel free to answer the prompts in the meditation in any way you want – short sentences, poetry, visuals, single words, or a dialogue. You can always choose to journal more deeply about specific images that emerge in the meditation at a later time.

> I am walking in the sun and the wind along a ribbon of iron shore in Anguilla. The sharp coral rock is filled with holes, jutting protuberances and razor edges. I am moving at a fair pace, balancing myself with light steps tentatively finding footing in the uneven territory. The path is the width of three fishing boats end-to-end with edges that meander with an irregular scalloping on both sides. On the left is the ocean – wet iron shore, tide pools, foam, occasional beach driftwood and plastic ropes and shoes that may have come from a boat hundreds of miles closer to Africa. On my right is a hill. The foreground is white sand and scrub bushes merging with a manzanita field – a thousand manzanita bushes bent and gnarled growing sideways away from the ocean breezes towards the hilltop. In amongst the thick-barked manzanita are one-foot barrel cacti flowering and thorny, touching nothing but the air around them.

> I am sitting on the left side, the side with ocean on the horizon. Deep blue and endless, the water line merges with the azure blue of the mid-afternoon sky and creates a domed world wrapped in my favorite colors, tangible to my eyes. My eyes feel caressed by the waves that come to me, always to me, as if I am their destination and their purpose. I can read what they are saying as they heave onto land and slip back to gather strength for their next caress.

> I am called to pick up the shell of a sea urchin, still green and rough before the sun bleaches it white. It is cool, wet, open on one side and closed on the other. I turn it over in my hand to expose the belly of the empty shell and see the five ribs expanding out from the top to the sides. I put it back, in the shelter of an iron shore shelf where water will come in and refresh it yet where few waves will be big enough to crush it against the rock. Here it will feel the sun and the moon swing across the sky and greet the small living and dead creatures that happen to be flushed in and out of its new home.

> This urchin shell is the inside of a spiny creature. It is a perfect structure, able to withstand relentless waves and storms. It can float and

be still, ride the waters of life and be comfortable on land where an infinite number of grains of sand blow across its bumpy hide. It is important to me because it has another life after the creature that was once inside and outside of it has changed form. It has integrity to its form. My creativity is that middle layer of my life, the one that holds the integrity of my form, the one that radiates symmetry and texture and that has a purpose in the world separate from the support it gives to the internal and external layers of me. Exposed, its purpose is beauty and simplicity. It is domed, encompassing yet porous. It is a tiny sifter of the basic elements of life connected to a bigger sifter of elements, and to a yet bigger sifter. Its five ribs tell me my creativity is connected to body, spirit, earth, sea, and sky.

This place is on my creative path because it is deeply peaceful and constantly in motion.

This scene is totally in motion – water, sky, wind. There are surprises in every cranny yet the surprises are part of the same cloth. Animal, vegetable, and mineral in harmony with odd man-made chemical products. The colors are subtle, but the entire rainbow is here in a shell or a plant or the sky at sunset. I can pause and look close and see a hundred separate stories or look at the mid-ground and see the history of the earth.

This place is on my creative path because it means life and motion and solitude.

My creative self senses belonging – it feels welcomed in its restlessness and invited to touch. It is invited to sit on the hard coral and the soft patches of sand. It recognizes the insignificance of one tiny creature and the value of that same creature in the beauty of the entire place. There are so many rough edges, so many possibilities for surprise and change, so many examples of biological ingenuity, so many proclamations of life thriving through adaptation and creativity.

I am attracted to this place because it takes no prisoners. It is all laid out for me, take it or leave it. There are no compromises, no shifts to accommodate my comfort, just raw being to accept or decline. I am attracted to it because it is always there when I go there. It has always been there and always will be there.

I am excited by the relentless waves, and the tenacious plants that never seem to tire of their necessity to crash to the shore or root deep against the winds. They are not hiding or leaving or procrastinating, they are being. This singularity of purpose frightens me; this acceptance of harshness, this constancy across all time scares me.

Why is this place on my creative path? Because it is I turned inside out. It is the place where I can go to expose the being inside. It is a place that expands my comfort with the diversity in my creativity, and with the jagged edges that co-exist, and in fact belong in me.

FORMULATING THE ESSENCE OF YOUR CREATIVE SELF

Your meditation journal can now become a valuable tool to help you gain insight into your "creative essence." Mine what you have written for clues about what matters to you by noticing words and images that jump out at you or that appear in multiple places.

The following exercises will help you gain awareness of your essence:

1. Go back to what you've written and drawn. Underline all the adjectives in your descriptions. If an adjective, for example, "translucent," appeared when you described the water in the brook on the side of the path and again when you described the petals of a sunflower in the rain where the wind put you down, underline it twice. If the same adjective appeared again when you described the eyes of the elk in the wood, underline it three times.

2. Make a list of the adjectives. Circle 4-6 adjectives that describe your natural creative self.

3. Put a check mark next to every object you've described. If an object appears in multiple scenes, add additional check marks.

4. Make a list of all the objects, noting which ones appear multiple times. Circle 3-5 objects that symbolize your natural creative self.

5. Repeat this process for the verbs in your story.

6. Now use the most compelling verbs, objects and adjectives you selected above to write one or two sentences that describe the essence of your natural creative self. For example, I took the words that stood out to me from this meditation exercise including "creative" "restless" "inside" "out" "sifted" "caressed" "exposed" "jagged" "sharp" "fragile" and "raw" and added concepts that summed up my feelings from the meditation: "unbounded" "cherished" and "strange" to create the following statement:

   My Essence Statement: My creative self, naturally so, is restless and unbounded. It brings the insides of things out to be sifted and caressed, exposed and cherished no matter how jagged, sharp, fragile, raw or strange.

MAKING A TOUCHSTONE TO REMIND YOU OF YOUR CREATIVE ESSENCE

1. Once you've done the meditation and examined its meaning to you, consider making a "touchstone" that helps you quickly recapture a sense of your creative self. The touchstone can take the form of any of the following:

- Collect pictures from magazines, postcards, your photo albums or other places that re-create the feelings you had when you walked your mental creative path. Create a collage or glue pictures in your journal or calendar.

- Collect natural objects that symbolize your creativity and your creative path. Place these objects throughout your home and workspace.

- Post the "essence of your creative self" statement you wrote where you will read it every day. The refrigerator; the cover of your day planner; above your computer…

2. Share your writing and touchstones with people who matter to you.

- Experience describing your essential creative self to someone without discounting or self-deprecating asides. Use images from your meditation.

Example 1:

See this rough piece of driftwood I collected? Its overall shape is jagged, but it is also soft and smooth when you touch it. My mind is the ocean. I love to tumble images for a poem and pare them into beautiful, clean, jagged shapes that are smooth and soft in a subtle way. My poetry takes the varnish off my experiences and exposes their essence to me.

Example 2:

It is no surprise to me that I am most proud of my digital photography after many years of doing film-based photography. When I drive through Vermont in October, I see every leaf and branch as a tiny dot of color and am overwhelmed by the massive patchwork of natural settings. Every tiny block, as small as you can make it when you squint your eyes is a unique point of color and light, a single pixel whose beauty and integrity is essential to the feel of the entire shot. I am a gatherer of pixels.

- Trust that revealing yourself to others will create opportunities. A plant flowering in isolation leaves no legacy because the bees and other natural supporters cannot find it. If you let yourself be known, supportive people will be drawn to you. Your natural creative self is part of an interconnected natural system; reveal yourself and see the connections emerge.

WHERE WILL YOUR CREATIVE SELF, NATURALLY SO, LEAD YOU?

Now that you've gotten to know your creative self from a new perspective, where will this new perspective lead you in your creative work? Listen to your own wisdom. Consider these questions as you reflect on your new vision of your creative self:

1. What does seeing your creativity as an incarnation of nature allow you to do?

2. What does believing yourself to be a natural phenomenon encourage you to do?

3. How do the natural attributes of your creativity appear in your creative work?

4. How might these natural attributes of your creativity show up differently in your work this week?

Consider the possibility that your creative self is an expression of nature at its most beautiful and as such, is inherently worthy of care and delight.

❖ ❖ ❖

Pamela Burke, Ph.D., is a creativity coach and workshop leader, writer and fiber artist in Monmouth County, New Jersey. She is the founder of Unbound Edge, Inc., a creativity, innovation, and organization development consulting business serving individuals, businesses and arts organizations. You can reach Pam to talk about your creative goals and how creativity coaching can expand your creative success at pburke78@comcast.net. Pam would like to acknowledge and thank the members of the Edge Group in Somerville, New Jersey for refining these meditations and sharing their insights.

Creativity Coaching Association Press
www.creativitycoachingassociation.com